The Cosmic Time of Empire

FLASHPOINTS

The series solicits books that consider literature beyond strictly national and disciplinary frameworks, distinguished both by their historical grounding and their theoretical and conceptual strength. We seek studies that engage theory without losing touch with history and work historically without falling into uncritical positivism. FlashPoints aims for a broad audience within the humanities and the social sciences concerned with moments of cultural emergence and transformation. In a Benjaminian mode, FlashPoints is interested in how literature contributes to forming new constellations of culture and history and in how such formations function critically and politically in the present. Available online at http://repositories.cdlib.org/ucpress.

Series Editors:

Ali Behdad (Comparative Literature and English, UCLA); Judith Butler (Rhetoric and Comparative Literature, UC Berkeley), Founding Editor; Edward Dimendberg (Film & Media Studies, UC Irvine), Coordinator; Catherine Gallagher (English, UC Berkeley), Founding Editor; Jody Greene (Literature, UC Santa Cruz); Susan Gillman (Literature, UC Santa Cruz); Richard Terdiman (Literature, UC Santa Cruz)

1. *On Pain of Speech: Fantasies of the First Order and the Literary Rant*, by Dina Al-Kassim

2. *Moses and Multiculturalism*, by Barbara Johnson, with a foreword by Barbara Rietveld

3. *The Cosmic Time of Empire: Modern Britain and World Literature*, by Adam Barrows

4. *Poetry in Pieces: César Vallejo and Lyric Modernity*, by Michelle Clayton

The Cosmic Time of Empire

Modern Britain and World Literature

Adam Barrows

UNIVERSITY OF CALIFORNIA PRESS
Berkeley · Los Angeles · London

University of California Press, one of the most
distinguished university presses in the United States,
enriches lives around the world by advancing
scholarship in the humanities, social sciences, and
natural sciences. Its activities are supported by the UC
Press Foundation and by philanthropic contributions
from individuals and institutions. For more
information, visit www.ucpress.edu.

University of California Press
Berkeley and Los Angeles, California

University of California Press, Ltd.
London, England

© 2011 by The Regents of the University of California

Library of Congress Cataloging-in-Publication Data

Barrows, Adam.
 The cosmic time of empire : modern Britain and
world literature / Adam Barrows.
   p. cm. — (Flash points ; 3)
 Includes bibliographical references and index.
 ISBN 978-0-520-26099-3 (pbk. : alk. paper)
 1. English fiction—19th century—History and
criticism. 2. English fiction—20th century—History
and criticism. 3. Time in literature. 4. Modernism
(Literature)—English-speaking countries.
5. Time—Political aspects. 6. Time—Systems and
standards. I. Title.
  PR830.T5B37 2011
  823'.80933—dc22   2010019955

Manufactured in the United States of America

20 19 18 17 16 15 14 13 12 11
10 9 8 7 6 5 4 3 2 1

For Tim Brennan

Contents

List of Illustrations ix
Acknowledgments xi

Introduction: Modernism and the Politics of Time 1
1. Standard Time, Greenwich, and the Cosmopolitan Clock 22
2. "Turning From the Shadows That Follow Us": Modernist Time and the Politics of Place 53
3. At the Limits of Imperial Time; or, Dracula Must Die! 75
4. "The Shortcomings of Timetables": Greenwich, Modernism, and the Limits of Modernity 100
5. "A Few Hours Wrong": Standard Time and Indian Literature in English 129
Conclusion: A Postmodern Politics of Time? Negri's "Global Phenomenological Fabric" and Amis's Backward Arrow 154

Notes 171
Bibliography 193
Index 205

Illustrations

FIGURES

1. A graphic illustration of the diversity of world time before 1884 / *32*
2. Fleming's model of the globe as the perfect timepiece / *33*
3, 4, 5. Illustrations of three radical clock-dial reforms / *120*

TABLE

1. The voting on Resolutions II and V at the International Prime Meridian Conference / *44*

Acknowledgments

This book began as an idea in a seminar at the University of Minnesota on nineteenth-century masculinities. The course was taught by Lois Cucullu, and the rigorous interweaving of popular and canonical texts with cultural theory that she modeled in that class set the groundwork for much of the intellectual work that I would do in the following years. I have dedicated the book to Tim Brennan, not only because he was my dissertation director on the project, but because he has served as a professional mentor and role model for me over the years. As an intellectual whose teaching and writing exemplify his honesty and political commitment, Tim has shaped my understanding of what it is possible to achieve in this profession. I was fortunate to benefit from the keen insights of Brian Goldberg and John Mowitt, who read the book as a dissertation and helped to shape its evolution. Also at the University of Minnesota I greatly benefited from frank and open professional interchanges with my graduate student cohort through a productive dissertation writing group. I am grateful to the members of that group, particularly Marie-Therese Sulit, Melanie Brown, and Diana Ostrander, each of whom read rough drafts of most of the chapters, often multiple times. Much of the early writing and research for this project was greatly assisted with the support of a William W. Stout fellowship and two consecutive Ruth Drake fellowships at the University of Minnesota.

I am grateful to have had the opportunity to present early versions of these arguments at professional conferences. In particular I was fortunate to participate in a seminar on simultaneity with Stephen Kern and others at the seventh annual Modernist Studies Association convention in Chicago, and I thank Edward Aiken for organizing that event. At the 123rd annual Modern Language Association convention, also in Chicago, I participated in a lively panel presentation on "Modernist Mean Time" organized by Jessica Burstein. My thanks to her and also to John Paul Riquelme, John G. Peters, and Carrie Preston, who offered encouragement and insight following that event. An abbreviated version of chapter 4 appeared in the journal *Modern Fiction Studies*. I am grateful to the Johns Hopkins University Press for their permission to reprint that material here. The archival research on which the arguments in chapter 1 are based was conducted during two trips to Library and Archives Canada in Ottawa, the first of which was funded by a Samuel Holt Monk/Moses Marston research award from the University of Minnesota. I am grateful to the staff, reference librarians, archivists, and freelance researchers at LAC for their assistance with this project.

As a first-time author I was fortunate to bring this book to completion under the guidance of the editorial board of the Flashpoints series. Thanks especially to Ed Dimendberg, who guided me gracefully through the process, to Hannah Love at the University of California Press, and to the external reviewers of the manuscript, whose attentive, fair, and rigorous responses to my work have helped to make this book what it is. Substantial revision of the manuscript was carried out at Salisbury University, and I thank my colleagues there for their support, as well as my new colleagues at Carleton University, who have enthusiastically welcomed me into their department. Thanks to my parents, Tom and Susan, for their unconditional love and support, to Bob and Amy, Henry and the late Dorothy Hill, to Denis and Cindy, Bob and Marlys, Beau and Nisha, Nick and Stefanie, and all those who have supported me over the years. Finally, to my wife, Darla, and son, Elliot, who know better than anyone what the costs of this project have been, I offer this book with my love.

Introduction

Modernism and the Politics of Time

A concern with time is intrinsic to the internal logic of modernity. "More than anything else," Zygmunt Bauman writes, modernity is the "history of time: the time when time has history" ("Time and Space Reunited," 172). Radically breaking with the authority and legitimacy of the past, modernity offers a totalizing vision of progress toward an illimitable future.[1] Its universal narrative of irrepressible global development presupposes a uniform scale of spatial and temporal measurement. In this context the legislative creation of world standard time at the International Prime Meridian Conference of 1884 stands as a signal moment in the history of modernity, providing a global grid whereby the minutest spatial unit and the most infinitesimal duration of time could be measured in relation to Greenwich, England. Convened in Washington, D.C., at the behest of a group of American metrologists and engineers with the Canadian industrialist Sandford Fleming as their spokesman, the goal of the Prime Meridian Conference was to establish the meridian of longitude passing through Greenwich as the spatial and temporal zero point for global cartography and civil time measurement. The issue at the conference was a particularly modern one: Did individual nations possess sovereignty over the regulation of civil life, down to the very intimate rhythms of temporal activity? Or was time, as Fleming insisted, transnational, universal, or, in his own terminology, "cosmopolitan"? Despite what one dissenting astronomer termed the "ancient and necessary barriers" of nations, time was conceivably the metaphysical principle that transcended all cultural and political division.² The Prime Meridian Conference would ultimately render Greenwich not only an international symbol of the British Empire, but also the cosmopolitan standard for measuring the very limits of modernity.

Although the conference made its recommendations in 1884, it took more than forty years for advocates of standard time to pressure individual nations to adopt the reforms.³ Between the 1880s and the 1930s a radical transformation thus took place in the synchronization of global activity that would facilitate commercial and military penetration into the remotest regions of space. The period during which Greenwich Mean Time became accepted, nation by nation, as Universal Time spans the period in English literary history typically associated with high modernism. As political and scientific representatives of "civilized" nations argued over the value of synchronized civil time, literary artists were experimenting with the representation of human temporality in ways that would radically alter prevailing aesthetic forms. *The Cosmic Time of Empire* situates that dominant aesthetic tendency of modernism within the context of the political and legislative battles over world standard time. Specifically I argue that representations of the Greenwich Observatory, Greenwich Mean Time, and temporal standardization more generally are tightly bound up in modernist texts with representations of an authoritarian management of bodies, communities, and nations. These associations between standardized time and manipulative forms of imperial control constitute a problem rather than a solution for the modernists, as they attempt to formally and thematically mediate between a host of competing temporal demands. The modernists negotiated, without ever necessarily resolving, a complex array of temporal models, alternately centered in the body, the mind, the state, the empire, and the globe. My argument thus depends on a central analogy between the substance of the debates at the Prime Meridian Conference and the experimental treatment of time in modernist texts, from Henri Bergson's philosophical treatises to the fiction of Virginia Woolf. Modernist literature dialectically enacts the same tensions between contextually embedded time and cosmopolitan time that fueled the debates at the Washington conference. Politicians, astronomers, philosophers, and artists during this period wrestled with contesting definitions of temporality in the light of a heavily funded campaign to definitively install Greenwich Mean Time as the one, true, "cosmopolitan" time. Indeed experimental modernist literature was not unique in its engagement with the public discourse of temporality. Modernist temporal experimentation was part of a larger fin de siècle cultural project to reshape and reexamine the limits and limitations of regimes of temporal management. That project, while intrinsic to the high modernist canon, also informs a variety of fictions not often considered modernist because of their genre, style, or country of origin. I explore the discourse of standardized temporality in works as seemingly disparate as a Victorian adventure novel, Bram Stoker's *Dracula* (1897), a South Asian anticolonial "Gandhi novel," K.S. Venkataramani's *Murugan, the Tiller* (1927), and a modernist classic, James Joyce's *Ulysses* (1922). Though they were published within the same thirty-year period, it is difficult to think of three texts more rigidly segregated by disciplinary boundaries. Yet all participate in the common cultural project of imagining the role of Greenwich Mean Time in the political construction of communities and nations, sometimes by naturalizing and sometimes by generating alternatives to standard time's global authority.

High modernism brings its own unique temporal demands to the discourse of global standard time, however, which tend to distinguish it from other works of its cultural and historical moment. As the modernist novel becomes more totalizing and encyclopedic in its aspirations, endeavoring to contain and connect diverse nationalities, discursive communities, and class fractions within one overarching, eschatological framework, it demands new narrative forms of conceptualizing time and space capable of managing those totalities. How does the novel maintain order when it reaches outside its generic, national, and linguistic boundaries, as do the novels of Joseph Conrad, James Joyce, and Virginia Woolf? In a sense this problem is similar to the one facing the architects of the standard time system, which was presented as the ideal map for reading the time and space of an increasingly globalized world. The aspirations of the literary modernists and the standard time advocates can thus be understood as fundamentally similar. Yet although standard time definitively "solved" the problem of globalization by simply unifying every space and time on the map as theoretically equivalent, these modernists refuse a homogenizing and philosophically abstract solution to the very real limits on temporal and spatial solidarity. The project of using British time to dictate a new global conception of space was unique to this historical period, as standard time advocates proceeded nation by nation to integrate the world into a system of Greenwich precision. To fail to recognize this new burden on British time in the decades between 1884 and 1930 is to miss the greater significance of direct modernist references to British time as well as modernism's larger transformations of standard narrative chronology, both of which indicate an engagement with questions of paramount public concern rather than a philosophical retreat into bourgeois, private interiority.

Modernist temporality has often been treated as a reactionary cultural formation expressing a deliberate retreat from crassly material or "political" engagements with questions of empire.[4] *The Cosmic Time of Empire* demonstrates, on the contrary, the degree to which modernist texts engaged with rather than evaded the enlistment of temporality in the imperial project, while simultaneously forging alternative models of temporality resistant to empire's demands. The modernist discourse of time, generally considered in purely philosophical or aesthetic terms, was thus always intrinsically politicized, bound up as it was with the problematics of imperial control and global conceptualization. At a time when imperial politics have become central in studies of modernism, I argue that it is possible, and productive, to rethink the politics of modernism through the politics of time.[5]

Standard time eliminated the discrepancy between a multitude of local times by dividing global space into twenty-four time zones, all synchronized to the Greenwich Royal Observatory, deviating from Greenwich by whole-hour integers.[6] Enabling the precise coordination of global activity, the system can in one sense be understood as the culmination of Enlightenment rationality, dispassionate scientific inquiry, and democratization. Indeed Clark Blaise has advocated that Sandford Fleming be considered an innovator alongside the likes of Darwin, Pasteur, and Edison.[7] Yet clock coordination was never purely the outcome of disinterested rationality. The ability to determine the time at two spatially distant locations has, perhaps inevitably, always been driven by the demands of international commerce and military hegemony. In the eighteenth century British naval power depended on exact knowledge of positioning at sea, a fact clearly recognized by the British Parliament when it passed the Longitude Act in 1714, offering a reward of twenty thousand pounds for anyone able to solve the problem of longitude. The story of John Harrison's claim to the prize money in 1773 for his invention of an accurate marine chronometer is well-known, but what is perhaps more noteworthy than the life story of this "lone genius" is the larger confluence of forces driving the demand for accurate global positioning, in Harrison's time as in the present day.[8] The Longitude Act followed closely on the heels of the annexation of

Scotland into Great Britain by the Acts of Union and was driven by naval pressures during the thirteen-year war of Spanish succession.[9] Accurate global positioning thus emerged as an acute need during a time when Britain was consolidating its national power at home and fiercely competing abroad for territories and resources. Time control was a crucial element in that battle for the control over spatial positioning. As Peter Galison writes in *Einstein's Clocks, Poincaré's Maps: Empires of Time*, the coordination of clocks that drove theoretical physics and communications technology alike in the following century was "never just about a little procedure of signal exchange," but rather was driven by "national ambitions, war, industry, science, and conquest" (38).

Standard time advocates of the nineteenth century presented themselves as public servants satisfying a clear and present demand from the industrial masses for hyperefficiency in time management. To an extent this was true. The architects of the Prime Meridian Conference certainly did not imagine or invent the nineteenth century's hyperconsciousness of temporal precision, nor did they single-handedly rationalize and reify time. These were processes rooted deep in industrial modernity and in urbanization, emerging from what E. P. Thompson characterizes as the "marriage of convenience" between Puritanism and industrial capitalism, which compelled workers to recognize time not as task-specific, but as a neutral commodity ultimately reducible to monetary terms (95). Thompson's account of increasingly time-thrifty factory owners forbidding their employees access to personal timepieces and keeping one master clock under lock and key clearly illustrates the structural inequalities built into the drive to standardize time. While Thompson recognizes an increasing faith in time discipline among English workers in their battle for ten-hour days and overtime pay, his study of time discipline clearly suggests that such discipline was not driven from below, but was imposed from above to accord with the needs of Taylorized factory production.

Hyperconsciousness of time was by no means restricted to factory workers and their employers. Peter Galison characterizes time synchronization as "a circulating fluid of modern urban life." As coordinated time in the mid-nineteenth century extended into "train stations, neighborhoods, and churches," it became a public service that "intervened in peoples' lives the way electric power, sewage, or gas did" (107). Certainly the increasing ubiquity of train travel in the lives of nineteenth-century Londoners made the Bradshaw guide to railway timetables a crucial necessity, a book as likely to grace the average Londoner's bookshelf as the Bible, the dictionary, and the almanac.[10] The guide's first issue, in 1839 (under the title *Bradshaw's Railway Companion*), was commonly satirized for its impenetrability, with lampoons produced as six-penny brochures and as stage pantomimes. (One satirist made the name Bradshaw synonymous with uselessness in the couplet "Almost as useless (howsoe'er you tried/To follow it) as any Bradshaw's Guide.")[11] These satires were largely a product of the 1840s and a reaction to the bewildering novelty of train travel itself. After his death in 1853 Bradshaw became a symbol of the powers of the railway age and was recognized as a pioneer in providing a key to navigating the new global landscape it created. When the trains were stopped because of a coal mining strike, an editorialist in *Punch* equated the bosses with Bradshaw: "But fallen is the pride of those/Who knew their Bradshaw, Perth to Tring;/And jubilant are Bradshaw's foes."[12] The circulatory fluid of standardized railway time was itself part of a larger late nineteenth-century drive for standardization across a range of social practices. Jennifer Wicke identifies the period between 1881 and 1901 as a time when the notion of a standard was "crystallized in disparate cultural practices and concretized as a cultural concept."[13] The increasing rationalization and reification of time during this period rendered time itself "palpable," as Mary Anne Doane argues. "Time was indeed *felt*," she writes, "as a weight, as a source of anxiety, and as an acutely pressing problem of representation" (4).

It was this anxiety over the maintenance and control of modern time that the standard time system promised to allay. Yet the solution advocated by the standard time architects at the Prime Meridian Conference was by no means a foregone conclusion, nor did it substantially represent the desires of even a majority of key European delegates in attendance. My aim in the first chapter of this book is to illustrate the extent to which arguments for the pressing necessity of a global system of time reckoning depended on deliberate misreadings and wild overstatements of the conclusions of the 1884 conference, which has been almost universally misrepresented as having given international sanction to the creation of a Greenwich-based civil time. There has never been a rigorous, book-length historical account of the Prime Meridian Conference, although Derek Howse, Ian Bartky, and Peter Galison have each devoted a chapter to it. Their accounts, however, are largely limited to the central rivalry between England and France, a rivalry that was vocal in the first few days of the conference but was by no means the most salient feature of the month-long debates.[14] My study of the conference proceedings and of Sandford Fleming's voluminous archive of personal correspondence at Canada's National Archives extends beyond Anglo-French rivalry to an investigation of more diverse European responses to world standard time. With the benefit of that archival research, chapter 1 is not merely a summation of existing historical research, but is more importantly a revisionist reading of the 1884 conference that brings to the surface peripheral voices previously silenced in the face of the more vocal antagonism between France and England. According to my reading a wide range of conference delegates protested the extension of Greenwich Mean Time into all but the most specialized subset of practices. The issue of the desirability of a universal adoption of the Greenwich longitude was deliberately and explicitly kept *off the table* in Washington by delegates from Germany, Spain, and the Ottoman Empire. Dissenting delegates forcefully defended the sovereignty of discrete national time reckoning and the sociocultural or religious foundations on which those national norms were based. These arguments illustrate the extent to which the inevitability of a universal standard time was by no means a foregone conclusion in the fin de siècle. In the first chapter I discuss the relevance of my archival research and chart out structural imbalances of power in the standard time system, using a proposed rail venture in northern Brazil as a case study of a community disenfranchised by its penetration. Standard time illustrates the maxim that, in Pierre Bourdieu's words, "unification profits the dominant" ("Uniting to Better Dominate," 1).

This revisionist reading of the history of standard time provides the foundation for a series of readings of texts by British and Irish authors written between 1884 and 1925. The near obsessive fixation with time in modernist fiction of this period has inspired a great deal of scholarship.[15] Yet the dominant critical tendency has been to treat modernist time as a purely philosophical exploration of private consciousness, disjointed from the forms of material and public temporality that standard time attempted to organize. This familiar narrative, though illuminating in many ways, fundamentally misinterprets the role of time in modernism by failing to recognize that what is far more characteristic of the discourse on time in the late nineteenth century and early twentieth is not the tension between public and private time, but rather the tension between national and global time. The discourse on time surrounding and informing the Washington debates bore no trace of any philosophical discrimination between individual time and collective time. A reactionary retreat from all forms of public, urban time tout court is more clearly evident in cultural products of the early and mid-nineteenth century, when railroads replaced stagecoaches and urbanization began to transform the economic and social dynamics of English life, than it is in the early twentieth century, by which time most English citizens, and certainly all Londoners, had long accepted the ubiquity of public, standard time as the "circulating fluid of modern urban life."[16] The impact of world standard time in England was not to alter the private sensation of English temporality. British clocks had, after all, been synchronized to Greenwich since the mid-1850s, and it is in Dickens rather than Conrad that one finds evidence of reaction to that move (in *Dombey and Son*, for example). What is significant about 1884, rather, is that it marks the date when England begins to *export* British time as a commodity to an entire globe newly dependent on Greenwich precision. For British authors, standard time provides a new way of conceptualizing the globe as spatiotemporally enmeshed with England. Global standard time as an imperial practice and Anglo modernism as a cultural practice share a common representational problem of conceptualizing and managing the relationship between global and local spaces. Texts of the period represent the unification of time and space in a common coordinate system even as they contest, and in some cases metaphorically dismantle, that unification. Global standard time was a tool of spatiotemporal representation that removed many of the formerly existent barriers to empire. As authors began to adopt this representational tool for their imaginative fictions they came ultimately to test its limitations and to offer counterrepresentations of space that would explore alternative forms of shared, public time, none of which could be easily manipulated within a common coordinate frame.

To make such an argument about British literary modernism, it is first necessary to contest the familiar narrative of modernism's affirmation of private, interior time consciousness, which has largely depended on an application of the theories of Henri Bergson to modernist literature, sometimes by the authors themselves but more often by literary scholars.[17] The political dimensions of modernist temporality have been misrepresented in a long-standing critical tradition that equates modernist time with the private, interior, and purely aesthetic pleasures of the Bergsonian *durée*. An implicitly Bergsonian reading of modernist time certainly informs the first chapter of Stephen Kern's very influential *The Culture of Time and Space: 1880–1918*, still the only rigorous attempt to theorize a relationship between standard time and modernist literature. *The Culture of Time and Space* remains the touchstone for studies of standard time and aesthetics;[18] thus a discussion of its critical assumptions at this point is particularly useful. Indeed it has now become virtually impossible to think of modernist time outside of the contexts of Bergson's philosophy and Kern's social history. To do so, however, is to generate potentially invigorating readings of modernist temporality and to avoid what I consider to be two common interpretive pitfalls in the critical literature. These pitfalls, which I label *temporal isolationism* and *temporal transnationalism,* both inform Kern's landmark study.

The introduction of standard time, according to Kern, was "the most momentous development in the history of uniform, public time since the invention of the mechanical clock" (4). Kern's definition of cosmopolitan, universal time as public immediately sets the stage for the assertion that modernism's oppositional stance will reclaim and champion an individualized private temporality. Although Kern designates the age's dialectical positions on time as "homogeneous" and "heterogeneous," the terms *public* and *private* recur more frequently in his treatment of literary texts. For Kern literary modernism's engagement with standard time is, without exception, an assault on public or national experience from a position of private, bodily, or transnational identity. Private time writes itself on the individual bodies of protagonists who exist in a local or national milieu that is "discordant," "sinister, or "superficial." Thus Oscar Wilde's Dorian Gray experiences "a sinister discordance between body time and public time," and Proust's Marcel is set apart from national scandals like the Dreyfus Affair and from his fellow bourgeoisie because he "moves at an irregular pace that is repeatedly out of phase with that of the other characters." A private, isolated act, Marcel's search of lost time impels him to turn within his own physical frame. According to Kern, "Proust learns to listen for the faint stirrings of memories implanted in his body long ago and destined to recur to him in unpredictable ways" (16). In this sentence Kern fuses what he understands as Marcel's private, bodily time with an ancestral "implanted" time controlled by cosmic "destiny" rather than by public or national events. Marcel is both temporally isolated within his corklined room and also temporally unified with his fellow humanity in a transnational sense. This is even clearer in Kern's reading of Leopold Bloom in Joyce's *Ulysses*. Bloom's heterogeneous and diverse experience of time may be "unique" within the social context of 1904 Dublin, but it is also related, in Kern's words, "to the infinite expanses of cosmic time" (17).

In Kern's work we see both of the interpretive traps between which I hope to chart a course. On the one hand we find an implicit understanding of literary modernism as affirming a private, temporal isolationism in the face of a degrading and superficial public sphere. The hypersensitive temporal perceptions of Dorian Gray, Marcel, and Leopold Bloom retreat from the corruption of the public sphere into a private disavowal of any but the most bodily, intimate temporal rhythms. On the other hand we find a seemingly paradoxical assertion that for all their temporal isolationism these refined private characters are capable, precisely because of their isolation, of achieving a cosmic or cosmopolitan union with a larger humanity not hindered by the determinations of nationally regulated clocks. This position, which I call *temporal transnationalism,* asserts a cosmic connection of individual bodies, isolated from their immediate contexts but finding union and communion in a cosmopolitan temporality. Kern's use of these two constructions of human temporality depends on a fusion or confusion of two independent traditions within modernist literary criticism. The *temporal isolationism* model draws on a reading of modernist temporality as exclusively Bergsonian, an allegation leveled against modernist writers by Wyndham Lewis as early as 1928. With his language of delicate temporal sensibilities, his disavowal of spatial and linguistic corruption, and his provocative metaphor of the durée turning away from its own shadow, Bergson staked out a reactionary retreat from the inherently corrupt world of shared, public values. The *temporal transnationalism* position draws on a more recent characterization of modernism as a predominantly metropolitan form, disengaged from and disenchanted with national contexts and eschewing all local determinations in favor of a cosmopolitan, liberal humanism. This characterization emerges largely from Marxist critiques of modernism's "exilic" condition by Terry Eagleton and Raymond Williams, for whom modernism's canonization is an attempt on the part of artists and scholars to avoid or evade the political responsibilities of national conflict.[19] While these two critical traditions have shed productive light on one aspect of modernist time consciousness, they have inadvertently led us to ignore the full range of late nineteenth- and early twentieth-century modernist engagements with temporality. I certainly do not mean to exorcise modernism entirely of its association with the subjective, the interior, or indeed the private. Such associations can, and inevitably will, be made. As David Harvey suggests, though, reference to private time becomes meaningful only within the context of the public discourses of time that I have been charting here (267).

My suggestion is that an extrication of modernist time from its association with Bergsonian isolationism and metropolitan transnationalism remains a crucial preliminary gesture in any study that hopes to move beyond the static image of a modernist consciousness forever shuttling between isolated individualism and jubilant cosmopolitanism.

In chapter 2 I discuss the implications for modernist scholarship of treating Bergson's particular version of modernist time as merely one of a vast array of competing models of temporality rather than as an indelible encapsulation of his age's zeitgeist. Situating Bergson's theory of the durée in *Time and Free Will* within the context of the movement to standardize world time (he was composing it as the delegates met in Washington), I suggest that Bergson's ambitious attempt to wrestle the qualitative and vitalistic time dimension away from the quantitative and mechanistic dimension of space is only truly meaningful within the historical context of the standard time movement, which after all promised to seamlessly unify global time and space in one grandiose cartographic gesture. Bergson, in a reactionary move, tries desperately to keep time and space *apart*, affirming the purely qualitative character of the former in contradistinction to the purely quantitative (and thus degraded) character of the latter. Yet Bergson's rear-guard response to the challenges of standard time's global vision represents only one of many attempts to sort out the implications of global standardization for human and narrative time in the fin de siècle. Placing his theories of time in dialogue with those of immediate contemporaries (some of them antagonists), such as Einstein and the delegates to the Prime Meridian Conference, I mean to suggest that Bergson's conception of a private durée in perpetual conflict with a degraded public sphere was by no means the only or even the most culturally dominant articulation of modernist temporality. Bergson's attempt to reconcile the pressing demands of global spatiotemporal representation is arguably both backward and inward looking in its orientation. His primary chosen interlocutor is the fifth-century BCE philosopher Zeno of Elea, whose famous paradoxes he attempts to disprove. Ultimately, *Time and Free Will* concludes with the assertion that genuine freedom requires us to "turn our eyes from the shadow which follows us and retire into ourselves" (233). Yet other modernists looked forward and outward in their attempts to reconcile their own experience of modern time with the dictates of the new global map. Foremost among these, as I have suggested, were the novelists of the age, whose work increasingly gestured hyperbolically outside of comfortable generic, national, and linguistic boundaries and who thus could not artistically or philosophically afford the luxury of Bergson's reactionary retreat from the muck and grime of the spatial public realm of contextually determined values.

The equation of Bergsonian temporality with all forms of aesthetic modernist time crucially informs a long-standing critique from the left of the bourgeois and decadent interiority of aesthetic modernism. This tradition, beginning with Georg Lukács in *The Meaning of Contemporary Realism* and achieving its most sophisticated articulation in Raymond Williams's collected writings on modernism, finds modernist writers mired, like Bergson, in the interior dimensions of a private time abstractly separated from historical change, place, and necessity. For Williams this subjectivism and abstraction was a function of that most phantasmagoric of modern entities, the cosmopolitan city, which, with its dizzying array of consumer pleasures culled from the far reaches of empire, promised the metropolitan modernist writer the intoxicating allure of being placeless and homeless, a global citizen without any of the burdens of mundane participation in the actual national polity. Yet if modernist writers tended in some senses toward a cosmic abstraction from localism, the discrete particularities of space, place, and nation equally exerted a powerful influence on their sensibilities. While critics on the left have attacked aesthetic modernism for its apolitical cosmopolitanism, modernism's enfant terrible of the right, Wyndham Lewis, accused the majority of his modernist contemporaries of being localist and nationalist to the point of fascism. Surprisingly, according to Lewis in his book *Time and Western Man*, it is their allegiance to Bergson that makes Joyce, Proust, Stein, Pound, and other writers such fanatical nationalists. Perhaps the first critic to associate modernist writers in toto with Bergsonian philosophy, Lewis provocatively identifies Bergson's obsession with temporality as little more than a cloak for regionalism and provincialism. I devote a substantial portion of chapter 2 to these claims because they hint suggestively at a modernist version of temporality dramatically different from the metropolitan transnationalist model. Situating Lewis's arguments within a constellation of fairly recent critical studies that pay close attention to modernism's tortured engagement with its own national contexts, I suggest that time in modernist writing is a far more fraught and ambivalent construct than it appears under the Bergsonian or metropolitan models. It was precisely because of their ambivalent and even tortured engagement with questions of private, national, and transnational values that the modernists were uniquely situated to interrogate the radical novelty and provocative disjointedness of standard time's reshaping of the globe.

The interest of modernist writers in the relationship between time, empire, and global space can perhaps more productively be traced to late nineteenth-century English literary models than to late nineteenth-century continental philosophy. Popular British narratives of empire in the 1880s and 1890s demonstrated a keen appreciation of the power of temporal standardization as a tool for the management of diverse spaces and populations. If the twentieth-century modernists, as I will argue, found standard time's homogenization of global space and time problematic, fin de siècle "imperial gothics" tended both thematically and formally to reinforce and naturalize standard time's power to unify the globe, bringing resistant populations and spaces within a precisely coordinated network. In chapter 3 I examine representations of temporal standardization and nonsynchronicity in a selection of popular adventure novels of the fin de siècle, all of which are explicitly concerned with the management of exotic spaces and bodies that initially resist any kind of spatiotemporal mapping. The title characters of H. Rider Haggard's *She* (1887) and Bram Stoker's *Dracula* (1897) refuse to fit into prescribed temporal and spatial limits. Ontological outsiders, largely because they are *temporal* outsiders, Ayesha and Dracula are literally deathless and ageless monsters resistant to the ultimate limits and limitations that human temporality would otherwise place on them. Yet despite the fundamental atemporality of these imperial outsiders and their cultural milieus, the narrative apparatus of the imperial gothic works stridently to contain and domesticate them within a clearly defined standardized spatiotemporal scheme. This happens not only thematically, with representations of actual instruments of spatiotemporal management, but also formally, at the level of narrative construction. In contrast to the ceaseless formal experimentation of the modernist texts of chapter 4, the imperial gothics enforce rigidly controlled narrative structures that tightly synchronize narrative chronology, eliminating rather than accommodating heterogeneous temporalities. The goal of these texts is to remove any threat to a vision of seamlessly unified space and time by narrating the extermination of temporal outsiders potentially threatening to the epistemological certainty of world standard time, situating them neatly within carefully plotted latitudes and longitudes. The management of exotic nonsynchronicities in the imperial periphery was thus an eminently cartographic problem, as I illustrate not only in readings of Haggard and Stoker, but also in an examination of Rudyard Kipling's cartographic strategies in *Kim* (1901) of assimilating and instrumentalizing "Asiatic" temporality, wedding it seamlessly to the imperial demands of British punctuality. Whereas modernist texts of the early twentieth century radically destabilized the coordinates of world standard time in their texts, late nineteenth-century adventure novels rigidly enforced them.

In contrast to the direct references to Greenwich that I identify in twentieth-century texts in chapter 4, the texts under consideration in chapter 3 are notable for their lack of reference to the Observatory itself or to the name Greenwich. Instead these texts represent railway time, the Bradshaw guide to train timetables, telegraphy, and other time-based technologies, as if they were independent of any national control or determination. Railroad time is not Greenwich or British time for Haggard, Stoker, and Kipling. It is simply *time*. Their texts do not expose the relationship between Greenwich and imperial power, as do the modernist texts in chapter 4. Rather they naturalize that relationship, rendering it invisible. Realizing, in aesthetic form, the ultimate goal of Sandford Fleming and the standard time advocates, these narratives render human time and Greenwich Mean Time equivalent and nonproblematic, smoothing over the intransigent alterity of those populations potentially resistant to the imperial manipulations enabled by a global common coordinate frame. In contrast modernism's efforts to stylistically reconfigure notions of social connectivity and temporal relationships will shatter both the form and the content of this marriage of convenience between Greenwich time and global temporality, in the process opening up spaces and times for alternative social configurations.

Chapter 4 constitutes the heart of my argument about the role of time in high modernist texts. Greenwich Mean Time is explicitly invoked in novels by Joseph Conrad, James Joyce, and Virginia Woolf as a hollow and often dangerously manipulative substitute for more socially and aesthetically productive forms of temporality. In these texts Greenwich time is situated within its larger political, commercial, and imperial contexts, bearing evidence of the extent to which Greenwich, by the early twentieth century, had entered modernist consciousness as a powerful symbol of authoritarian control from a distance and of the management of diverse populations. Exposing what Conrad's character Comrade Ossipon calls "the shortcomings of timetables," these modernists sought to dislocate their own treatment of human temporality from its enlistment in the standard time system by resituating temporal processes within more meaningful, contextually determined and variable social patterns. These three texts are particularly useful for a study of standard time and modernism because, in making direct reference to Greenwich Mean Time, Greenwich coordinated clocks, or the Greenwich Observatory itself, they bring to the surface latent tensions over temporality within a larger body of modernist fiction not as explicitly or obviously concerned with Greenwich. As with any attempt to situate imaginative literature within the extraliterary contexts of imperialism, political legislation, or scientific innovation, however, these readings of British novels inevitably raise the problem of mediation. To what extent is it possible to suggest that the world-historical transformations of global standard time, managed not by artists but by scientists, politicians, and industrialists, had any kind of impact on a handful of writers, alone in their studies, as they crafted their narratives?

Extensive consideration of the problem of mediation between literature and science is a nearly routine move in the best studies of this nature, which self-consciously walk a fine line between atomistic and zeitgeist accounts of mediation. While the atomistic approach can be tediously local (combing over authors' journals to find direct references to contemporaneous developments in history), the zeitgeist approach can be irresponsibly global, claiming simply, for example, that "time was in the air" in the fin de siècle, as Clark Blaise repeatedly does in his book on Sandford Fleming.[20] For Michael Whitworth the disadvantage of the atomistic approach is that it can only "report utterances" on the part of individual authors, without determining "their relation to any larger system." Alternately zeitgeist approaches, Whitworth writes, are incapable of "discriminating between different social networks," erroneously assuming that "an entire society would have been saturated uniformly in . . . new knowledge" (*Einstein's Wake*, 18). This more general methodological tension becomes particularly acute in studies of modernism and empire, which, as Patricia E. Chu explains, have had to wrestle with definitions of modernism as simultaneously an aesthetic and a historical phenomenon (55). Astradur Eysteinsson's oft-quoted statement of the central paradox of modernist studies is thus particularly relevant in theorizing the relationship between modernism and empire, as Chu suggests. Eysteinsson asks "how the concept of autonomy, so crucial to many theories of modernism, can possibly coexist with the equally prominent view of modernism as a historically explosive paradigm."[21] When modernism has traditionally existed as a literary category primarily because of its purely aesthetic features, how is it possible to maintain the category of modernism while opening up its aesthetic autonomy to larger social networks?

Attempts to resolve this paradox in studies of modernism and technology have often tended toward a stark opposition between the purely aesthetic cultural product and the anti-aesthetic forces of technological growth, always and everywhere opposed to the liberty and autonomy of creative expression. According to this paradigm, modernism implicitly opposes technology, imperial or otherwise, in an attempt to maintain its aesthetic autonomy. This kind of oppositional approach is characteristic of Kern's treatment of the relationship between modernist art and standard time, as numerous critics have observed.[22] For Sara Danius, Kern's discussion of public and private time in modernist art is representative of a larger tendency in modernist scholarship to see modernism as a *reaction* to modernity, paralleling, echoing, or contesting its development. According to this paradigm, Danius writes, "aesthetic modernism tends to be understood as external to modernity" (33). In her study of technology and modernism she proposes a model of mediation according to which technological modernity is *constitutive* of modernist art, internal to it rather than external. According to Danius modernist aesthetics is "immersed" in the technological, economic, and social conditions of the late nineteenth century and early twentieth. The aesthetic strategies of the modernists are thus analogous to and informed by technological strategies of reconfiguring social relations. "Even if high-modernist practices often sought to transcend or even cancel what was thought of as public time, instrumental reason, and the logic of commodification," Danius writes, "it can nevertheless be demonstrated that those art forms were affected, enabled, and to some extent even caused by those developments" (10).

Danius's constitutive model of the relationship between modernist aesthetics and technological modernity can be productively brought to bear on the thesis proposed by Fredric Jameson in his landmark essay "Modernism and Imperialism," a work that has crucially informed my conceptualization of the subject of this book. In his essay Jameson identifies the formal contradiction unique to modernist writers between 1884 (the date of the Berlin Conference) and the First World War as a problem of global cartography. Locating "a significant structural segment of the economic system as a whole" outside of the home country, imperialism in its advanced stage confronted the modernist writer with the conceptual and experiential limitations of his or her own spatial experience. Unable to grasp the functioning of the global economic order as a whole, because unable to imagine the "life experience and life world" of the colonies overseas, the modernist faces a problem in cognitive mapping. Modernists such as E. M. Forster, according to Jameson, "solved" this problem by stylistically invoking the language and imagery of infinity, a style that served as the "place-holder" for the "unrepresentable totality" (58). Jameson's essay, the first to theorize a relationship between modernism and empire, has been criticized, often validly, from many quarters.[23] Yet his identification of global mapping as the central problem of the modernist period remains highly provocative and endlessly productive. Cartography as an organizing metaphor usefully identifies the period's obsession for charting, classifying, and manipulating distant space. Certainly my thesis that British fiction between 1884 and 1930 is characterized by a tension over spatiotemporal mapping strategies owes much to Jameson. What is missing from his account, though, is an acknowledgment of the existing technologies of representation that would have aided the modernists in their mapping strategies, ameliorating the kinds of cognitive or existential gaps that led them, in Jameson's view, to fall back on mystical invocations of infinity when confronted with global space. Jameson quite rightly invokes 1884 as codifying a new world economic order because of the Berlin Conference, but he unsurprisingly ignores the International Prime Meridian Conference, which occurred nearly simultaneously in that same year. World standard time not only enabled the efficiency of advanced global imperialism, but more important (for a study of aesthetics), it provided English citizens with a conceptual tool for cognitively reading that new imperial space as intrinsically unified with England through the hyperprecision of Greenwich time. Jameson ignores the network of means by which English modernists could fill in their conceptual gaps about the functioning and experience of the global economy. One such means was certainly the new world map, with Greenwich as its spatiotemporal zero point. In this sense my treatment of the relationship between the aesthetics of modernism and the technological and juridical innovations of the standard time system employs a constitutive model such as the one advocated by Danius. World standard time crucially informed modernist conceptions of time-space coordination, even as modernist aesthetic strategies challenged its limits and limitations as a representational tool.

In chapter 1 I present London *Times* newspaper coverage of the Prime Meridian Conference as well as discussions of the standardization of time in a number of late nineteenth-century journals. In chapter 4 I offer a meticulous analysis of the *Times* coverage of an attempted bombing of the Greenwich Royal Observatory in 1894. This body of evidence is intended to suggest that Greenwich's role in managing global space was widely publicized in the fin de siècle, substantiating the claim of Conrad's Mr. Vladimir that the "whole civilized world" had heard of Greenwich. It is not entirely necessary to my argument, though, to prove that each of the writers I discuss followed this coverage. Conrad almost certainly read the *Times* reports of the bombing, but beyond this I do not claim. Nor do I mean to argue that each representation of Greenwich in the modernist novels under consideration shows evidence of an intentional, direct response or reaction to the Prime Meridian Conference. Rather they bear evidence of the extent to which Greenwich had entered the consciousness of the modernists as a powerful symbol of authoritarian control from a distance and of the management of diverse populations. National pride over the institution's position and consciousness of the symbolic resonance of being the new global time zero began to mark references to Greenwich in the early twentieth century, as a number of provocative references to the institution indicate. Randall Stevenson, for example, notes a jubilant reference to Greenwich Mean Time in Arthur Wing Pinero's 1885 play, *The Magistrate*.[24] By far the most famous incident, though, is Martial Bourdin's attempted bombing of the Observatory. As I argue in chapter 4, Conrad's disavowal of any public knowledge of Bourdin's motivations is belied by coverage in the *Times* that clearly indicated a public awareness that the Observatory was associated with intense political controversy. Journalists in 1894 expected their readers to know why the Greenwich Observatory, with its symbolic and actual control over temporal rhythm, was a potential target for foreign and domestic dissidents. Michael Newton has demonstrated as much in his discovery of documents in the Royal Greenwich Observatory archives suggesting that between 1880 and 1885 the Home Office had examined the Observatory for its vulnerability to dynamite attacks. "Clearly," Newton writes, the Observatory had been considered "a possible target" well before the alleged attack (141). Similarly Karen Piper has uncovered documents attesting to Scotland Yard's reaction to an alleged plot by prominent suffragettes to disable the Observatory. British police guarded the building in 1915 because of a report that suffragettes had been overheard on a tram car saying, "Wait till they start on the Greenwich Observatory; London, without time, will cause them to wake up" (37). If Greenwich's spatiotemporal privilege is a mere historical anachronism today, at the height of the British Empire its status as time zero seemed the crowning symbol of empire's assumed authority to measure, regulate, and delimit the uneven temporalities of global modernity.

A necessarily global phenomenon, world standard time's greatest impact was arguably on populations whose temporal standards and models were radically different from those of the imperial centers. In chapter 5 I turn to contemporaneous literature produced by English-language, subcontinental Indian writers in order to investigate the politics of time from a colonial context. In the case of India the relationship between modernism and empire was necessarily dependent on the conditions of modernization. The railway and telegraph lines, both their physical presence and their interaction with preexistent models of temporal rhythm, play central roles in such texts as S.K. Ghosh's *The Prince of Destiny* (1919) and K.S. Venkataramani's *Murugan, the Tiller* (1927). The possibility of a politics of anti-imperial time in India depends on the extent to which technological modernization is assimilated and adjusted to cultural constructs of the West and the East. *The Prince of Destiny* is a particularly revealing text in its juxtaposition of a temporally standardized, anti-imperial revolution against a cultural construction of the East as a timeless, "cosmopolitan," and counter-revolutionary entity. In India, where the stakes for a viable politics of time were particularly acute, its complex and ambivalent interaction with politically inflected cultural models of Eastern values made its realization equally as fraught as it was in the imperial centers. Extending my history of standard time and narrative beyond the national borders of Great Britain, this chapter intervenes in postcolonial debates over the role of nonsynchronous time in constituting a viable project of countermodernity, cautioning against the dangers of essentializing a unique Indian temporality linguistically or narratively incommensurable with standard time's grid or Western narrative's conventions. Whereas Meenakshi Mukherjee in *The Twice Born Fiction* has argued that early Indian fiction in English often simply romanticized timelessness and the heroic past, I contend that the tensions between competing representations of time in early Indian fiction are rooted in an awareness of the socioeconomic transformations that accompanied standardized transportation and communication networks. This chapter does not presume to be an exhaustive study of the role of Greenwich in English-language Indian novels. Such a task would require a book-length study of its own. My intention is to suggest how the conclusions of my study of standard time and British literature might open up potentially invigorating investigations of the politics of time in early twentieth-century literature of the global South. If modernist time has been wrongly construed as isolationist, antinational, and antimaterial, postcolonial time has similarly been misconstrued in terms of brash contrariety: contra modernity, contra history, contra nationality. This construal of postcolonial temporality offers the tantalizing notion of time as a realm of sheer *jouissance* and anarchical rhythm, but it forecloses a host of important questions about the mechanics of temporal imperialism, questions that were quite clear-sightedly explored in the narratives of Ghosh and Venkataramani. These early English-language Indian writers placed culturally incommensurable models of time and timelessness in tension with industrial manifestations of standardized temporality, demonstrating an acute awareness of the cultural and political violence accompanying standard time's incursion into the subcontinent.

Time has remained strangely untheorized in many strains of contemporary cultural theory, having given way to place and other cartographic constructs.[25] Since the 1970s the more visible and enduring theories of power have been predominantly concerned with analyses of space rather than time.[26] The contemporary theoretical landscape is rife with spatial paradigms, models, and diagrams, from Michel Foucault's panopticon to Gilles Deleuze and Félix Guattari's rhizomes and plateaus. The globalized world is often conceived diagrammatically, as a system of borders (permeable or impermeable), territories (sovereign or subject), networks (of capital and communication), flows (of information and immigrants), and various models of postpanoptical forms of surveillance.[27] When time enters the discussion it is often only as that which globalization has already made obsolete. It has been "compressed," "distantiated," or "shattered" with the simultaneity and instantaneity of contemporary forms of communication.[28] This shift from the chronometric to the cartographic suggests that, at the end of history, all that matters is the extent and reach of an irrepressible modernity as it gradually enfolds the world map. Yet struggles over standard time in the early twentieth century reveal the radical instability of that globally synchronized modernity, dependent on a continual colonization of social time requiring extensive capital investment, technological modification, legislative sanction, and cultural saturation. The elimination of time as a resource, a limit, or arguably even a viable field of research is a continuous site of political struggle rather than a fait accompli. *The Cosmic Time of Empire* provides a preliminary chapter in the history of that politics of time, representing the standardization of world time, along with the struggles over its implementation and its cultural representation in the art of the early twentieth century, as a necessary and inaugural moment in the history of globalization.

CHAPTER 1

Standard Time, Greenwich, and the Cosmopolitan Clock

One of the "hallmarks of modernity," writes Henri Lefebvre in his 1974 study, *The Production of Space,* is its "expulsion" or "erasure" of time. Inscribed in spaces and in social relationships in the premodern, time in modernity is subordinated to the economic and expelled from the political. In deliberately violent imagery Lefebvre writes that time in modernity "has been murdered by society" (96). If this separation of time from space was so dramatic and violent, why, Lefebvre wonders, did it not cause an "outcry"? How did it become "part and parcel of social norms"? "How many lies have their roots" in the separation of time from social spaces (96)?

In this chapter I present a reading of the 1884 Prime Meridian Conference, the event at which a world standard time based on the Greenwich prime meridian was internationally sanctioned. Careful analysis of the debates of 1884 reveals the extent to which modernity's "murder" of time did in fact generate prodigious resistance. Dissenting delegates at the conference protested the assimilation of time into an empty, universal value system, asserting the sovereignty of social norms of time within nations and the sociocultural or religious components of temporal relationships on which those norms were based. These protests were not an instance of the familiar modernist gesture toward a valorized primitive time. Indeed the primitive or premodern is nowhere invoked in the debates. Rather they were affirmations of time's social value staged from *within* the heart of the modern. To recapture and revitalize these arguments, which received no press coverage in 1884 and no mention in the handful of historical accounts, is not simply to register a historical footnote of the feeble protests of geopolitical sore losers. It is to offer instead an opening up of the possibilities of temporal politics from within the modern. In later chapters I argue that modernist literary artists explored dynamic and complex reinscriptions of social time within the spaces of modernity. Speaking the name of Greenwich in relation to the political, the commercial, and the imperial, modernist artists punctured a hole in modernity's edifice of temporal neutrality, in the process reimagining networks of temporal relationships in their prose that were becoming increasingly untenable within the spaces of modern life.

"ANOTHER INJUSTICE TO HIS BLEEDING COUNTRY":
THE MISPLACED IDEA OF STANDARD TIME

To locate modernity's erasure of social time in a single event in 1884 would be highly specious historical argumentation. Clearly the emptying out of social time was the work of several centuries, involving the de-theologizing of time among Enlightenment *philosophes,* the discourse of immutable physical laws that Newton's *Principia Mathematica* enabled in the seventeenth century, and the denigration of the artisanal laborer's irregular work rhythms that E. P. Thompson describes in his essay "Time, Work-Discipline, and Industrial Capitalism." These are all part of the broader historical canvas onto which a portrait of the suppression of social time would have to be painted. Still, if one wanted an exact date at which the erasure of social time became a *global* phenomenon (and modernity, as Anthony Giddens has argued, is intrinsically the globalization of organizational institutions [*The Consequences of Modernity,* 63]), one could do worse than point to Wednesday, October 15, 1884, when one major international conference was well under way and another was in a critical early stage. On that day the reader of the London *Times* could see on the same page, columns apart, an account of the first major vote of the Prime Meridian Conference and an account of the upcoming Berlin Conference on West Africa, an event England was watching carefully because of the potential threat it posed to the monopoly of trade on the oil rivers of the area later named Nigeria. Here, on one day, were accounts of arguably the two most important legislative events of fin de siècle imperialism: the Berlin Conference, at which the protocols were set for the territorial subdivision of Africa for future exploitation, and the Prime Meridian Conference, at which the protocols were set for the creation of a globally synchronized time that would substantially enable that exploitation.

The proximity of these two events to one another should give pause. One event, universally recognized as the symbol and enactment of European colonial greed and imperial hubris on a grandiose scale, occurred within months of an ostensibly disinterested, scientific, and politically neutral event meant to eliminate "barbarous" time-keeping practices.[1] The one conference legitimated territorial dominance and commercial monopoly under the banner of free and fair trade; the other legitimated the construction of a universal time system dictated from the center of imperial power under the banner of convenience and progress. In both cases national pride and unfair advantage were attributed solely to the continental powers, with England taking up the wearisome burden of the needs of future generations. "Wherever the British flag flies," the *Times* correspondent wrote of the Berlin Conference, "trade is free to all comers. British commerce seeks only a fair field and no favour." While Germany and France demanded "commercial freedom for all nations on the Congo," their practices in West Africa were marked by a "reciprocal guarantee of advantages." Britain, on the other hand, had come by its monopoly of trade on the oil rivers fairly. If trade on the lower Niger was controlled by "a monopoly of British merchants," the correspondent wrote, "this is due to no favouring tariffs or exclusive privileges, but to superiority in enterprise, capital, and skill." Fair trade was desirable on the Congo, over which England exerted no influence, but not on the Niger. "To place the Congo under an international commission would be a step in advance," the *Times* reporter continued, but "to put the Niger under the same kind of control would be as clearly a step backwards."[2] Fair trade, in other words, was fine for other nations, but not for England, which was above petty international lobbying for favor. England possessed skill and enterprise as ontological virtues above and beyond the sphere of the political.

Three columns over, in its report of the Prime Meridian Conference, the *Times* represented England, in a different context, as the marker of apolitical superiority. Here again opposition to England's advantage could be attributed only to petty nationalism: "Nothing but extremely sensitive national feeling could have stood in the way of the adoption of the English line [meridian]." That Greenwich, the site of an observatory and not a national capital, was to be the source of the prime meridian should have been enough to assuage "national pride." England's interests *coincide* with those of "geography, navigation, and science generally," just as its monopoly on the Niger signaled the triumph of capital and trade generally. To pose the question of political or commercial advantage in the case of the prime meridian was to court absurdity and caricature. In his stage adaptation of *The Secret Agent* Joseph Conrad would capture this rhetoric of bewilderment in the face of political attacks on the sacrosanct realm of astronomy. "I can't see how [astronomy] can have any connexion with politics," a socialite muses after the botched bombing of the Greenwich Observatory, "those anarchists must be simply mad" (*Three Plays*, 134).

The need to find political oppression in even the march of scientific progress marked one as a nationalist ideologue or a half-wit, as the correspondent for the *Times* clearly suggested in his primer on basic astronomy, provided for the common London reader on the eve of the Prime Meridian Conference. In this report the *Times*, recognizing that "it is a matter of common experience that adult readers may retain but faint recollections of what they knew as schoolboys," provided a capable overview of the rotation of the earth on its axis, the mean solar day, John Harrison's chronometers, and the dominance in terms of tonnage of Greenwich-based navigation. While the need for a universal Greenwich-based meridian is a matter of "schoolboy" logic, a simple syllogism, the role of opposition to such simple logic is assigned, at the end of the article, to a stage Irishman, who sees oppression even in the contours of simple logic: "There is a familiar story of an Irishman who came on business to Liverpool, and was half-an-hour late for an appointment. He exhibited his watch in evidence of his punctuality, and when it was explained to him that he had local time, and that the sun rose half-an-hour later in Ireland than in England, he bitterly protested against the arrangement as another injustice to his bleeding country."[3]

The anecdotal Irishman foolishly sees immutable astronomical relationships in terms of political power, and national oppression in even the most objective of scientific processes. James Joyce, in the "Lestrygonians" section of *Ulysses*, will echo this Irishman's protests in the context of Irish subordination to England, as Leopold Bloom recalls the half-hour (actually twenty-five-minute) difference between Greenwich time and the time at the Dunsink Observatory in Dublin. Joyce retells this story in terms that make the political manipulation of astronomical neutrality explicit, with Bloom imagining himself forcibly expelled from the Dunsink Observatory for even posing the question of temporal difference. Salman Rushdie in *Midnight's Children* also dramatizes a debate over the political manipulation of time, as two characters discuss the proposed half-hour difference between India and the newly formed Pakistan:

> "It was only a matter of time," my father said, with every appearance of pleasure; but time has been an unsteady affair, in my experience, not a thing to be relied upon. It could even be partitioned: the clocks in Pakistan would run half an hour ahead of their Indian counterparts. . . . Mr. Kemal, who wanted nothing to do with Partition, was fond of saying, "Here's proof of the folly of the scheme! Those Leaguers plan to abscond with a whole thirty minutes! Time Without Partitions" Mr. Kemal cried, "That's the ticket!" And S. P. Butt said, "If they can change the time just like that, what's real any more? I ask you? What's true?" (86–87)

While Rushdie's characters take seriously the symbolic violence of manipulating national time, the author of the *Times* article on the anecdotal Irishman mocks the linkage of territorial control with the processes of astronomy. To raise the question of the Irishman is to court absurdity. The elimination of multiple prime meridians is simply an elimination of unnecessary confusion, a view that remains the dominant understanding of the conference. In his report of October 14 the *Times* correspondent writes that the vote for Greenwich will make the Prime Meridian Conference "memorable to scientific history if it has put an end to one worse than useless diversity."[4]

The reporter's distaste for diversity may strike the twenty-first-century reader as inherently offensive. The notion of temporal diversity, or in more familiar postcolonial terms, hybridity and heterogeneity, has become a favored locus for a liberatory politics of difference.[5] Rather than stage a critique at the level of ontological difference, however, I would like to explore the material and social manipulations of standard time that are obscured by this loaded rhetoric of ontological diversity. As I have been attempting to demonstrate, the *Times* reporter tries to foreclose any kind of meaningful debate about the politics of Greenwich standard time by marking any opposition as a naïve expression of petty nationalism or cultural diversity. Fighting this rhetoric by championing cultural heterogeneity simply by virtue of its diversity would be to accept the reporter's terms and to miss his key act of rhetorical subterfuge, which asks the reader to equate a British institution with the immutable laws of science, progress, fair trade, and civility, while cloaking the immense material disadvantages that equation will naturalize. Why was there no "outcry" against the murder of time, as Lefebvre asks? Because the terms of the debate were defined in such a way that no rational person could fail to take the dominant view. Battling the rotation of the earth on its axis in favor of inconvenient cultural diversity would, after all, be quixotic in the extreme.

This equation of the needs of British commerce with the immutable laws of Nature is part of a larger narrative of technological determinism, which Merrit Roe Smith has traced back to the Enlightenment, but which reaches its apogee in the period of the fin de siècle, when the belief that "technological developments determine the course of human events" had become "dogma" (7). The *Times* reporter's castigation of the Irishman for railing against the natural law of British commercial dominance represents what Bruce Bimber has called a "nomological" account of technological development, according to which development is not culturally or socially determined, but proceeds according to "inexorable logic." The progress of technology in nomological accounts, Bimber writes, is "naturally given and independently drives social development" (84). A corollary to the nomological account of technological determinism is that its products (railways, steel-production facilities, etc.) will produce the same social effects regardless of human needs, judgments, or cultural differences.

The question of agency is a crucial problem in accounts of standard time, which, when it makes even a cursory appearance in accounts of time in the fin de siècle, appears as a technologically determined fact emerging inevitably out of the orderly march of scientific laws rather than as the political intervention of a handful of advocates to facilitate the operation of global commerce. As a case in point, Patricia Murphy, in her account of time in the Victorian period, writes that "the railways" responded to inconsistency in local times "by attempting to standardize time" (13). Who does she mean by "the railways"—its engineers, its administrators, or the actual iron rails themselves? This may seem a petty quibble over an otherwise illuminating treatment of the subject, but the use of "the railways" in lieu of any actual person (W. F. Allen, secretary of the Railway Time Convention, who proposed a Greenwich-based North American rail synchronization in 1883, would be a prime candidate) is symptomatic of a larger confusion over the sources of temporal standardization. Allen himself argued that his proposal did not represent the overwhelming needs or opinions of "the railways" in any kind of global sense,[6] but his role in standardization is eclipsed in Murphy's account and others, his individual agency transformed into that of the rails themselves.

The notion that the standardization of global time was a step in the long orderly march of inevitable scientific discovery is clearly argued by one of standard time's chief architects, Sandford Fleming. In the introductory paragraphs of his essay "Time-Reckoning for the Twentieth Century" Fleming represents the process leading from temporal diversity to uniformity as one of order, simplicity, and efficiency. His account disavows any personal agency on the part of the creators or beneficiaries of the standard time system. Yet rhetorical demands to endow his twentieth-century world with actors continually belie this attempt, as "civilization" (345) later becomes "men of business" (347), and "the highest authority" sanctioning the system is revealed to be not God, but U.S. President Chester Arthur (345). This is not to suggest that I am simply advocating substituting individual names for institutions and countries in a kind of microcritique of macro-analysis, a process that, as Thomas Misa argues, simply reinscribes determinism at the level of the individual. Rather my point is that the disavowal of human agency in the social production of time is precisely one of the major outcomes of standard time's replacement of the manipulations of particular actors within institutional settings with an ephemeral entity simply called *time*.

In an 1892 pamphlet advocating Greenwich-based standard time for the world, Maj. E. Noel of the rifle brigade, in deliberately militaristic language, labels time the enemy of international convenience and suggests that standardization can effectively neutralize its power: "Time is ever passing on, or, as we say 'flying' and we call him 'the enemy'; but, although we cannot detain this flitting enemy, we can in any case regulate his flight and make it subservient to international convenience" (4).[7] The enemy, in Noel's terms, is not a particular configuration of human time, expressed and embedded in specific communities or forms of labor, but a metaphysical entity that Noel seems to have paradoxically caught in the physical crosshairs of his rifle, ready to blow it away, but gradually conceding the necessity of hobbling it in the foot for the sake of the international community. Although it could be argued that standard time's role in the process of social disembedding and exploitation is a fairly minor corollary to more pressing and tangible issues of commercial dominance, political corruption, and underdevelopment, all of which certainly predate the incursion of standard time, it would be a mistake to underestimate the power of standard time in naturalizing and making invisible these larger processes of global inequity. An abstract, irrefutable standard time assumes the ontological burden of justification for imperial and neo-imperial dominance. It is time that now becomes the enemy, an enemy traced by standard time advocates not to 1884, but back into the far reaches of antiquity. The demands on time that accompany standardized rail technology are just the latest manifestation of, for instance, Kronos devouring his children, a bogeyman that standard time did not create and that in fact its hyperefficient system had taken leaps and bounds toward beheading for the benefit of the global community.[8]

If time itself is the enemy, how does one fight it? This contest between a metaphysical oppressor and the physical outcomes of its cultural and economic oppression is clear in the experience of the former colonies, where British demands were equated with the laws of science and nature. In Ngũgĩ wa Thiong'o's novel *Petals of Blood* (1977) a community of Kenyan farmers is dispossessed of its ancestral homeland because the farmers default on interest payments for loans the new government has forced them to accept. "Only one condition," they are told: "Payment had to be regular. Easy" (318). Just as the old woman Nyakinyua is unable to persuade the populace to violently resist an oppressor they cannot definitively locate ("Who would they fight now? The Government? The Banks?" [327]), the question of defaulted interest payments similarly confuses the source of oppression. Rather than fight the unfairly structured system that requires the owners of land to lease it from those who stole it, the dispossessed would have to fight time itself. They would be railing against the logically indisputable fact that the fifteenth of the month comes when it comes. In making such an argument they would be no better than the Irishman who finds political oppression in the fact that the sun rises half an hour earlier in Britain. The system that harnesses commerce and culture to a synchronized time is culturally specific and untranslatable to the context of a 1960s agrarian Kenyan village. We might think of standard time, as it makes its way around the world in the decades after 1884, in terms of what the Brazilian literary critic Roberto Schwarz has called a "misplaced idea," a cultural production that emerges out of acute tensions and developments in one country and is then transplanted onto another society in such a way that the seams show, creating a temporal Frankenstein's monster. Greenwich Mean Time, however, is not just an idea, but a cultural construct accompanied by a massive technological infrastructure that supports, enforces, and justifies it—the railways in the nineteenth century, for instance, or the Global Positioning System in the current era.

Theoretical and experimental work on the cultural specificity of particular constructions of time has been done in the past fifteen years, not by the continental, linguistic theorists favored in literary studies, but by sociologists operating under a new transnational paradigm best outlined and represented by John Urry's study *Sociology beyond Societies*. Under this new paradigm sociologists have been attempting to read outside of national contexts, posing questions instead within a global framework. What we learn from Urry, or from Barbara Adam's body of work on "multiple times," is that time is not a universal constant, but varies widely in experience and expression from one society to another, depending on a dense network of variables, from a society's dominant form of labor, to its codes for social organization, to cultural and religious factors.[9] Time is embedded, in other words, within a social community, produced by and inseparable from a grid of contextually determined variables. Pierre Bourdieu, in his landmark study of indigenous Kabyle peasants in Algeria, for example, notes the "indifference with regard to punctuality" and a disregard for the clock that renders Kabyle temporality distinct from North American or European standards. For the Kabyle, Bourdieu writes, "the parts of the day are lived as different appearances of the perceived world, nuances of which are apprehended impressionistically: 'when the sky is a little light in the East,' then 'when the sky is a little red,' 'the time of the first prayer,' then 'when the sun touches the earth,' 'when the goats come out,' 'when the goats hide,' and so on" ("Time Perspectives of the Kabyle," 223). Time told by the moment the goats come in from the stream is qualitatively different from time given by the millisecond from an instrument ("the devil's mill," as the Kabyle call the clock), whose operations are regulated by an unseen employer.

With the advent of Greenwich time social temporality is degraded to a second-order reality, while the abstract, neutral, universal constant of Greenwich-based time is projected as an immutable law, a truth of Nature discovered by science and independent of the various judgments, needs, and activities of the communities forced to restructure themselves according to its image and dictates. In the case of the Kikuyu farmers forced to conform to the notion of monthly interest payments, Greenwich time is not seamlessly integrated into the village, but rather forces a confrontation. For GMT to successfully operate as a beneficent tool for the Kikuyu, they would first have to dramatically reconfigure their mode of labor, religious beliefs, and codes of social organization. In short, all of the components that go into the production of time would have to be realigned. In the first three parts of *Petals of Blood* we see that the community's sense of time is not amenable to the notion of standardization, with its concomitant monthly interest payments. The Kikuyu farmers have been accustomed to think in terms of the annual agricultural yield, in anticipation of which they practice considerable belt-tightening self-sacrifice, an impossible attitude given the demands of regular monthly payment.[10]

The fetishization of clocks and watches in the late nineteenth and twentieth centuries is a special instance of the fetish character of commodities. Time is wrested from the specific labor with which it is intrinsically connected and applied uniformly to all labor without discrimination to extract maximum profit for minimum investment.[11] Time exists because of the movement of the earth and is felt variably by humans according to the nature of their labors. The transformation of labor-specific temporality into the rigidly controlling and uniformly ticking cosmopolitan clock is not the only or worst of the transformations of nineteenth-century capitalism and twentieth-century globalization, but it is perhaps the most intimately experienced, as time bridges the mechanical and the human, the quantitative and the qualitative.

COSMOPOLITAN TIME: THE SATISFACTION OF AN UNFELT NEED

Nineteenth-century standard time advocates insisted that time's indeterminacy, ephemerality, and diversity were oppressive stumbling blocks to the global community, and that a new system of time reckoning could rescue the hypothetical common traveler, whose social and commercial interests were imperiled by the existing lack of uniformity in time management. To evaluate these claims I turn first to the general arguments of the standard time "apostles," before moving specifically to the substance of the Washington debates of 1884.

One of standard time's most prolific and persistent advocates was Sandford Fleming, a Scottish-born engineer who moved to Canada in the 1840s and became a leader of Canadian industry and science. An admirer of Thomas Carlyle, Fleming internalized the elder Scottish sage's ethos of production, absorbing himself in a series of grand imperial projects.[12] From the 1870s on he tirelessly circulated his argument among world leaders in support of uniform civil time reckoning based on Greenwich time. This "cosmopolitan" system, he argued, would benefit not only "men of business" but also the "entire family of man"

FIGURE 1. A graphic illustration of the diversity of world time before 1884. The source of this illustration is unknown, but Sandford Fleming had a copy of it in his private papers. Sandford Fleming Fonds, "Standard Time. Pictures and Charts," box 123, folder 51, Library and Archives Canada, Ottawa.

("Time-Reckoning," 349). The unification of civil time was intended to do away with all deviance in the minutes and seconds of clocks around the globe (dramatically illustrated in figure 1), with set time zones deviating only by whole-hour integers from the time determined by calculations at the prime meridian. Fleming called for the transformation of the Earth itself into a perfect cosmopolitan clock, as he demonstrates in an illustration for his essay "Longitude and Time-Reckoning" (figure 2).

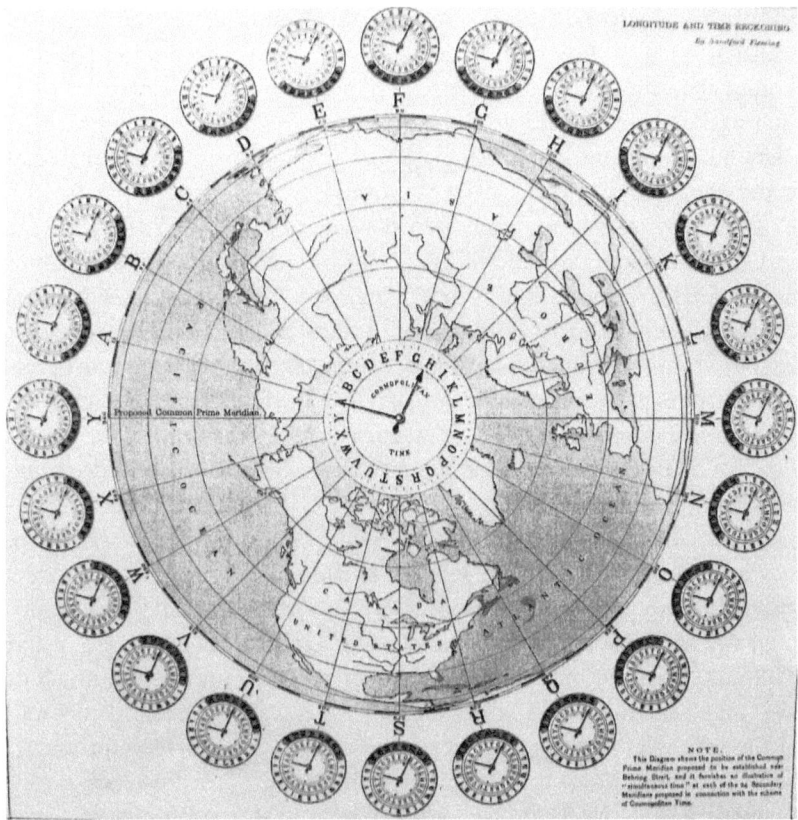

FIGURE 2. Fleming's model of the globe as the perfect timepiece. The center of the globe reads "cosmopolitan time," and each zone is assigned a letter of the alphabet (excluding J and Z). From Fleming, "Longitude and Time-Reckoning."

Cosmopolitan time was the only time that existed, Fleming believed. It was the metaphysical principle that transcended all division. Single and indivisible, the same for a Canadian entrepreneur as for an Australian aboriginal, time could be measured with "the nicest precision."

At the heart of these constructions of cosmopolitan temporality was a worldview that saw little value in nation-based models of social organization. Fleming had no particularly nationalist investment in Greenwich itself, advocating Greenwich simply because it was the most likely candidate given its established position in nautical almanacs. As Albert Lefaivre would put it at the Prime Meridian Conference, England's "power and riches" would fade,[13] rendering Greenwich's spatiotemporal privilege a mere historical oddity, which is indeed what it is today. Not everyone was as sanguine as Fleming about the merits of transnationalism, however. Charles Piazzi-Smyth, astronomer royal of Edinburgh, argued in response to a paper Fleming circulated in 1879 that national sovereignty was the real issue. Piazzi-Smyth claimed that Fleming was "running full tilt against common sense and universal experience" in proposing a transnational system of time that would necessarily disrespect nations, which were, he wrote, "directly Divine institutions enacted by God himself." In characteristically dramatic and near-biblical rhetoric, Piazzi-Smyth derided "the dread international conference which transcends all mere radical politicians in seeking ever by blood and fire to destroy most completely the ancient and necessary barriers between the nations, and to form all mankind into one vast, headless society."[14] The Russian astronomer Otto Struve of the Poulkova Observatory argued against Piazzi-Smyth's claims, declaring that "the geographer" was "by account of the nature of his occupation" a "cosmopolite" who saw no "subdivisions" in space. This was, however, purely true of "the learned world alone."[15]

Aside from a growing consensus of "the learned world" of astronomers, the drive for a universal standard time, outside of cartography and railroad operation, met with indifference or antagonism from much of the "civilized world." As Peter Galison argues, telegraph companies and clock manufacturers had to work overtime to market their products, *creating* rather than satisfying an existing need. According to Galison, Leonard Waldo, who ran the time service in Boston beginning in 1877, believed that the community had to be "unconsciously educated to the desirability of a uniform standard of time" (109). In Hartford, Connecticut, Charles Teske complained, "It is like awakening the dead out of their sleep, to get people interested in this matter" (Galison, 110). Waldo endeavored to create a consumer demand for clocks that could eliminate errors of hundredths of a second, but to his dismay there was simply no practical purpose for such hyperprecision among ordinary travelers. "Train operators and passengers," Galison writes, "surely did not need clocks more accurate than human reaction time" (112). Sir George Airy, astronomer royal at the Greenwich Observatory in 1879, was seemingly accurate in his assessment that standard time was not "what the mass of people want" (Galison, 120).

To be sure, advocates for standard time in popular science journals of the 1880s argued that a demand for hyperprecise time was intrinsic to modern humanity, but these claims were unsubstantiated by evidence and often self-contradictory. Edmund Engler of Saint Louis wrote for *Popular Science Monthly* that "individuals as a matter of convenience" require "the exact time of day to the second" because of "the increased value of time when measured by the number of events or the magnitude of operations which modern ingenuity is crowding into a given interval." Yet he admitted that standard time satisfies what is presently an "unfelt" need (304). The editor of *The Sidereal Messenger* argued that standard time would increase "safety to life and property," but he provided no evidence of an increase in railway fatalities.[16] Indeed W. H. M. Christie, arguing for "Universal Time" in *Popular Science Monthly*, claimed that the public was largely indifferent to any deviation in the time on their watch dials. Christie claims to have found that "in rural districts on the Continent arbitrary alterations of half an hour fast or slow are accepted not only without protest but with absolute indifference" (796). This accords with W. F. Allen's account of how the revolutionary American "Day of Two Noons" was met by the public: "The people quietly acquiesced, reset their watches a few minutes faster or slower, and for the most part soon forgot that any but 'standard time' had ever been in use" (145). Whether working by artificial light or in the fields, Christie continued, laborers were largely unconscious of time at all. "Those who work in collieries, factories, or mines would doubtless be unconscious of a difference of half an hour or more between the clock and the sun, while agriculturalists would practically be unaffected by it, as they can not have fixed hours of labor in any case" (796). While standard time advocates argued that their reforms responded to the demands of the modern individual, they invariably represented that individual as a member of an acquiescent herd with little sense of any time at all, mechanical or natural—a "sleeping dead," in Teske's terms, which could be manipulated with little resistance.

If public apathy regarding standard time was so high, how did the 1884 International Prime Meridian Conference reach its consensus on a Greenwich prime meridian? The answer lies in the conference proceedings, which have been misrepresented by historians of the event as bearing evidence of a unified consensus over the new time system.[17] At the conference, however, the *application* of the Greenwich prime meridian was a fraught issue. W. F. Allen recognized this when he contested Fleming's misrepresentation of the Washington conference two years later. Writing to the American Metrological Society's president, J. K. Rees, about one of Fleming's papers, Allen argued:

> It would be inferred from what Mr. Fleming says, that the "International Meridian Conference" recommended the "Universal Day" for all purposes unqualifiedly. The actual recommendation was "IV: That the conference proposes the adoption of a Universal Day for all purposes for which it may be found convenient and which shall not interfere with the use of local or other standard time where desirable."
>
> There is room for a wide margin of opinion as to what constitutes "purposes for which it may be found convenient." For scientific purposes generally, its adoption is desirable; but for "civil" use, I am inclined to think it would produce as much, if not more, inconveniences than it would obviate.[18]

While Allen seems to be retreating from his earlier arguments in favor of a "total abolition of the use of local time by the public," as he had written in 1884, his view on the necessary limitations of the use of Greenwich-based time, stated clearly in this 1888 letter to Rees, represents the dominant view held by delegates at the conference, where the scope of "cosmopolitan" time had in fact been dramatically restricted, as I will demonstrate.

THE PRIME MERIDIAN OF LONGITUDE: "A RELATIVELY UNIMPORTANT AFFAIR"

I begin my analysis of the 1884 Prime Meridian Conference with the provocative assertion that it did not in fact achieve the goal for which it is credited. It did not advocate the use of the Greenwich meridian as a universal time-reckoning tool. As even Derek Howse recognizes, but does not explain, the most important consequence of the conference (the adoption of time zones) was not included in the wording of any of the resolutions (152). Ian Bartky, for this reason, labels the conference "a failure," though he neglects to explain why the conference failed.[19] Sandford Fleming brought to the event a powerful arsenal of arguments representing over a decade of research and rhetoric, and his arguments were all defeated. It is that defeat which I consider here, because it represents an example of resistance from within modernity, however unsuccessful, against the global suppression of social time.

The conference began on the first of October and ended on the first of November, with thirty-three representatives from twenty-one nations in attendance. Fleming, one of four members of the British delegation, quickly grew disenchanted with the direction the Washington debates were taking, as we learn from his private correspondence to the president of the conference (a draft of which is in his archived papers in Ottawa). Fleming recognized by the second day of the conference that the delegates had veered away from the topic of time reckoning and into a consideration of longitude as a purely cartographic tool. He tried again and again to introduce language into the official resolutions that made *time reckoning* central and to focus debate on universal time, but to no avail. The five resolutions of the International Prime Meridian Conference were as follows:

I: That it is the opinion of this Congress that it is desirable to adopt a single prime meridian for all nations, in place of the multiplicity of initial meridians which now exist.

II: That the Conference proposes to the Governments here represented the adoption of the meridian passing through the centre of the transit instrument at the Observatory of Greenwich as the initial meridian for longitude.

III: That from this meridian longitude shall be counted in two directions up to 180 degrees, east longitude being plus and west longitude minus.

IV: That the Conference proposes the adoption of a universal day for all purposes for which it may be found convenient, and which shall not interfere with the use of local or other standard time where desirable.

V: That this universal day is to be a mean solar day; is to begin for all the world at the moment of mean midnight of the initial meridian, coinciding with the beginning of the civil day and date of that meridian; and is to be counted from zero up to twenty-four hours.

The American delegate Lewis Rutherford reminded delegates on the first day of debates that the conference was called to establish *both* "a prime meridian and a universal time" (28).[20] Jules Janssen of France, though, immediately qualified this by asserting that the desirability of a prime meridian was felt only "by geographers and navigators," thus focusing the debate on a specialized subset of uses (29). Fleming interjected by reading the American act of Congress calling the convention, which stated that the meridian was "to be employed as a common zero of longitude *and* standard of time-reckoning throughout the globe" (33). To Fleming's dismay, however, the debates continued that first day to treat longitude as a purely geographical tool, never mentioning the desirability of a universal time-keeping system. Over the long weekend before the conference reconvened Fleming drafted a proposal of seventeen recommendations, which he submitted to Admiral Rodgers, president of the conference, in hopes that they would be submitted to all delegates. In his note to Rodgers Fleming wrote, "The determination of a Prime Meridian admits of the establishment of a much-needed time system for the world, and I respectfully submit that such system *cannot well be lost sight of* in a wise selection of a meridian proper to be employed as common zero" (italics added).[21] Delegates, Fleming saw, were "losing sight of" the real issue. By beginning with the selection of the prime meridian, the conference had put the cart before the horse, neglecting to address the much larger issue of cosmic time. In his recommendations he suggested that the conference approach its task by debating, in descending order of importance:

1. The regulation of time
2. The reckoning of longitude
3. The adoption of a prime meridian

Longitude should not be "considered apart" from time reckoning, Fleming wrote, but instead should "be denoted by the same terms as those applied to Cosmic Time." The recommendations did not reach the delegates by their next meeting, on the sixth, and time reckoning was still off the agenda that morning. Janssen argued that because longitude was purely an issue for geography, the need for an accurate astronomical observatory at the site of the prime meridian was being overstated. "Initial meridians for geography," he claimed, "need not be fixed with quite such a high degree of accuracy as is required by astronomy" (46). Hyperaccuracy, he continued, "could not be expressed on maps" (68). His remarks concluded that day's brief session, which had again considered longitude purely from a cartographic perspective.

When the conference reconvened one week later Fleming was the first to speak, although his recommendations had still not been delivered to the delegates. He attempted nevertheless to correct the conference's oversight of universal time. "Besides the benefits which would accrue to navigation," he argued, "are advantages of equal importance in connection with the regulation of time" (76). The question should be approached by delegates "in no narrow spirit"; rather they should act as "citizens of the world" (75). He then attempted his most radical intervention into the conference proceedings by proposing to have the language of Resolution II changed from "meridian for longitude" to "a meridian proper, to be employed as a common zero in the reckoning of longitude *and the regulation of time throughout the world*" (87). The amendment provoked immediate negative responses from delegates who, prior to that point, had not spoken.

Baron Von Alvensleben of Germany argued that in Fleming's amendment "two questions are mixed up together." "The first thing for us to do," he argued, "is to fix upon a prime meridian; the second thing to settle is the question whether the adoption of a universal day is desirable or not. If we adopt this amendment, these two questions are involved in one vote. Therefore I think that they should be divided, for they are not appropriate in the form in which they are presented" (88). Juan Valera of Spain claimed that he had been empowered by his government only to accept Greenwich "as the international meridian for longitudes" and that any further resolutions were beyond his instructions or authority. He had accepted Greenwich for longitude, Valera continued, only in an attempt to convince England and the United States to adopt the metric system. He speculated further that Italy's delegate was "similarly situated" (88). General Evans of the British Royal Navy, one of the biggest thorns in Fleming's side at the conference, agreed with Germany that the prime meridian was "simply a question of the reckoning of longitude as now employed by seamen of all nations": "I think it would be well to keep that fact separate from the reckoning of time" (106). Evans would later attack Fleming for equating time and longitude: "Mr. Fleming made the remark that he could not disassociate longitude from time. If he had mixed with seamen he would have found out that there is very frequently a well-defined difference between the two in their minds. Longitude with seamen means, independently of time,—space, distance. It indicates so many miles run in an east or west direction. Consequently, I am not able to look upon longitude and time as being identical" (128). We must remember that Fleming's notion really was radical in the nineteenth century. Time had never been united to longitude in the way that he was suggesting. It was necessary to use time in order to find the position of the longitude, and local times were determined by the longitude of the nearest national observatory, but the notion that a cartographic tool like longitude could be used to dictate a world time that everyone would use to regulate their daily activities was quite novel. The history of the unification of the longitudes involved using accurate time to discover spatial position, not the reverse. John Harrison's chief problem had been to find longitudinal positioning at sea, and his chronometers used temporal simultaneity to determine spatial positioning.[22] The problem was not *What time is it there?* but rather *Where am I?* Delegates could be forgiven for thinking of longitude first and foremost as a tool for solving spatial and not temporal problems. The Greenwich Observatory had provided time service in England and set chronometric standards for vessels at sea, but this was a function of its role as a world-class observatory, not of its position at a particular meridian. Longitude had formally been a reference tool for those drawing or using maps. It was a spatial practice, not a temporal one. All other "civil" times simply derived from the nearest observatory in their nation, irrespective of what longitudinal point it might occupy in any larger spatial scheme. For locales with no access to observatory signals the sundial provided the nearest accuracy required by human activity. Fleming's notion of taking a spatial cartographic system like longitude and wedding it to a world-unifying time-keeping and time-transmission system was profoundly radical. This was the real revolution of standard time, and yet it was never made clear at the conference. It took decades for nations to realize that the old understanding of longitude as a purely specialized tool for a narrow range of disciplines had been overturned.

After a speech by the French delegate Lefaivre, which brought the discussion back to "astronomy, geodesy, and navigation," Fleming's amendment was voted out (91). Longitude and time had been officially *separated* at the Prime Meridian Conference. Germany, Spain, and Italy, though all three voted for Greenwich as prime meridian for longitude, would abstain from or vote down any resolution that attempted to set the parameters of a universal day.[23] Fleming, still hoping to redirect delegates to his cosmic time system, proposed the formation of a committee to study the issue, which was also voted down. Remarkably the measure to separate longitude from time reckoning, arguably the most important vote of the conference, has not been mentioned by any historian.[24]

When the resolutions regarding the desirability of a universal day finally came under consideration days later, delegates were careful to advocate its use only for specialized purposes rather than for general adoption. Albert de Foresta of Italy recommended that their language specify that the universal day was designated "for certain scientific needs and for the internal service of great administrations of ways of communications, such as those of railroads, lines of steamships, telegraphic and postal lines" (135). In the end the resolution on the universal day passed largely because of the great latitude of interpretation it allowed.

It specified that the universal day would "not interfere with the use of local or other standard time where desirable."

When the debates moved on to defining the details of the next resolution, the European delegates felt that interpretive latitude diminishing. On October 20, the sixth day of the conference, the Spanish delegates, in a move that neither Clark Blaise nor Peter Galison acknowledge, staged a blockade on any further discussion, a move they themselves described as "radical."[25] Ruiz del Arbol moved that an official resolution be adopted to specify that the Greenwich meridian *not be used* for time reckoning. While delegates had "accepted the meridian of Greenwich to account the longitudes," Arbol argued that "the introduction of any new system of time-reckoning is far more scientific and important, and liable to great difficulties and confusion in the future." The Spanish delegates requested an official resolution that would state in no uncertain terms that the conference "abstains from designating" the Greenwich meridian "to reckon the universal time" (158). Arbol pleaded with delegates not to "make a premature declaration, which will be an authoritative one as emanating from this congress, an apparently insignificant reform, but in reality one of very great importance" (162). He spoke for the majority of European powers (as the voting on Resolution V later indicated) when he stated unambiguously, "According to my views, the meridian of longitude is relatively an unimportant affair. But if you adopt a meridian for time, it will be very difficult to alter it in the future. . . . I understand it [sic] very well that it is proposed to confine this principle to certain subjects . . . avoiding dangers in communications, in navigation, in railways, and in transmitting telegrams" (163). The Spaniards drew heavily on the Judeo-Christian significance of time measurement, a claim hitherto confined to the rhetoric of Charles Piazzi-Smyth, who had been arguing for Jerusalem as the only acceptable site to bear such obvious symbolic weight.[26] It cannot be overemphasized that Arbol's claim that longitude was "relatively unimportant" in relation to time measurement is simply incomprehensible given Howse's, Blaise's, and Galison's readings of the conference, none of whom recognize that the relationship between time and longitude had not been established to the satisfaction of the delegates.

J. C. Adams attempted to answer the Spanish delegates by insisting that to "count longitude from one meridian and time from another" would sacrifice "simplicity" (162), but it was General Strachey's diplomatic counterargument that carried the day. He simply deferred to the wording of the previous resolution, in which it was clear that "this *so-called* universal day [notice the new qualifier] will not interfere in the smallest degree with any purpose for which time is employed in civil life" (164–65). Arbol's resolution was voted out, on the grounds that the previous resolution already allowed nations control over how universally to apply the "so-called universal day."

In a long speech following this vote Rustem Effendi of the Ottoman Empire declared his support of the Spanish objections, insisting that the resolution should "leave to each country the greatest latitude possible in adopting a universal hour" (179). It is in Rustem's speech that the foundation of a powerful critique of Fleming's "cosmopolitan" system is best articulated. Although the speech was quickly dismissed by the president of the conference, the voting patterns afterward suggest that it received the tacit approval of a substantial body of delegates. "The question of a universal hour," Rustem argued, "is not of equal interest and importance to all" (178). Owing to their size, it was clear that the United States, Canada, the British Empire, Russia, and Germany stood to gain the most from the system. "But there are," he continued, "other countries, like France, Spain, Italy, Scandinavia, etc. that may content themselves with a national hour, owing to the small difference in time within their dominion" (179). Given the nature of their labors and cultural practices, Rustem said, the Ottoman Empire desired great latitude in time reckoning. "The majority of our population is agricultural," he argued, "working in the fields, and prefer to count to sunset; besides, the hours for the Moslem prayers are counted from sundown to sundown" (180). Echoing his Spanish colleagues' emphasis on the immense cultural significance of time measurement, he implicitly resisted the civil Greenwich day as the symbol of a suspect universalism that favored only the major industrial and territorial empires of America and England at the expense of the needs and interests of a region with distinct cultural values. Over a century later Rustem's objections have by no means been put to rest in the Muslim world. In 2008 Sheikh Youssef al-Qaradawy, along with a host of Islamic scholars at a conference in Qatar, called for the abolition of Greenwich Mean Time, imposed "by force" during the height of the British Empire, in favor of a Mecca-based time for the Muslim world. Though predictably mocked in the Western press for its evidence of Islamic pseudo-scientific backwardness, the Qatar conference nevertheless suggests the persistence of deep cultural rifts over the symbolic power to measure and regulate the rhythms of modernity.[27]

After Rustem's speech Resolution V was put to a vote. On the surface V seemed like a trivial resolution, specifying only whether the universal day should begin at midday or midnight. Reading the proceedings carefully, however, it is clear that Resolution V, perhaps too late in the day, served as the first point at which serious objections were made to the very principle of cosmic civil time that Fleming had hoped the conference would approve. If we regard the voting results in that light and recognize the extent to which the voting on Resolution II (concerning the Greenwich meridian for longitude) had been considered "relatively unimportant," we begin to understand that claims of "substantial unanimity" at the conference were indeed misleading.[28] The majority vote was favorable to the resolution by 14 to 10, but the margin was close, and the countries abstaining or voting no were largely the major European powers: France, Germany, Italy, Austria-Hungary, Sweden, Switzerland, Turkey (table 1).

To appease the abstaining delegates General Strachey and Lewis Rutherford reiterated on the final day of debates that local time was still sovereign. "There was, of course," Strachey said, "never any intention of employing the universal day so as to interfere with the use of local standard time" (197). "Our universal day," Rutherford concurred, "is not to interfere in any way with the use of civil or other standard time" (198). Fleming, watching his dream of a consensus over cosmic time irretrievably thrown out, attempted one final intervention, but Admiral Rodgers immediately interrupted him with the near-withering statement that Strachey's remarks had been intended "to avoid a discussion upon a subject that could hardly lead to any satisfactory conclusion. If however Mr. Fleming desires to address the conference, he will be at liberty to do so." Fleming, fully understanding the command to be silent despite the ostensible invitation to speak, merely stated, in the last substantive sentence of the 1884 conference, "I shall not insist upon speaking" (198). The conference effectively ended with Fleming cowed into submission, his vision of cosmopolitan time reckoning shelved and Greenwich relegated to the status of a "relatively unimportant" scientific tool.

If the 1884 conference went into the history books as the date on which universal civil time reckoning was legislated, it was largely due to the efforts of the standard time apostles in the succeeding twenty years to misrepresent what actually happened in Washington. In campaigning in country after country for the adoption of the universal civil day, Fleming and others made no mention of Rutherford's and Strachey's

TABLE 1. THE VOTING ON RESOLUTIONS II AND V AT THE INTERNATIONAL PRIME MERIDIAN CONFERENCE

	Resolution II (on a Greenwich Prime Meridian / Meridian for longitude)	Resolution V (on the parameters of a universal day)
Austria-Hungary	Aye	No
Brazil	Abstain	Aye
Chile	Aye	Aye
Colombia	Aye	Aye
Costa Rica	Aye	Aye
France	Abstain	Abstain
Germany	Aye	Abstain
Great Britain	Aye	Aye
Guatemala	Aye	Aye
Hawaii	Aye	Aye
Italy	Aye	Abstain
Japan	Aye	Aye
Liberia	Aye	Aye
Mexico	Aye	Aye
Netherlands	Aye	Abstain
Paraguay	Aye	Aye
Russia	Aye	Aye
San Domingo	No	Abstain
Salvador	Aye	(not present)
Spain	Aye	No
Sweden	Aye	Abstain
Switzerland	Aye	Abstain
Turkey	Aye	No
United States	Aye	Aye
Venezuela	Aye	Aye

International Conference Held at Washington. For the Purpose of Fixing a Prime Meridian and a Universal Day (Washington, DC: Gibson Bros., 1884).

declarations of the sovereignty of local time, nor of the convention's consistent rejection of Fleming's language of cosmic time. Instead 1884 was presented as a diplomatic precedent, with the voting over the "relatively unimportant" resolution on longitude suddenly the only outcome of the conference, burdened with a weight that the delegates insisted it should not bear. The European blockade of the universal day was never mentioned. It does not appear in any of the three major studies of the conference.[29] In the end Fleming's misrepresentation of the conference, for which even W. F. Allen chided him, was the version for the encyclopedia. By 1916, when Turkey, the last abstaining nation at the conference, had given in to Greenwich-based time zones, civil standard time was a reality in Europe and it no longer seemed to matter what had really happened at a conference then thirty-two years old.

Around the world, as individual nations were urged by standard time apostles to conform to the recommendations of the 1884 conference, those recommendations were increasingly misrepresented as unequivocally advocating the Greenwich longitude for all purposes. Throughout Europe the discrepancy between a specialized scientific use of the Greenwich meridian and its use for all human purposes (as Fleming would have it) was the key point of contention. In the meeting on the issue at Berlin delegates wondered what possible advantage could accrue to agriculture, for instance, especially for farmers "of moderate and small pastures." Ernst Pasquier, who advocated for standard time in Belgium, wrote Fleming that although he believed Germany would adopt the Greenwich longitude, it would be "only for the interior service of the railways" since "the extension of this time to civil life meets in this country a strong opposition."[30] In his own country of Belgium too, Pasquier wrote in 1891, the problem was in "the extension of the system of zones with regard to civil life."[31] That the Belgian Academy could look favorably on "the system of hourly divisions with Greenwich as the meridian" but reject the idea that it be adopted in "civil life," as Pasquier had written a year earlier, suggests how few people really agreed with Fleming as to the value of a specialized tool like longitude being used to regulate civil time.[32]

The disembedding of social time was thus founded not on international consensus, but on subterfuge and misrepresentation. It was, further, not a move devised by the British Empire, but by transnational investors who used (or misused) the "dread international conference" (in Piazzi-Smyth's terms) to synchronize countries to precisely coordinated capital flow, as I argue below. Standard time began as a civil campaign by American and Canadian engineers. The British Admiralty was indifferent and world political leaders apathetic. It was unclear what benefit would accrue to civil life by temporally synchronizing global human activity. The researcher confronting Fleming's archives of letters to and from world leaders is inevitably struck by his boundless and tireless devotion to a cause in which few could see any real value. An English official in Trinidad speculated, for example, that the entire movement was an impractical and purely symbolic display of intellectualism: "It gives no doubt satisfaction to certain minds to introduce scientific calculation into the details of daily life, just as it may please the modern Frenchman to reflect that his market purchases are regulated by a unit which astronomers use in their grand world measurements, but the average Englishman is hard to convince of the practical gain of these requirements."[33] Whether motivated by delusions of grandeur, as the Trinidadian official suggests, or neutral scientific objectivity, one thing was clear early on that has received little attention in the histories of standard time and that brings us nearer to the significance of the movement. It was illustrated at the earliest of the international conferences on the prime meridian, held in Venice in 1881. At the conclusion of that conference it was recommended that an international commission be established to investigate not only "the question of longitude but especially that of hours and dates." The commission would be composed, the report concluded, "of scientific members, such as geodesists and geographers and of persons representing the interests of commerce."[34] The bedfellows of the standard time movement were not science and politics, or science and the military, but science and commerce. Forty-four years later Virginia Woolf, in *Mrs. Dalloway*, would trenchantly encapsulate the standard time movement in her vision of a "commercial clock" giving out Greenwich time "gratis" with the names of petty sock merchants inscribed on the clock face instead of the numbers of the hours. At Venice the official inauguration of internationally unified time made this connection between science and commerce explicit.

What is particularly modern about standard time is that it facilitates the unification of global markets to the penetration of capital. The "dread international conference" sanctioned the coordination of capital flow with transcontinental railways, telegraphy, Pacific or "Empire-girdling" cables, and imperial intelligence bureaus, all of which Sir Sandford Fleming was instrumental in advocating and implementing. Perhaps the best illustration of the coordination of these technological innovations for the interests of Western capital was the disastrous Brazilian scheme in which Fleming and a group of American investors were involved only four years after the Washington conference. Brazil, along with San Domingo, had joined the French blockade against the adoption of Greenwich in the "relatively unimportant" Resolution II. When we understand Fleming's investment in the monopolization of South American resources, as well as his concerted attempts to open up foreign markets for import and export of commodities in which he held substantial stock, such as sugar and cement, we begin to understand the interrelation between temporal precision and transnational capitalism more clearly.

FLEMING AND THE PARA SYNDICATE: THE BRAZILIAN
MISADVENTURES OF STANDARD TIME'S ARCHITECT

In the autumn of 1888 one of Fleming's many grandchildren sent him a card proudly displaying the twelve-year-old's first hand-drawn map. It was a color-coded map of the continent of South America, with the longitudinal lines clearly marked.[35] It must have made the patriarch proud to see one of his offspring acknowledge his role not only in standardizing those lines, but also in representing the fertile land that Fleming was that very year attempting to open up to American and Canadian capital. Fleming had become chief engineering consultant and investor in a body called the Para Transportation and Trading Company, which proposed a mammoth opportunity for investors in building a railroad across northern Brazil and the upper Tocatins River, leading to a silver mine in Goyaz. Striking an agreement with the conservative ruling party of the region, American investors, led by J. J. C. Abbot, R. J. Kimball, and G. W. Hooker, secured a contract that granted them a ninety-year monopoly over the silver of Goyaz. In a memorandum to potential investors the Para syndicate called for what was, at that time, the astonishing sum of ten million dollars for the project: three million for the mine and seven million for the railroad.[36] The railroad was the riskiest part of the venture, given the unevenness of the terrain and the large number of immigrants who would have to be settled in the region for its construction. Fleming received, via Kimball, a series of reports on the region by the syndicate's representative, chief engineer J. R. Paulin, who also reported directly to Fleming in Ottawa. Paulin provided a detailed breakdown of the region's potentially exploitable resources. In addition to "large quantities of rubber trees" and 28,000 hectares of chestnuts, "the soil," Paulin wrote, "is very rich and seems to grow everything they plant pell-mell": "I have no doubt that if a good class of immigrants could be introduced into the country even in small numbers, that in a few years they would raise a large quantity of products for exportation. . . . Intermittent fever [is a problem, but] seems to attack the natives a great deal more than strangers and that I would attribute mostly to their negligence and carelessness."[37] Engineers Middleton and Reynolds similarly reported that native populations settled in the region, although "not to be trusted," were easily manipulated because "all those indians have a mortal terror of firearms." Confirming Paulin's reports on the region's fertility, the men wrote that "nuts of different kinds" were "abundant," including "many scented nuts that would no doubt, if the country were opened up, find a ready market."[38]

In the beginning of 1889, though, the Para syndicate began to run into a series of problems, beginning with the alleged profligacy of some of its representatives in Brazil, one of whom Abbot claimed was practicing "extortion" on the investors "in respect of his festivities."[39] In May of that year no part of the railroad was yet in place, as the syndicate was having difficulty placing its bonds. The "rascally Brazilians," Abbot wrote, were not evidencing their sufficiency to guarantee the bonds because "never having built any railroads or guaranteed any such bonds" the province of Para had no established credit on the market.[40] In the end, though, Para's crash was not the result of immoral agents or insufficient credit, but the political sovereignty of Brazil itself. On the first of November Kimball wrote a frantic letter to Fleming in which he announced that a change in political power in the region had resulted in a complete nullification of the syndicate's monopoly over resources: "When the laws were passed confirming to us the contract, the 'Conservative' party was in power, and our enterprise was opposed by the 'Liberals,' who are now in power. . . . All level minded people here unite in stigmatizing the action as most illegal, unconstitutional, and outrageous, a clear betrayal of trust and forfeiture of credit." The "evident intention" of the newly elected party in Brazil was to "defeat the entire project."[41] In an enclosed clipping from the *Rio News* an editorialist derided the newly elected prime minister's "declared hostility" to the mining project and represented the act as "a gross breach of faith" that "will cause heavy losses to those who have invested money in the enterprise."[42] While top-secret plans were floated to launder the invested money into various pseudo-companies to cut losses, the situation was declared "well-nigh hopeless" in 1890.[43]

It is not, of course, surprising that we should find Canada's most prominent engineer and entrepreneur involved in investment and development in South America, but the relative recency of the Prime Meridian Conference in relation to the Para venture invites close scrutiny. Here, after all, was one of the great architects of world standard time involved in a scheme that employed the very transportation and communication technologies that necessitated standardization in order to draw resources from the one nation that had joined France in abstention at Washington. The interplay of rail technology with monopolistic exploitation of foreign resources and the marshaling of staggering sums of American capital could not be clearer than in the Para episode.

The Brazil venture was not unique in this respect, however. All of Fleming's vast global telecommunications and transportation projects were tied up with highly lucrative commercial ventures in which he was personally invested. The trans-Canadian railroad he charted in the 1870s was extended into a region of the Rockies declared open by the governor to highly profitable anthracite mining, which the railroad transported back to Alberta for immense profit. Fleming and one of his sons were involved in a lengthy and ultimately successful suit over the rights to that anthracite in the first years of the twentieth century.[44] Similarly, as Fleming advocated for and invested in his most grandiose scheme of an "Empire-girdling" cable that would telegraphically connect Canada to Australia, he was also investing enormous sums of money into cement stock and instructing another of his sons, well-placed in the Western Canada Cement and Coal Company, to find a means to export their cement to Australia.[45] The standardization of transportation and communication within a common coordinate system would be immediately followed by massive flows of capital across borders previously considered impenetrable. Fleming, in this sense, was truly forward-thinking. He cared little for the political or imperial aspect of his projects, though he could invoke the empire quite earnestly for rhetorical purposes. During the period in which he was planning to connect the Pacific Cable via small islands in the Pacific he was contacted by English agents to enlist his support in pressing for political action on sovereign islands. An English former political prisoner of the Hawaiian government, for example, wrote a dramatic letter to Fleming in 1895 in which he tried to convince Fleming of the "magnificent opportunity" for the British government "to take advantage of the conditions which justify her intervention in behalf of her abused and dragooned subjects to also secure such concessions in the way of cable privileges as will facilitate the construction of the Pacific Cable." The Hawaiian islands, the writer continued, "are now available to be won or lost." Fleming's draft of a reply was understandably circumspect.[46] It may be unclear whether Fleming would have had any means to instigate a British-Hawaiian war, but it is patently clear that he was very interested in separating questions of political sovereignty from those of commercial investment. Let the island be governed by whatever nation cares to do it, Fleming thought, so long as it allows capital to flow unimpeded.

Fleming made as much clear when he said of the Fanning Islands, another proposed site for connecting the Pacific cable, that "it was not the sovereignty of the islands that is being sold, but simply the freehold interest." This public statement inspired a reaction from one politician in British Columbia, who wrote to Fleming that it would not be safe to let the Fannings fall into any other hands than those of the British government. The Fannings could not, the correspondent claimed, fall into the regrettable position of Anticosti Island, which was "in the hands of a great French capitalist."[47] In Fleming's world of cosmopolitan time, though, political imperialism took a back seat to commercial imperialism, which would, he believed, solve larger social and political problems.[48] Commercial interests could work in Fleming's favor when it came to time reform as well. The secretary of Lloyd's of London, for example, hoping to strike a deal on supplying stores for all ships along the Pacific cable route and knowing of Fleming's passion for temporal uniformity, wrote that Lloyd's would pressure the Admiralty to adopt uniform civil time at sea if Fleming could promise the company a monopoly on stores of "victuals" and medicine for ships docked at the Fanning Islands.[49]

To return to the Para syndicate in Brazil, we see that Fleming's faith in uniform and coordinated capital flow above and beyond any considerations of political expediency was not always successful. The nations were not uniform, nor was upper Brazil the Canadian Rockies or its government subject to Queen Victoria. The enormous contempt and disdain expressed in letters about the "careless natives" and "rascally Brazilians" who had signed away the rights to their own resources to men who made no secret of their plans to tyrannize over them with rifles and resettlement programs did not in this case go unchallenged. The Liberal Party of Brazil could keep the northern capitalists at bay for the moment, but the history of the South American continent would bear witness in the twentieth-century that Fleming's vision of uniform capital penetration would carry the day. One might consider the Para syndicate's Goyaz concession a likely source for Joseph Conrad's fictional Gould Concession in *Nostromo* (1906), if not for the fact that such ventures in South America were so alarmingly ubiquitous in the period. To penetrate the barriers of national sovereignty, temporal and spatial coordination of transportation and communication had to be firmly in place. If military and political leaders of the day were obtuse to this trend of modernity, the "industrial public" was not. The 1884 Prime Meridian Conference, then, stands as one of the key events at the onset of modernity, forecasting, at the height of British imperialism, the postimperial politics of the global market. Without realizing it, delegates had ratified the creation of a universally coordinated civil time, designed primarily for the cosmopolitan investor in his commercial ventures around the globe.

The parallels with the present globalization age are manifest here, with many of the major components already in place. As Bourdieu has argued, the national barriers to the unification of a world economic field have historically been both geographical and juridical in character: "These limits, at once technical and legal, to the extension of the economic field tend today to weaken or disappear as a result of different factors: partly purely technical factors, like the development of new means of communication like air transport or the Internet; partly from more properly political or juridical-political, factors, like liberalization and deregulation" ("Uniting to Better Dominate," 1). The extension of Western capital across geographical and national barriers through the means of communication technology is as much characteristic of the 1889 Para syndicate in Brazil as in the present day. Rail and telegraphy enable the erasure of geographical diversity and particularity in support of a uniform, homogeneous communication grid, with coordinate systems mediating and ameliorating cultural and spatial divisions. The rail is coordinated by standard time in order to efficiently transport silver from its owners to multinational companies. All this was ratified, from a scientific and political perspective, by an international conference at which space had supposedly been declared theoretically uniform. The only difference between the Goyaz of 1889 and the typical South American nation of today is that in 1889 small nations still had a degree of power and autonomy to reject dependency on American investment without crippling their position in world markets. Without a world bank to enforce their interests, Abbot, Kimball, and the other investors had to make a failed effort to enlist the U.S. government in retributive measures against the Brazilian Liberal Party.

The coincidence of standard time with world finance was clearly evidenced in 2001, when the prime minister of Thailand proposed a losing measure to change his country's standard time to correspond to that of Hong Kong so that Thailand could benefit from precise coordination with the Hong Kong stock market.[50] Temporal standardization and efficient maximization of profits have always gone hand in hand. On the cosmopolitan clock all labor is controlled within a fraction of a second. Fleming himself, as a major investor in Canadian cement, had expressed an interest in Frederick Taylor's stopwatch research into labor efficiency. Fleming had ordered copies of Taylor's book *Concrete*

Costs, which applied Taylorization to cement manufacturing and processing.[51] Fleming's push for the twenty-four-hour clock was motivated by a desire to eliminate all idiosyncratic variations in temporal maintenance. The world itself was to be transformed into one great cosmopolitan timepiece in which there would finally be no excuses accepted for any deviation from the great movement of the ticking globe. The seamless unification of space, capital, and time was legislated in 1884 in Washington, even though the majority of the legislators who participated in that event would have been shocked to know that this was in fact what they were being asked to do.

CHAPTER 2

"Turning From the Shadows That Follow Us"

Modernist Time and the Politics of Place

The 1884 Washington conference did not demonstrate the global consensus on universal civil time that Sandford Fleming and his apostles had hoped it might. Despite Fleming's lofty rhetoric of cosmopolitan time for all purposes on earth, European delegates, as we have seen, were quick to keep separate the issues of cartographic longitude and universal civil time. The American delegates, Rodgers and Rutherford, diplomatically insisted in their concluding remarks that each government would have complete latitude over what uses, if any, it would make of a Greenwich-based civil time. For Fleming this capitulatory language was deeply frustrating. If the global map was to be temporally and spatially unified, it would have to happen universally. If not, the bewildering heterogeneity of discrete local times around the globe would be as problematic as before. More important the nonunified nations would be resistant to the construction and implementation of communications and transport technologies designed for the flow of capital and raw materials.

Resistance to standard time's unification of global time and space for the fluid mobility of capital across national borders was most powerfully expressed at the conference in terms of simple noncompliance. Delegates clearly recognized the imperial advantages of synchronizing temporality to a system of global cartography, and the dissenters' objections were predictably (and justifiably) couched in national and cultural terms. The Turkish delegate invoked the agricultural mode of production of the Ottoman Empire as well as the importance of Muslim practices of time measurement. The Spanish delegates deferred to the Christian significance of event dating and the variable extents of each nation's geographical expanse. Their criticisms, in short, were not expressed in *individual* or *psychological* terms. Standard time was never considered, in Washington at least, as an impingement on a preconceived, existentially authentic, private temporality, but rather as a potential violation of national sovereignty and cultural values. Time was imbricated with communal practices and modes of production, not with interior psychology.

Discussions of temporality in literary modernism, however, have tended to treat time in the early twentieth century as a narrowly circumscribed philosophical preoccupation of the elite, as if meditations on the organization and measurement of time were little more than parlor games inapplicable to any real world of shared values and practices. That view certainly summarizes Wyndham Lewis's blistering attack on many of his contemporaries in *Time and Western Man* (1928), a book I discuss in some detail below. Although many of Lewis's aesthetic and political views have had little real purchase in the past eighty years, his allegation that the writers now considered canonical modernists were slavish devotees of the temporal philosophy of Henri Bergson has stuck fairly well in the collective critical consciousness. We are more inclined to think of modernists as leisured quasi-philosophers in regard to their interests in time than as writers actively engaged with the pressing temporal dimensions of national, social, and political autonomy. Yet that is precisely what I mean to demonstrate in later chapters. To make this claim it is first necessary to reexamine not only the role of Bergsonism in modernism, but also the function of place and location in the modernist imagination. The modernist classics have conventionally been celebrated for their ability to transcend the banal or even crippling determinations of space and nation. In their cosmopolitan avoidance of the pitfalls of nationalism and their celebration of universal or at least transnational values the modernists demonstrated their disdain for narrow provincialisms and petty regionalisms. In this sense Bergson, declaring the entire dimension of space a corrupting influence on the dynamic temporal flux of the durée, could indeed be considered the period's governing conscience. Yet modernism's ostensible transnationalism has as much to do with a dominant tendency to see the metropolitan city as the exemplary locus for modernist production as it has to do with the philosophy of Bergson. The cosmopolitan city

(London, Paris, Berlin), with its lavish and dizzying array of consumer goods culled from the far reaches of empire, instilled in the modernists an illusory sense of being removed from the petty constraints of local or national belonging. The early twentieth-century urban experience was the modernist experience par excellence, capturing the sheer energy and chaos of modernity, realizing in its daily phantasmagorical transformations the kind of flux and vitality that might approximate the pure, unadulterated Bergsonian durée.

I certainly do not mean to reject these critical assumptions, nor to deny the power of the many readings they have generated. I do mean to suggest, however, that if modernism had a tendency toward valorizing the placelessness of the cosmopolitan, it was often equally as drawn toward inhabiting and reconfiguring the intimate and the shared public spaces of the local and the national. Location emerges in modernist fiction as a problem to be solved, not as a barrier to be overcome or an enemy to be destroyed. The readings of novels by British, Irish, and Indian authors that make up the remaining chapters of this book focus close attention on the extent to which those texts engage with unique and discrete problems of precise spatial and national locations. Those engagements with place and space are generally incomprehensible under the Bergsonian and metropolitan modernist models. In this chapter I make the theoretical case for a place-based politics of modernism, both by contextualizing Bergson's arguments as merely one of a range of competing visions of time and space in the fin de siècle (including Einstein's relativity theory and the cosmological humanism made widely available in popular science books) and also by examining the role of localism and provincialism in modernist writing, situating my own arguments within a constellation of fairly recent critical studies that appreciate modernism's fraught engagement with its own national contexts.

If Sandford Fleming clearly identified time as the cosmopolitan principle that could transcend petty spatial affiliations with nations and locations, Henri Bergson saw time as a subjective possession that could not be located or graphically spatialized without violently corrupting its essence. Bergson's *Time and Free Will* (1889) was being composed as delegates met for the Prime Meridian Conference in Washington, and significantly "the astronomer" recurs in his text as an ever-present villain, eagerly transforming the purely qualitative experience of time into a quantity that can be divided and measured. Fleming's cosmopolitan time, which flows smoothly and continuously, the same for all creation irrespective of place and position, was anathema for Bergson.

To represent time as a "homogeneous medium" was, for Bergson, to confuse quantity with quality: "Time enters into the formulae of mechanics, into the calculations of the astronomer, and even of the physicist, under the form of a quantity. We measure the velocity of a movement, implying that time itself is a magnitude. . . . It is said . . . that the time which our clocks divide into equal portions . . . must be a measurable and therefore homogeneous magnitude—it is nothing of the sort, however" (107). Using a pendulum clock as an illustrative symbol, Bergson argues that the hand of the pendulum marks only a single oscillation at a time, "counting" discrete "simultaneities." It is the ego, "enduring" in duration, that connects the succession of simultaneities and projects its own duration onto the pendulum's movements. The subjective mind, however, operates "without relation to number," existing instead as a "continuous interpenetration of conscious states." The ego is composed purely of succession with no external referent, whereas the clock is purely external motion with no inherent succession. The ego's identification of its own duration with what happens on the pendulum clock is merely a confusion of "pure" or "true" duration with a homogeneous space that, unlike the ego, can be spatially represented and quantified. If the clock is a "symbolical representation of duration, derived from space," subjective or pure duration has no spatial dimension at all, but must necessarily borrow one in order to represent itself in language.

Bergson here denigrates language itself as a corruption (albeit an unavoidable one) of a subjective and extralinguistic durée. The resources of language are utterly inadequate to give expression to the infinitely variable and fluid experiences of sensation: "We instinctively tend to solidify our impressions in order to express them in language. Hence we confuse the feeling itself, which is in a perpetual state of becoming, with its permanent external object, and especially with the word which expresses this object. In the same way as the fleeting duration of our ego is fixed by its projection in homogenous space, our constantly changing impressions, wrapping themselves round the external object, which is their cause, take on its definite outlines and its immobility" (130). The problem with inanimate objects (which for Bergson include words as well as stones and clocks) is that they seduce us into a false and easy identification, in which our ceaselessly changing subjectivity, qualitatively attuned to discriminate among a vast array of sensations, is fixed and halted. We chain ourselves to words as Prometheus to a rock. Bergson's use of "taste" in his comments on language, immediately invoking Proust and his madeleine for the contemporary reader, illustrates the extent to which the durée is an exclusively private domain, corrupted by the vulgarity of any kind of social organization or shared value system. Notice the disdain for the "common" and "rough" in favor of the "delicate" in the following passage: "The word with well-defined outlines, the rough and ready word, which stores up the stable, common, and consequently impersonal element in the impressions of mankind, overwhelms or at least covers over the delicate and fugitive impression of our individual consciousness" (132). Bergson identifies the "spatial" with a kind of plebeian or proletarian "rough and ready" world of "common" shared values. It is not difficult to understand what Georg Lukács and other critics would later disdain in this language of the individual's discriminating and inexpressible realm of valorized sensation that held itself loftily above any vulgar common expression.

If we recognize that the key innovation of the standard time system was to inextricably affix temporality to a cartographic system of spatial longitudes, then we must acknowledge that Bergson's critique of homogeneous time is situated right at the crux of the technobureaucratic debates of his age. Bergson's argument is ultimately no more complex than that of Adm. F.J.O. Evans at the Washington conference, who insisted that the spatial practice of measuring longitudes was distinct from the practice of time measurement. Time is not space, Bergson declares, and in making the declaration he affirms a certain solidarity with the Spanish delegates to Washington, who were quick to recognize the crucial cultural importance of universal time measurement in distinction to the "relatively unimportant" spatial practice of drawing longitudinal lines. In a telling metaphor Bergson signals the military dimension of mapping time in spatial terms. It is not possible, he writes, "to follow the progress of psychic activity . . . like the march of an army on a map" (180). In Bergson's language of the "rough and ready" or "common" world of shared value, however, we find none of the Washington delegates' awareness of time as dependent on cultural practices or modes of production. Intervening in age-old Western dichotomous thinking (his main foil is Zeno and his paradoxes), Bergson is charting the durée as a human universal, irrespective of any external circumstance. He confronts the hegemony of the "astronomer's time" with a radically divergent multiplicity of interior states that cannot be meaningfully represented graphically. The anarchy of the interior is ultimately figured as the proof and evidence of free will, which Zeno's spatializing paradoxes attempted to contravene.

In a global environment in which multinational investors were borrowing scientific legitimacy to assert a seamless unity of temporal and spatial orientation Bergson was attempting an ambitious and reactionary *wresting apart* of time and space, affirming the purely qualitative character of the former in contradistinction to the purely quantitative (and thus degraded) character of the latter. It is for this reason that he would later consider his work on time more fundamentally radical than that of Einstein, whose special theory of relativity he would accuse, in *Duration and Simultaneity,* of reinforcing a Newtonian universal time, even as it ostensibly rejected such a system. For Bergson, Einstein's theory was inapplicable to any meaningful theory of temporal perception because it missed the fundamental distinction between qualitative temporal perception and the quantitative measurement of clocks. Einstein's argumentative use of coordinated clocks in the special theory of relativity was a mathematical exercise producing paradoxical results divorced from any perceptual reality. His famous moving clocks, alternately speeding up and slowing down, were "purely mathematical entities," Bergson asserts, interesting only insofar as one is willing to "dissolve things into relations" and regard "every reality, even ours, as a confusedly perceived mathematics" (64). Einstein's mistake was to equate the person with the clock and the relationship between people with the relationship between electrically synchronized clocks. Only when one is willing to admit the synchronization of the flow of one's own durée with the instantaneous reading on the clock dial does the synchronization of clocks have any bearing on reality. Without this "intuitive simultaneity," Bergson writes, "clocks would serve no purpose. They would be bits of machinery with which we would amuse ourselves by comparing them with one another; they would not be employed in classifying events; in short, they would exist for their own sake and not to serve us" (55). Bergson accuses Einstein of doing nothing more than playing games with coordinated clocks, an exercise that produces clever mathematical results that nevertheless have no bearing on actual human time. In transforming people into interchangeable clocks, placed alternately on speeding rockets and passing trains, Einstein does not affirm a perceptual pluralism but in fact manipulates reality from the perspective of a privileged observer able and willing to construct "a mathematical vision of the universe in which everything will be converted from perceived reality into useful scientific representation" (96). In this sense, then, Einstein's intervention into Newtonian mechanics, far from doing away with the notion of a single, privileged time, "calls for it and gives it a greater intelligibility" (113).

Bergson's larger implication is that Einstein's theories are founded on a mechanistic, technologically coordinated universe, in which people are only mathematical ciphers. The relationship between global technological coordination and relativity theory has been the subject of several recent studies, which have attempted to place the abstraction of Einsteinian theory within larger turn-of-the-century developments in telecommunications. Peter Galison demonstrates how relativity theory, despite its common representation as "purely intellectual" and "hovering in a cloud of abstractions" (26), was in fact deeply rooted in the burgeoning technology of clock coordination around the turn of the century, specifically through Einstein's work as a patent officer in Bern, a center for the "invention, production, and patenting" of clock synchronization technology (31). Michael Whitworth has similarly compared Einsteinian simultaneity to the simultaneity produced by telecommunications technology, both of which produce, in modernist fictions, "incongruous juxtapositions" (*Einstein's Wake*, 194). These parallels between relativity theory and the coordination of world time through technological innovation suggest that Einstein's cosmological view emerged out of, and not in contradistinction to, standard time's unification of discrete temporalities. If the Washington delegates equated time with longitude, Einstein pushed that equation to its mathematical limits, while Bergson simply refuted the equation.

Space "corrupts" time, Bergson argues, and in doing so it corrupts "at its very source our feeling of outer and inner change, of movement, and of freedom" (74). Time must be freed from the "alloy" of spatial conception (100). If Einstein's theory required humans to be interchangeable with synchronized clocks, Bergson disavowed identification with any external temporal standard. This quasi-mystical advocacy of disengagement is particularly clear in Bergson's conclusion to *Time and Free Will*, where he writes that regaining a "genuine free self" would require that we use a "strenuous act of reflection" to "turn our eyes from the shadow which follows us and retire into ourselves" (233). There could be no better illustration of Bergson's position than in this ascetic command to disavow our very shadows, the markers of our relation to the sun. Rather than affirm a primitive sundial or a national determination of solar position, Bergson retreats from the very acknowledgment of the sun's determination of temporal rhythm. Rather than resist the co-option of solar or communal time into a system of synchronized capital flow, Bergson disavows any communal time as degraded, spatial, and impersonal. The durée may be a universal human possession, but the anarchical character of one's own experience of the durée cannot, *by definition,* be communicated or shared. Bergson's is thus not an affirmation of psychic universality, but an extreme form of psychic isolationism, a refusal to recognize any basis for communal solidarity through shared temporality.

For Lukács the Bergsonian obsession with "subjective" time was bound up with modernism's disavowal of place and historical transformation. In his late readings of contemporary realism Lukács argues that modernist aesthetics were not simply "experimental gimmicks" but signaled an engagement with deeper philosophical problems:

> A case in point is the problem of *time*. Subjective Idealism had already separated time, abstractly conceived, from historical change and particularity of place. As if this separation were insufficient for the new age of imperialism, Bergson widened it further. Experienced time, subjective time, now became identical with real time; the rift between this time and that of the objective world was complete. Bergson and other philosophers who took up and varied this theme claimed that their concept of time alone afforded insight into authentic, i.e. subjective, reality. The same tendency soon made its appearance in literature. (*The Meaning of Contemporary Realism,* 37)

Lukács clearly expresses the basis here of the materialist critique of modernism, which is accused of mimicking a philosophical trend against history and particularity, in favor of an abstract and subjective interior temporality. Whereas Kant's subjective idealism recognized the phenomenal world as existent if inaccessible to subjectivity, Bergson's "widening of the gap" degrades and debases the material world as inauthentic in relation to the fugitive interior time-world. Whereas the great realist texts worked out "the complex tissue of man's relations with his environment," the avant-garde text separates man from exterior processes and thus, despite its dizzying and flamboyant sense of motion, produces a vision of subjectivity that is fundamentally static and changeless. Lukács is not blind to the appearance, in Joyce's *Ulysses* for example, of a barrage of exterior sensory sights and smells that intrude on interior subjectivity. However, all the minutiae of 1904 Dublin is for Lukács merely a backdrop to Bloom's or Stephen's or Molly's sovereign subjectivities. The very encyclopedic accumulation of naturalistic detail evinces the author's ultimate disengagement with such detail. Lacking any governing perspective according to which relevant or meaningful details are to be organized, the author merely stockpiles a heap of random and indiscriminate objects. The modernist backdrop is a world into which one is "thrown" in the Heideggerian sense, rather than a world with which one is intimately and inextricably engaged. It is, then, largely a continuation of late nineteenth-century naturalism, which, as Lukács argued in *The Historical Novel,* similarly treated history as a mere extravagant backdrop (as in Flaubert's *Salammbô* [1883–92]).

Lukács's representation of modernist literature as divorced from the material world and introverted into Bergsonian subjectivity has obvious political implications, which have been worked out most thoroughly by Raymond Williams in his description of "metropolitan modernism" in *The Politics of Modernism.* Williams illustrates how high modernism's formal shift depends on the changing character of major cities from closed societies to "open, complex, and mobile" centers marked by massive immigration. The major modernists, themselves "exiles and emigrés," drew on multiple traditions to forge new forms: "Liberated or breaking from their national or provincial cultures, placed in quite new relations to those other native languages or native visual traditions, encountering meanwhile a novel and dynamic common environment from which many of the older forms were obviously distant, the artists and writers and thinkers of this phase found the only community available to them: a community of the medium: of their own practices" (45). Modernist language changes with the metropolitan perception of its character as a medium rather than a social custom. Torn from their national and cultural usage, words become strange and distant, capable of being "shaped and reshaped" (46).

With Williams we find a modernism that eschews national culture in favor of an international metropolitan perception. The psychic flux of urban perception mediates cultural divides without reference to national structures. The durée becomes transnational, vitalistic, and independent of any particular location or context. Jed Esty, in his book *A Shrinking Island,* identifies a shift from this metropolitan moment back to a fixation on the local and national in the 1930s and 1940s in England; his argument draws heavily on a reading of high modernism's transnationalism. "The canonical works of high Modernism," Esty writes, "represent subjectivity by shuttling between individualizing and universalizing discursive modes, between *psyche* and *myth*—a cosmopolitan short circuit that often bypasses social configurations such as classes, genders, and nations" (105). The cosmopolitan artist in the metropolis, with unprecedented access to cultural materials from all over the world, is thus able to incorporate local elements while generally *rising above them*. It is important to note, though, that even in Williams's articulation of metropolitan modernism, the character of the modernist city and its exiled artists was never conceived as static. Williams, with his characteristic awareness of ceaseless historical transformation, suggests that even among the canonical émigré artists the lofty position of alienated transnational did not hold stable for long but transformed into various types of political and national commitments. While Picasso and Brecht directly supported communism and Wyndham Lewis and Ezra Pound moved toward fascism, Williams reminds us, Eliot and Yeats made "their muffled, nuanced treaty with Anglo-Catholicism and the celtic twilight" (34). It is in fact postmodern artists or critics, Williams argues, who freeze modernism in a moment of "radical estrangement" in order to valorize their own desire to "leave [their] settlement and settle nowhere" (35).[1]

With Lukács's modernism of Bergsonian psychic isolationism and Williams's modernism of cosmopolitans in interchangeable centers, we find a cultural formation that is capable of engaging with its contexts only as background for a valorized existential urban angst. The cultural elite that expresses this angst loftily transcends any and all debased national engagement. If standard time was making the world one uniform grid, this view of modernist politics would seem to implicate modernism as a salutary counterpart to a homogenization of global perception, despite its illusion of dizzying and immeasurable temporal flux. *Ulysses* is the key text in this scheme of modernism, with its cosmopolitan Wandering Jew, Leopold Bloom, affirming the human values of love and forgiveness in the face of, for instance, the seemingly violent and narrow rage of the Irish nationalist citizen in the "Cyclops" episode. For Lukács, Joyce's Dublin was merely a container for the supremely universal human subjectivity, which might find itself as easily transplanted to Paris or Jerusalem. Lukács's attack on the meaningless encyclopedic clutter of the Dublin backdrop in *Ulysses* directly echoes Wyndham Lewis's earlier attack on Joyce in his vituperative opus, *Time and Western Man*. Significantly, though, Lewis finds in the Bergsonian Joyce not a universal psychic isolationism from the material and national, but *the exact opposite*. For Lewis, Joyce's invocation of time as a unifying principle in *Ulysses* quickly degenerates into a vulgar parochialism, celebrating "local color" and retreating from Lewis's own rosy vision of a postwar European cosmopolitanism that is happily classless and raceless. Whereas Lukács's foundational reading has been influential in understanding literary modernism as having transcended the local and national materiality of culture, Lewis, drawing on the same textual evidence, reaches dramatically different conclusions that have only recently begun to be explored in modernist scholarship. When Lewis's reading of *Ulysses* is juxtaposed with Lukács's, a more complex and ambivalent model of modernist nationalism emerges.

In *Time and Western Man* Lewis provides an analysis of the collective "mind" of his contemporaries, against whom he stakes himself as *The Enemy* (the title of the magazine in which Lewis serialized *Time and Western Man*). The mind of the writers, philosophers, and scientists of the 1920s, Lewis writes, is a "time-mind" in that it is childishly preoccupied with the whimsical fluctuations of a highly personal sensation of temporal experience. That Lewis considers the Bergsonian durée as the chief culprit behind the droves of time-obsessed children who dominate the literary landscape is clear when he designates the "present period" as having been inaugurated at "the birth of Bergson." The fixation of literary artists on time is associated in Lewis's text with nearly every evil known to modern man. It creates and is created by spoiled aristocrats (Proust), faux-naïfs posing as infants (Stein), and simpletons who follow the herd (Pound). The time-cult is also easily subsumed under advertising, Lewis claims, although the operation of this subsumption is never quite clear.[2]

Lewis enjoins his readers, once they have glimpsed the flux and chaos of the time-mind, to shut the door on it and "lock it on the outside." Ultimately the time-obsessed, like overprivileged children, use time to escape what Lewis simply calls "reality." They renounce a commonsense relationship with the world in favor of a Protean psychology that removes itself from any recognizably solid ground. What Lewis actually means by "reality" or "concrete" ground is unclear. Throughout he hints that he will counter the degenerating influence of time with a properly "spatializing" attitude toward the "plastic" or "graphic" world. The number of pages he devotes to a clear articulation of this spatializing position is disproportionate to its weight in his argument (twenty pages out of nearly five hundred). When he does illustrate a spatial attitude toward reality his language becomes quasi-mystical, describing the mind's subjugation to the rigid and implacable solidity of the object. "Our" world, Lewis writes, is one of stasis and stability, which the Bergsons, Einsteins, and Joyces seek to wrest away or degrade. Lewis's counter to the time-cult is a kind of space-cult, in which what is glorified is the object that is beyond time, or at least is not noticeably touched by temporality: "On a still day consider the trees in a forest or in a park, or an immobile castle reflected in a glassy river; they are perfect illustrations of our static dream; and what in a sense could be more 'unreal' than they? That is the external, objective, physical, material world (made by our 'spatializing' sense) to which we are referring" (425). Equating the wild forest with the domestic park and natural phenomena with the man-made military structure of the castle, Lewis imagines a "concrete" world as given to us intact and immobile, with no trace of its use and abuse in human history.

Thus far Lewis's critique of Bergsonian abstraction is unsurprising. Of more immediate interest is his provocative, if somewhat abortive attempt to unite the "time-mind" with questions of political commitment. This is best expressed in his chapter on Joyce. According to Lewis, Joyce, despite his protestations to the contrary, engages in a version of nationalistic and nostalgic evocations of "local color." Anticipating Lukács, Lewis derides the naturalistic tendency in Joyce to pile heaps of random and indiscriminate detail into the text, forming "an Aladdin's cave of incredible bric-a-brac in which a dense mass of dead stuff is collected." The reader of *Ulysses* is confined "in a circumscribed psychological space into which several encyclopedias have been emptied" (89). What unifies all of this matter is its *deadness*. Joyce recuperates twenty-year-old "rubbish" that is valuable only insofar as it captures the particularity of a region in place and time: Dublin, June 16, 1904. For Lewis, the Bergsonian durée, for all its mystical vitalism, expresses the temporal equivalent of a spatial provincialism and intolerant nationalism. His comments are worth quoting at length:

> This psychological time, or duration, this mood that is as fixed as the matter accompanying it, is as romantic and picturesque as is "local colour," and usually as shallow a thing as that. Some realization of this is essential. *We can posit a time-district, as it were, just as much as we can a place with its individual physical properties.* And neither the local colour, nor the local time of the time-district, is what is recorded *sub specie aeternitatis*, it is unnecessary to say.
>
> Both may, however, become obsessions, and are so, I believe, today. But that is merely—that is my argument—because people are in process of being locked into both places *and* times. (This can be illustrated, where place is concerned, in the way that Signor Mussolini is locking the Italians into Italy, and refusing them passports for abroad).
>
> We are now sufficiently prepared and can educe the heart of this obscure organism that so overshadows contemporary thought, by showing its analogies. That the time-fanaticism is in some way connected with the nationalisms and the regionalisms which are politically so much in evidence, and so

intensively cultivated, seems certain—since "time" is also to some extent a region, or it can be regarded in that light. We have spoken of a *time-district,* and that is exact. Professor Whitehead uses the significant phrase "mental climate." This is by no means a fanciful affiliation; for *time* and *place* are the closest neighbors, and what happens to one is likely to be shared by the other. And if that is so, the *time-mind* would be much the same as the geographic one, fanatically circumscribing this or that territorial unit with a superstitious exclusiveness, an aggressive nationalist romance. Has not time-romance, or a fierce partisanship on behalf of a *time,* a family likeness, at least, with similar partisanship on behalf of a *place?* (83; emphasis in original)

For Lewis the contradiction between Joyce's professed disdain for Irish nationalism in *A Portrait of the Artist as a Young Man* and his clear exploitation of "Irishness" as an informing conceit or identifying "color" is ultimately irreconcilable. "Everywhere the people become more and more alike," Lewis writes. "Local colours, which have endured in many places for two thousand years, fade so quickly that already one uniform gray tint has supervened." The artificial recapitulation of aggressive nationalism compensates for this "reality" of cosmopolitanism, just as the disappearance of class in 1920s England (a highly debatable claim) produces an "artificial class-consciousness" (78). The "time-cult" of Joyce, Proust, and Stein are the dregs of a naïve resistance to a salutary cosmopolitanism that, in Lewis's view, was sweeping aside all petty, aggressive nationalisms. Like the Italians locked in Italy by Mussolini, the time-obsessed modern writers of the 1920s were being locked into discrete time districts by Bergson, marketing their petty provincialisms for literary profit even as they insisted on a transcendent universalism in their politics and aesthetics.

There is a profound observation buried in Lewis's polemic, one on which he fails to elaborate. The argument that Bergson and the "time-cult" of literary modernism are clandestinely national as opposed to the properly spatial artist, whose world outlook is progressively cosmopolitan, runs counter to the "metropolitan modernist" model provided by Raymond Williams. For Williams modernism's obsession with the urban metropolis was part of a larger attempt to mediate between psychic individualism and a cosmic human collective, while sidestepping the intervening stages of political, national, and cultural organization. Lewis sees in this heightened perception, however, merely a jargon cloaking a fiercely regional provincialism. The obsession with time is in fact a stylistic ruse that thinly disguises a fixation on a district—a minutely and exhaustively catalogued national milieu (as in

Joyce's encyclopedia of 1904 Dublin). It would be possible to marshal a series of examples that might illustrate Lewis's point (an argumentative burden that Lewis himself unfortunately never assumes), and indeed there is a strain of contemporary scholarship that has tended to be skeptical of reiterated assertions of modernism's antiprovincialism. Alex Davis and Lee M. Jenkins, in their edited collection of essays, *Locations of Literary Modernism,* argue that an intense investment in place, region, or nation among a range of modernist writers has unjustly led to their "peripheralisation or marginalization" according to the prevailing critical paradigm (6). The Hugh MacDiarmid scholar Robert Crawford has argued that it is only "cursory" accounts of modernism that insist upon its "cosmopolitanism and internationalism" at the expense of the "equally important side of modernism that is demotic and crucially 'provincial'" (Davis and Jenkins, 10). Indeed the canonical English metropolitan modernist texts shy away from the dizzying blur of urban perceptions that might universalize the cities they paint. Joyce argued that *Dubliners* could never have been titled "Londoners" or "Parisians" (Nolan, 29). T. S. Eliot's "unreal" London might be any metropolitan wasteland, if not for *The Waste Land*'s uniquely English idiom and densely allusive British literary references, from the opening echo of Chaucer's General Prologue through the Thames maidens to the echoes of Shakespearean and Renaissance revenge tragedies. To be sure, German, Italian, Greek, and Sanskrit are overlaid at crucial moments, but are nearly dwarfed by the text's (and its author's) overwhelming Anglophilism. In *Mrs. Dalloway* we are always aware that we are in London, not Paris, Berlin, or Vienna. Woolf's street itineraries are meticulously mapped, as some peripatetic critics of the novel have discovered on walking tours, and Big Ben's presence persistently fixes the reader on a uniquely British cultural symbol.[3] Sara Blair has demonstrated that Bloomsbury, typically represented more as a cultural "aura" than as a material site of cultural production, can be fruitfully situated within the specific local dynamics of the Bloomsbury district's uniquely "variegated texture" (825).

In resuscitating Lewis's critique of the Bergsonian artist as clandestinely local and anticosmopolitan I do not mean to dismantle Williams's model of metropolitan perception, which remains a crucial entry into modernist aesthetics. Nor do I by any means wish to affirm or resurrect Lewis's political stance (though it has already been resurrected in contemporary neoliberal thought). Instead I hope to inflect Williams's model of a cosmopolitan modernism with a concurrent tension in the Anglo-modernist tradition, away from psychic cosmopolitanism and toward unique and discrete engagements with national or local politics and culture. I do not mean to suggest, however, that such engagements are unique to British writers. In the textual readings that make up the remaining chapters of this book I discuss the ways that British, Irish, and Indian authors all explore the temporal politics of place and position, an exploration I see as characteristic of the larger modernist discourse on time. The extreme positions of temporal isolationism (the durée turning away from its own shadows) and temporal transnationalism (a cosmopolitan humanism that disdains the local or provincial) by no means capture the full range of temporal politics characteristic of modernist art. I am certainly not alone in making this assertion. In his 1985 study, *Mapping Literary Modernism: Time and Development,* Ricardo J. Quinones argues that although modernism in its early phase flirted with an escape from historical certainty into mythic universality, it gradually became dissatisfied with gestures of escape and began to offer new models of reengagement with history and society. Perceptual pluralism was for Joyce and Woolf a problem, not a solution, Quinones argues: "They too feared that susceptibility to the many facets of experience might result in a barren cosmopolitanism" (222). Bloom's cosmopolitan distance is as much satirized as it is celebrated in *Ulysses* (in his role as hapless cuckold, for instance), while Woolf's relationship to social forms of temporality is not purely resistant, but profoundly ambivalent. The trains and clocks of London in *The Waves* are not entirely demonized as mechanistic, but are in part recognized as a necessary force for stabilizing identity and value (232). One might argue that even in the earlier *Mrs. Dalloway* the striking of Big Ben serves as an impetus for a kind of social connection that it suggests but only inadequately fulfills. The seeming "inwardness" of modernist character is, for Quinones, in its very "openness" and ambiguity a window onto the author's representation of an external social environment (249). Unlike Lawrence's Gerald Crich, with his unyielding and dominating will, characters like Bloom and Clarissa, by refusing, in Clarissa's words, to "say of herself, I am this, I am that," open themselves up to a unique imaginative empathy for characters like Septimus Smith, a man distant in class, gender, experience, and space.

In her study of Joyce and nationalism Emer Nolan has similarly criticized the dominance of the "metropolitan modernist" model as an overdetermined neglect of a modernist text's nonmetropolitan contexts. Nolan begins with the passage from Lewis that I cited earlier and asserts that it "issues a unique and valuable warning" that has been "simplified and ignored" in subsequent Joyce scholarship (13). The warning is that we not read Joyce as categorically rejecting Irish nationalism in favor of "international standards" simply because he depicts characters who are intensely critical of their nation. Stephen, in both *A Portrait of the Artist as a Young Man* and *Ulysses,* is more accurately understood as caught in a "painful deadlock" rather than a "detached ambivalence" in relation to Ireland (130). Cosmopolitanism is a problem for Joyce, not a solution, something Lewis shrewdly observed (perhaps precisely because he himself was writing, as Nolan suggests, from a "racist, colonialist" view).[4] According to Nolan, Lewis understands, as few Joycean critics have, that "Joyce's Ireland hovers elusively between province and metropolis, past and future" (13). Stephen is never given an exclusive or dominating voice in either *Portrait* or *Ulysses.* In both texts he is put in active and sometimes violent conflict with oppositional stances that quite often expose his own narrowness or intellectual coldness. The retreat of an Irish writer from his nation for a European pan-culturalism is, Nolan rightly observes, "consistently foregrounded as the *content* of [Joyce's] writing, and not just as its context" (44). Joyce "professes aestheticism, but does not write aestheticist literature." Instead he often grants more exuberance and comic vitality to the nationalist antagonists of Stephen or Bloom than he does to his detached artist protagonists. Joyce further invests such antagonists with informed and reasonable political positions, which often had in fact been earlier expressed by Joyce himself in essay form. Thus in *Stephen Hero* Stephen's cosmopolitanism is roundly dismissed by Hughes, who proclaims in a public speech, "A man that was of all countries was of no countries." Stephen's expressions of international aestheticism are "the subject of general comment and controversy," and his "assertion of artistic autonomy," Nolan continues, "is assaulted and defended, continuously thematized and understood as politically charged from the outset" (44).[5]

In Nolan's reading we find a modernism that is constitutionally incapable of turning its back on its contexts, despite Pound's or other critics' insistence that such a turn, on Joyce's part particularly, constitutes its greatest claim to international recognition. It would be equally inaccurate to insist on any easy engagement with nationalism in modernist literature,[6] but Nolan's language of the "painful deadlock" captures modernism's tortured wrestling with its own national contexts. Modernism's inability to resolve its own politics of place manifests itself stylistically, particularly in the early modernism of Joseph Conrad and Ford Madox Ford, in a language of frustrated ambiguity—as, for example, in Conrad's repetitious use of the words *unfathomable* and *unknowable*. Pericles Lewis reads such ambiguities in Conrad's *Heart of Darkness* as manifestations of a characteristic modern struggle between transnational, liberal humanist values on the one hand and an awareness of the biological inheritance of national "character" on the other. The racial dimension of the "English character," he argues, creeps in through the prodigious gaps in the concepts of "humanity, decency, justice, efficiency, liberty, devotion to ideals," and ultimately provides a more lasting glue for social solidarity than does lofty cosmopolitanism. The great mystery as to why Marlow seeks out and identifies with Kurtz is ultimately deferred to an expression of shared national and racial characteristics. Liberal, transnational ideals such as "justice," Lewis writes,

> depend so completely [for Marlow and for Conrad] on a particular English character, which is the product of historical accident (or good luck), [that] they are incapable of being exported to the rest of the world. When the devotees of an English-style liberalism attempt to apply it to places and peoples unsuited by character to liberal self-government, the result is either a fanatical idealism tinged with egalitarianism *a la* Kurtz that takes down all institutions or a bureaucratic and hypocritical nightmare like the Company's in which the strongest take advantage of the weakest while cloaking their motives in the form of law and liberalism. (124)

Conrad is painfully aware of the inadequacy of forcing one set of national values on all of humanity on the grounds of an enlightened and benignant liberalism. His figure for such grandiose projects of globalized Enlightenment is the colossal Kurtz, whose ideals quickly degenerate into eugenics. Similarly in Joyce's use of Parnell's story in *Portrait* or Proust's use of the Dreyfus Affair in *The Guermantes Way* Pericles Lewis sees a characteristic modernist fixation on racial determinations of identity. By "racial" Lewis means "the intimate relationship between the individual and his ethnic group which [for Joyce and Proust] precedes all cultural ties and fundamentally conditions the individual's experience. It is more primary than culture, but it necessarily implies a combination of historical, cultural, biological, and spiritual conditions" (41). Lewis's treatment renders intelligible Stephen's famous diary entry at the end of *Portrait* in which he refers to "the uncreated conscience of my race," a statement that Lewis suggests had been incomprehensible under the "conventional critical wisdom that associates modernism with individualism, cosmopolitanism, or a rejection of society" (8).

These tensions between a racialized, national English character and a global worldview tinged with liberal humanist value define not only the discourse of literary modernism, but also the discourse of standard time, or more specifically of astrophysics and its accompanying cosmological world picture. The popular discourse of astronomy in the early twentieth century could be construed as yet another bolster to modernism's alleged cosmological humanism and its accompanying antinationalist politics. The profusion of astrophysical tools and astronomical knowledge, garnered in lavishly funded eclipse expeditions in the Victorian period, produced its own minor literature of fiction and nonfiction devoted to exploring the philosophical lessons that were to be gained by a newfound awareness of the vastness of space and the relative recency of human history and culture. Scientific popularizers such as James Jeans and Arthur Eddington dominated a corner of the English book market with such titles as *The Universe around Us* and *The Nature of the Physical World*. In these texts, often accompanied by photographs of a seemingly endless cosmos, the authors elaborated on the cosmological *longue durée*, in which "a day of almost unthinkable length stretches before us" (Henry, 46). Leonard Woolf, reading Jeans's books, described how "depressing and humiliating" were human aspirations and struggles in the face of "universes of myriads of stars flaming through space" (Henry, 47). In her book on astronomy and modernism Holly Henry argues that the discourse of cosmological time and astronomical discovery inspired Virginia Woolf to take a larger worldview that was above "fascist, or nationalist politics" (158). Yet Henry is forced to admit that Jeans's own conclusions about the lessons of the heavens were stridently racist and nationalist. Jeans apparently used the example of the dinosaurs, who "failed to retain their supremacy," as justification for his support of a British eugenics project, by which the nation could "prevent the moral, mental, and physical wreckage of today from reproducing itself." The only way to prevent humankind from suffering the fate of the dinosaurs would be to assiduously practice "the weeding out of the unfit." Britain, Jeans alleged, wrongly "saves" its babies "indiscriminately—good and bad, strong and weak, healthy and diseased" (Henry, 149). If the most successful astronomer (in terms of book sales) could read the stars as supporting the preservation of the British race, why should we assume that modernist writers were reading them in more salutary ways? Henry equates Virginia Woolf's global worldview with that of an Apollo 9 astronaut whose views of the globe from space inspire a lofty contempt for fanatical nationalism, represented unsurprisingly by "hundreds of people in the Mideast killing each other over some imaginary line that you're not even aware of and that you can't see" (108). Henry may find this sentiment enlightening, but it is unlikely to appeal to Palestinians, who might resent the rendering of their struggles as "imaginary." One could argue that a global worldview is simply the equation of one's national, racial view with the logic of the cosmos, precisely the equation that is made, as I argued in chapter 1, between standard time and empire.

When astrophysics was so heavily funded by territorial empires for the consolidation of their power, as Alex Soojung-Kim Pang demonstrates in his book, *Empire and the Sun,* it would be highly unlikely that the discourse would produce the kinds of disinterested global humanism that Henry finds so uncomplicatedly universal. "Victorian astronomers knew," Pang writes, that "reliable observations of eclipses could not have been made outside the spheres of European civilization and technology" (143). Far from seeing themselves as independent thinkers fighting national prejudice, astronomers knew that, as Charles Pritchard wrote in 1871, "the mighty empires now consolidated in the far west and south would not exist" without the ceaseless footwork of astronomical investigation (Pang, 143). Pang's investigation of the situatedness of astronomical fieldwork within "the world of railroads, telegraphs, plantations, government bungalows, and regimental headquarters" (142) is a healthy corrective to Henry's discourse analysis of the salutary transnationalism of cosmological knowledge, with its accompanying worldview that so quickly glosses, as does Henry, "nationalist" with "fascist" politics. Historical ignorance does not equal global insight, as Woolf herself recognized in gently satirizing Clarissa Dalloway's inability to say where the equator is located or to discriminate between Turks and Armenians.

If the humanist, cosmological view dramatically restricted the scope and aspirations of human history, it also depended on the notion of a single, unitary world time, with one point of origin and one clear trajectory. The arrow of entropy, the cooling of the sun, the expansion of the universe, and other physical laws that stupefied the minds of Jeans's and Eddington's readers all seemed to confirm the unidirectionality and inevitability of temporal processes.[7] Standard time presumed the even and orderly unfolding of human time as a river with one source, one outlet, and one even rate of flow. "Time," Sandford Fleming wrote, resembles a mighty river, whose unvarying stream passes before us. Such a river is unchangeable, yet continually changing. Volumes of water always advancing are replaced by new volumes in perpetual succession, and yet the river continues one and the same ever flowing unity. The passing stream of time is much the same, and the problem presented to us is to keep a proper record of its flow. It is perfectly obvious that the principles which should govern should be such as to secure complete accord in the detail of its measurement independently of locality. All peoples are concerned in the attainment of harmonious results, and therefore it is important that they shall acquiesce in the employment of the same unit of computation and in counting the measurements from one common zero. ("Time-Reckoning," 348–49)

Fleming's extended stream-of-time metaphor accomplishes two key objectives. First he equates standard time's flow with "harmony," "advancement," "unity," "might," and "succession." Time sanctions, and in fact *is,* the orderly progression of lineage and linearity, the universal guarantor that, so long as humanity "acquiesces" to measure it, the flow of history will produce uniform results for all. Second he disavows the notion that time might be intrinsic to human activity, bound up with its codes and structures. The role of humanity is to passively "record" and "measure" an entity extrinsic to them and indifferent to the particularities of their "locality."

In its abstraction from the particularities of locality standard time could be understood as a kind of totalizing historicism, promoting uniformity and homogenization. Peter Osborne in *The Politics of Time* writes that the notion of modernity demands an engagement with the question of "one time, one history." Appeals to an "immanent" unitary history depend on the standard time system, which placed every planetary action on the same scale of measurement: "Capitalism has 'universalized' history, in the sense that it has established systematic relations of social interdependence on a planetary scale (encompassing non-capitalist societies), thereby producing a single global space of temporal co-existence or coevalness, within which actions are quantifiable chronologically in terms of a single standard of measurement: world standard time" (34). Osborne, however, disagrees with the claim that standardized capitalist time has produced a unified globe. Both standard time and its revolutionary countermodel of "socialism as the unification of history" wrongly depend on a "totalizing" view of what constitutes humanity. Rejecting capitalist world standard time as a unifying principle because it insufficiently accounts for the ontological nature of "humanity," Osborne instead turns to the phenomenology of Martin

Heidegger (inflected through Paul Ricoeur) for a more thorough treatment of that ontology.[8]

In a sense Osborne's turn to "ontological difference" as a bulwark against humanism, singularity, and uniformity (a move by no means confined to his own work) could be understood as yet another version of the dialectic between temporal isolationism and temporal transnationalism that I have been charting in the context of modernist scholarship and cosmological discourse. The single, uniform flow of "cosmic time" is the ultimate metaphysical support for temporal transnationalism in aesthetics and politics, while a celebration of difference is yet another manifestation of the temporal isolationism that had been embodied earlier in Bergson's theory of the durée. Whereas the cosmological worldview too readily equates specific national prejudices with global reality (nationalism is fascism in disguise, borders are imaginary, human activity is inconsequential), ontological difference just as easily translates into isolationist disavowals of any common ground as "mere historicism." Is it possible to chart a course between these two visions of time and history? I suggest that the charting of such a course is exactly what distinguishes the modernist project from earlier narrative representations of time and from later postmodern versions of temporality. Modernism represents a crucial stage in the history of the transformation of world time. Neither subsumed under global standard time's uniformity nor retracted into a psychical, fluid, interiority, modernist temporal subjectivity exists somewhere between conformity and isolationism. Precisely because of their ambivalent, even tortured engagement with national contexts and questions of shared value the modernists were uniquely situated to interrogate the radical novelty and provocative disjointedness of standard time's reshaping of the globe. The modernist project of dialectically negotiating the divide between temporal uniformity and temporal heterogeneity was perhaps best articulated theoretically by Ernst Bloch in his writings on the noncontemporaneous in the 1930s. While recognizing the persistent and undeniable reality of temporal heterogeneity, Bloch nevertheless refused to counter the uniform homogeneity of capitalism ("the great unbroken Pan" [115]) with a celebration of anarchical, isolationist "difference."

"Not all people exist in the same Now," Bloch provocatively begins his essay on the noncontemporaneous, and it is clear by the end of his disquisition that all people *should*. Bloch valorizes the "Now" as the authentic moment of driving, revolutionary contradiction and castigates noncontemporaneous class fractions such as "youth," "the peasantry," and "the urban centre," all of which tend to move to the political right as they look away from the present. For Bloch, however, a temporally standardized revolutionary project need not necessitate a sacrifice of temporal diversity or an alliance with the enemy. As did Sandford Fleming, Bloch represents time and history as a river, but his river is significantly different from Fleming's:

> Everything flows, but the river comes from a source every time. It takes matter with it from the regions through which it has run, this colours its waters for a long time. Equally for that new form there are remnants of an older one, there is no absolute cut between today and yesterday. There is no totally new work, least of all the revolutionary kind; the old work is merely continued more clearly, brought to success. The older paths and forms are not neglected with impunity, as has been shown. Dreams in particular, even the most wakeful ones, have a past history, and they carry it with them. Among backward strata these remnants are particularly strong and often totally musty, but even the revolutionary class honors its precursors and still heeds them. The old forms may help, if correctly deployed, with the new. (132)

Bloch's river is not unchanging and uniform, nor is it "independent of locality." On the contrary, the river of time carries with it the remnants of the past and the traces of the "regions through which it has run." The sources of time are the struggles and dreams of independent communities, all of whom create and "colour" the waters of time. Rather than positing an abstract, universal origin and end-point of development, Bloch's river charts a course between temporal incommensurability and standardized homogeneity by emphasizing regional temporal particularity. The imperative is to recognize the diverse heterogeneity of temporal experience while refusing to give up the ideals of interdependence, communication, and shared value.

Bloch's metaphorical river provides a useful emblem for the representations of temporality that I chart in the following chapters. The modernists were neither lost in the heady ether of temporal transnationalism nor sealed in interiorized enclaves of temporal isolationism. They did not celebrate the private and revile the public. Rather their avant-garde negotiations of temporality charted a course down Bloch's river, reshaping the public foundations of temporal organization, even as they resisted the enlistment of that public time for imperial projects of commercial and military expansion.

CHAPTER 3

At the Limits of Imperial Time; or, Dracula Must Die!

The 1884 Berlin and Prime Meridian Conferences eliminated material and conceptual barriers against spatiotemporal globalization. Setting the protocols for imperial rivalry in West Africa and beyond, the Berlin Conference would enable the Western powers to fill in with their imperial colors the "white patch" of Africa, which Conrad's Marlow describes as having been a "blank space of delightful mystery" before it was "filled . . . with rivers and lakes and names" (*Heart of Darkness*, 142). The Prime Meridian Conference would simultaneously unify the diverse temporalities of the world, ensuring that one could never lose the proper Greenwich time, no matter how far from home one strayed. This demystification of global space in the fin de siècle generated among popular fiction writers a reactionary move to recapture the mysterious and occult spaces of the globe, resistant to the scientific rationality of the modern age. Patrick Brantlinger argues that writers of the "imperial Gothic," such as H. Rider Haggard, Bram Stoker, Arthur Conan Doyle, and H. G. Wells, responded to the rationalization and unification of the globe by recuperating irrational and incommensurable experiences of mysticism and disunity, projecting the dark spaces of the mind and spirit worlds onto exotic locales somehow missed by the cartographers of empire. The adventure novelists of the 1880s and 1890s were mapmakers who projected onto global space their own dreams and nightmares, rather than projecting onto it a rational grid of railways and telegraphs. In imperial Gothic fiction, Brantlinger writes, "Africa,

India, and the other dark places of the Earth become a terrain upon which the political unconscious of imperialism maps its own desires, its own fantastic latitudes and longitudes" (246). Like Fredric Jameson, Brantlinger identifies cartography as a major source of anxiety for the writers of the late nineteenth century and reads aesthetic production as driven by transformations in the conception of global space.

It was not only global space that was being transformed in the fin de siècle, however, but global time as well. Just as the adventure novels of Haggard depended on topography uncharted in any official map, they also depended on dramatically unsynchronized exotic populations. If the imperial Gothics drew fantastical spaces of the imagination, they primarily populated those spaces with temporally deviant or discordant inhabitants. This is by no means surprising, given that the anthropological imaginary, as Johannes Fabian has argued, has long depended on a denial of common temporality between cultures.[1] Conrad's equation in *Heart of Darkness* of a trip down the Congo River with a trip into the ancient past typifies the conception (by no means eradicated today) that populations not aligned with Western socioeconomic models are somehow temporally anachronistic, examples of the prehistoric paradoxically coexisting with the modern. The writers of imperial Gothics and their intrepid heroes, while often flirting dangerously with temporally going native and giving themselves up to the nonsynchronicities of the exotic, ultimately erase those nonsynchronicities, bringing the time of the exotic up to date and imposing rigid chronological exactitude on deviant populations. This happens both thematically, in terms of representations of temporally synchronized technologies (clocks, railways, telegraphs), and also formally, with narratives that insist upon an often tight synchronization of chronology as well as closure to threateningly open-ended temporalities. Brantlinger's argument that the imperial Gothics primarily resisted the technobureaucratic processes of the imperial age in favor of the irrational processes of the occult can be tempered somewhat by recognizing that one of the major technobureaucratic pressures of the age was the synchronization of global time. To this pressure, at least, the writers of imperial Gothic succumbed, enforcing temporal synchronization upon and divesting foreign populations of the power to control their own temporality.

To a certain extent the late nineteenth-century adventure novel depended for its pleasures on an evocation of discrepant times not capable of being measured by the clock or by Greenwich Mean Time. The average London reader of H. Rider Haggard, caught up in the precisely timed routines of urban labor and leisure, no doubt longed for the more expansive and task-specific temporalities of Allen Quartermain and Horace Holly, men of independent means, able to give up months of their lives to exploration and adventure. Haggard knew this, and knew better than to transform his stories into puritanical treatises on the virtues of temporal precision. Yet despite its expression of a longing for temporal experience outside of the limits of Greenwich time, Haggard's fiction suggests a compensatory pull away from the temporally exotic and toward the comfort and familiarity of Greenwich time, naturalized throughout his texts as a healthy, normal counterbalance against the violence and sexual danger of the nonsynchronous. Moreover Haggard is not alone among fin de siècle writers in negotiating this balancing act. In this chapter I consider three examples of the narrative management of temporally deviant outsiders in the late nineteenth-century fiction of empire. In Haggard's *She* (1887), Bram Stoker's *Dracula* (1897), and Rudyard Kipling's *Kim* (1901) the title characters each typify a version of temporal exoticism. Haggard's Ayesha and Stoker's Dracula are timeless creatures existing on the peripheries of empire, challenging the standards and limits imposed by the conventions of British time. The narrative thrust of the imperial Gothic is to eliminate every vestige of the challenge these characters present to unified world time by temporally fixing them within familiar latitudes and longitudes. While dependent on the exotic thrill of these atemporal characters, the texts ultimately harness them within a comfortable narrative trajectory, ensuring readers that the threat they pose to the global temporal order is eminently manageable through readily available tools. If Haggard's and Stoker's fictions constitute strategies of managing and containing threatening exotic temporality, Kipling's *Kim* disavows the existence of such a threat altogether by representing the British Raj as an efficiently functioning hybrid of English punctuality and exotic timelessness. Kipling's faith in the efficacy of the Great Game, with its cartographic aspirations to manage and contain the "great, grey, formless" subcontinent, enables him to conceive of spatiotemporal harmony where Haggard and Stoker saw only stark opposition. Kim, simultaneously the perpetual adolescent and the masterful sahib, is capable of both performing tasks according to the strict dictates of English punctuality and of falling back, "Oriental style," on formless and unmeasured exotic temporality. For Haggard, Stoker, and Kipling the narrative management of global space involved a confrontation with temporal nonsynchronicities. In this sense their project mirrors that of the global standard time advocates at the

78 | Chapter 3

Prime Meridian Conference, who similarly understood that deviations in the measurement and expression of temporality posed deep structural problems to the unification and management of global space. It is not my intention to claim that these writers were directly responding to the debates surrounding the Prime Meridian Conference. Rather I hope to show the extent to which the representation of global space and foreign populations in late nineteenth-century narrative constituted an explicitly temporal problem. Managing the exotic within narrative involved a confrontation with temporal nonsynchronicity, and the burden on the novel was to formally contain, unify, or otherwise ameliorate the tensions that nonsynchronicity provoked. The generic constraints of the adventure novel were themselves uniquely suited for such a project, depending on a linear narrative structure and clearly defined thematic closure. The adventure novel thus implicitly standardized experience, ensuring that the threat of nonsynchronicity never exceeded appropriate bounds. This is in stark contrast to the modernist texts I consider in chapter 4, each of which thematically and formally creates aesthetic space for nonsynchronicity. Modernist novels call direct attention to the role of Greenwich Mean Time in curtailing and foreclosing heterogeneous temporal experience, revealing the role of Greenwich in managing imperial space. In contrast, the word *Greenwich* appears rarely in the texts under consideration in this chapter. Rather than expose the relationship between Greenwich and imperial power, these adventure novels naturalize that relationship, rendering human time and Greenwich Mean Time equivalent and nonproblematic, smoothing over the intransigent alterity of those populations potentially resistant to a global common coordinate frame.

In one sense adventure writers expressed distaste for the bureaucratic rationalism of the clock, imposing its dull, unimaginative order on the more healthy and vigorous rhythms of the outdoors. At the same time, though, at the farthest reaches of imperial space the clock could provide comfort and stability in the face of alienation and violence. In his autobiography Sir Henry Morton Stanley expresses this love-hate relationship with the British clock. In middle-age, his African adventures long behind him, Stanley settled into the routines of parliamentary life and bemoaned its rigid schedule. The "asphyxiating" atmosphere of the House of Commons, with its hours of meaningless labor, Stanley complains, makes it "impossible to obtain air or exercise" (502). Forced to endure hours of tedious argumentation in the House, Stanley imagines the more loquacious MPs condemned to an unusual clock-based punishment: "Some of them, I wish, could be taken to the Clock-Tower, where they could wrangle with Big Ben to their hearts' content" (503). In contrast to this association between clock towers and punishment, however, he recalls a moment in his youth when a clock symbolized the pleasures and comforts of a temporary home. Sent as an illegitimate child to a workhouse at a young age, Stanley and other boys escaped and made their way as fugitives to a stone cottage, where a woman gave them bread, treacle, and buttermilk. Stanley paints his nights spent outside as a fugitive in clearly Gothic colors, describing the "spectral inhabitants" of the darkness and a "whiff of ghostly wings" (36). In contrast to these Gothic terrors he recalls how the "homely clock" of the kind woman in the cottage, "with its face crowned at the top with staring red flowers, ticked loudly during the pauses of [his] narrative." Juxtaposing this "homely clock" with an image of the woman suckling her baby, Stanley notes that the benevolence of the image "stands out unfading" in his memory (37). If the clock could curtail the vigor and spontaneity of imperial adventure it could also provide "homely" comforts and elicit associations with domesticity, maternal love, and bodily sustenance.

Tension over the virtues and detriments of temporal precision certainly characterizes the work of H. Rider Haggard, whose entire oeuvre depends on an imaginative reconstruction of tribes lost to history. In one sense temporal precision functions as a tool of imperial power in Haggard's work because it serves as a weapon against the atemporal exotic, lost in prehistory and extending changelessly into the future. Haggard's explorers export values of justice and democracy to these premodern civilizations, often inadvertently and accidentally (since the main goals of the adventures are typically self-satisfying treasure hunting or identity questing). They thus function as globalizing agents, intervening against hopelessly local worldviews. Their agency is figured in astronomical terms, as if a proper cartography of empire demanded a realignment of cosmic phenomena. Empire comes from the heavens in Haggard, rather than from a discrete national origin. In *King Solomon's Mines* (1885) Allen Quartermain and crew represent themselves as "men from the stars" and, in an often-imitated scene, predict a solar eclipse in order to shock and awe the natives.[2] Relying on an almanac and an accurate knowledge of the correct Greenwich time, Quartermain correctly predicts that a total eclipse at "11.15 Greenwich time" (172) will "put out" the sun (174). Described as an "ardent astronomer" as he waits for the eclipse (184), Quartermain uses his astronomical powers to inspire the antimonarchical Kukuana faction to "do away with" the evil practices of the land (176). Representing their own desire for mastery over exotic populations in terms of the demands of the cosmos, Haggard's adventurers align "backward" tribes with the processes and policies of Western imperialism.

Ayesha, the deathless queen in Haggard's later novel, *She,* is also figured as intractably local in her worldview, despite her thousands of years of life experience in the pre-Christian era. "I dwell among the caves and the dead," she tells Holly, "and naught know I of the affairs of men, nor have I cared to know" (143). The plains and caverns of Kôr are impenetrable labyrinths that seal off their inhabitants from any contact with the outside world. Unmapped they are also virtually unnavigable. Holly recognizes the impossibility of finding his way unaided through the "network of marshes which, stretching for scores and scores of miles, formed a stronger and more impassable fortification round the various Amahagger households than any that could be built or designed by man" (169). In their final adventure in the "Temple of Truth" Holly describes the adventurers as "nearly blinded and utterly confused" by the mists and vapors of the temple (272). Hidden within her geological labyrinth unmapped by the Western powers, Ayesha also hides from conventional methods of historical dating, inhabiting a temporality based on occult powers, memory, and emotional events rather than the clock. Temporally ossified in the moment when she killed her lover, Kallikrates, she inhabits a changeless eternity of youthful beauty and endless remorse. Defying "time and evil," in Vincey's words, Ayesha equates "five minutes" in Leo's presence with "sixty generations that are gone" (200). Her time reckoning is based on events rather than the revolution of the Earth around the sun. Preserving her dead lover's corpse Ayesha also preserves her memories "in a grave that [her] own hands have hollowed" (143). In one sense her gendered defiance of the dictates of rational temporality is seductive to the British adventurers, just as the gendered space of the lost mountains of Kukuanaland in *King Solomon's Mines,* notoriously represented as "Sheba's breasts," is similarly inviting. Ayesha briefly wins the explorers over to her conception of temporality. Holly, realizing that his three weeks in Kôr feel like thirty years, argues explicitly for an event-based method of dating. "Truly time should be measured by events," he exclaims, "and not by the lapse of hours" (315).

Yet despite the seductiveness of Ayesha's discordant temporality, the general thrust of the narrative is to definitively date her by, bluntly, killing her off. In the odd climactic scene in which she transforms into a wizened monkey under the influence of the flame, Ayesha finally carries the visual markers of her actual temporality. Transformed into a shriveled mummy, as indeed she should have been at two thousand years of age, she is also described as a "monkey," a clear indication of her own primitive empire's devolution in the eyes of the Western world. Haggard himself claims to have felt remorse at enforcing this abrupt end on a character with whom he confesses to have been in love. The dictates of the tale, however, demanded such an ending. Her fate, he writes, was "necessary to the moral" and required him as a writer to "steel" himself "to bring her to such an end." According to Haggard, his moral is a Christian one, rendering her fate as a character predestined. Ayesha, representing "intellectual Paganism" or "modern Agnosticism," "lifts herself up against the Omnipotent." "Therefore," Haggard concludes, "at the appointed time she is swept away by It" (Monsman, 199). Temporal deviance is here represented as defiance of the Christian order, which dispenses with such upstarts at the precisely "appointed time." Haggard as a writer represents himself as begrudgingly doing the business of God by eliminating his character, in the same way that Quartermain and company act as agents of the heavens in "putting out the sun" in the eclipse scene. In both cases the precisely timed elimination of temporal anachronism is presented as analogous with Heaven's work. This is the moral core of much of Haggard's writing, expressed by Holly as a "natural shirking . . . from the things that are above Nature" (246). Submitting to the will and the rhythm of the heavens is a humble Christian duty, equated with the humility that accompanies Western democracy. Just as Holly and Leo declare that they must relinquish their control over their nation to "the votes of the lower and least educated classes of the community" (255), Holly also realizes, in the face of the night sky, his own inability to alter the course of the heavens. Staring at the "glittering points" in the "immense arch of heaven," he reflects on his own insignificance, in the knowledge that when "his hour comes" he will "pass humbly, whither he knows not" (118). The rising and setting of the sun is the symbol itself of life's inevitable end, of "the earthly beginning, and the end, also" (57). The heavens remind us of our mortality and our place within a larger system, lessons from which Ayesha shields herself in her sunless caverns, defying the temporal limits of existence.

If Haggard's Christian moral necessitated the extermination of timeless exoticism, the adventure novel was well suited for satisfying such a purpose. Demanding satisfying plot resolution and the restoration of moral and social order, the adventure novel tends toward an irrevocable linear resolution of plot points and extraneous loose ends. Killing the most complex and ambiguous characters (Gagool, Ayesha, Quartermain himself) and sealing off the sources of occult mystery (the diamond mines and the Temple of Truth) often generated problems for the prolific Haggard, who had to write countless prequels in order to bring back his most popular characters and locales after their definitive extermination in previous books. Yet the genre demanded the elimination of ambiguity. The dilemma of the adventure novel is initially posed in terms of impenetrable obscurity, represented often in Haggard's novels by artifacts bearing unreadable symbols and layers of textual commentary in dead languages and ancient script. The dozen or more pages in the third chapter of *She* devoted to the "uncial Greek" script inscribed on the sherd of Amenartes produce little more than an effect of inscrutability on the reader, with pages devoted to the ancient script, the modern transcription, and the English translation. The daunting task confronting the adventurers is thus represented in terms of translation. Ultimately the adventure novel promises an exact translation of all threatening obscurity into the more readily comprehensible tropes of the genre. For Daniel Bivona *She* both thematically and structurally "reinforces aesthetically the prohibition against return and regression." Denying the "cyclical plot" of a return to prehistory by sealing off the cave to the temple at the end of the novel, Haggard "commits his heroes to mortality and the linear plot of imperial heroism" (81). Ayesha's seductive immortality and her event-based temporal orientation are starkly eliminated as viable options within the world order that the British bring to the obscure corners of the Earth. Haggard's heroes are astronomers, predicting the exact moment of the eclipse of backward societies and acting in the name of a national temporal order they equate with that of the cosmos.

Lost in unmapped and unnavigable territories far from the grid of transport and communication technology, with neither Baedeker nor Bradshaw to guide them, Haggard's adventurers have their work cut out for them. Bram Stoker's *Dracula,* published ten years later, imagines an atemporal exotic villain like Ayesha *within* the English metropolis, and thus subjected to a full arsenal of standardized temporal technology. Stoker's international coalition of vampire hunters use tools of temporal synchronization as weapons against the vampire, whose very ontological being initially frustrates any attempt at temporal control or representation. Stoker's novel, like Haggard's, manifests anxiety over the difficulties of spatiotemporally representing dark, mysterious, and unmapped corners of the Earth, in this case an Eastern European region beyond the scope or even interest of empire.[3] Transylvania is a repository of both religious fanaticism and biological degeneration (simultaneously embodied by the Czech and Slovak peasants with "painfully prevalent" goiters kneeling before shrines [15]). The region produces, as an integral agent of its cultural lore, a figure that is timeless, living for generations and fluctuating in appearance from an old to a young man depending on his level of blood consumption. The anxiety that Dracula produces in the vampire hunters is that, unlike Jonathan Harker in Dracula's castle, who knows "the span" of his life, Dracula's existence is limitless, open at both ends, and thus ontologically unthinkable. The ability to aesthetically represent foreign space is bound up in Stoker's text with the employment of formal strategies of temporal maintenance and the definition of *natural* as that which can be spatiotemporally located within a common coordinate system.

Transylvania and its famous inhabitant initially prove resistant to spatial mapping. As Harker learns when he prepares for his visit to Castle Dracula, no accurate maps of its exact location exist. "There are no maps of this country as yet," he writes, "to compare with our own Ordnance Survey maps" (10). Harker's early journal entries are themselves a topographical and anthropological record of his expedition into the uncharted. He records every minutia, from the gastronomic details of his meals (even copying recipes for his fiancée) to national demographics. His efforts to spatially map his foray into Transylvania anticipate Stoker's larger narrative project to *temporally* map its ontologically timeless inhabitant. The beast's temporal indeterminacy must be eliminated by assigning it a temporal full stop. Stoker's project, aligned with that of standard time generally, is to enlist temporal devices in order to fix the vampire in time. In fact the narrative technique of *Dracula* itself will produce a temporal version of the military ordnance surveys that Harker lacks. It contains the temporally unrepresentable within a rigidly synchronized time frame.

In *Dracula* the power of the timetable is unquestioned. Memorization of train departure times is employed by human and vampire alike, with Dracula's death and subsequent transformation into a chronological text signaling the power of British time to eliminate extraneous and unassimilated details. ("All needless matters," we are told in the prefatory remarks, "have been eliminated" [5].) As a weapon against temporal indeterminacy the vampire hunters produce a written text that coordinates the exact times of their individual experiences to the minute, leaving no temporal gaps through which the Count is allowed to slip. (He often strikes his victims as they sleep, in a state wherein temporal orientation is difficult.) The text that we read as *Dracula* is presented as bits of diary entries, letters, telegrams, and newspaper clippings that have been stitched together in careful chronological order. These multiple narrative fragments come, as Jennifer Wicke notes, from "radically dissimilar and even state-of-the-art media forms," situating the novel more firmly within the dynamics of modernity rather than within older Victorian "diaristic and epistolary" traditions ("Vampiric Typewriting," 579–80). Wicke observes that Mina's shorthand dictation of Harker's story is equally as radical as Dr. Seward's gramophone cylinders: "Shorthand . . . in fact participates in one of the most thoroughgoing transformations of cultural labor of the twentieth-century, the rationalization (in Weber's sense) of the procedures of bureaucracy and business, the feminization of the clerical work force, the standardization of mass business writing" (581). The technobureaucratic rationalization of the standard time system is thus mirrored in *Dracula* by the standardized mass cultural media which the novel purports to have synthesized into one "mass of typewriting." This is the labor that Harker and Mina perform as a prelude to the expedition to Transylvania. Their "whole connected narrative" is produced, as Mina writes, by "knitting together in chronological order every scrap of evidence they have" and is then passed among the hunters for study (199). It translates into a uniform typewritten font the individual idiosyncrasies of handwriting style or vocal pattern, a translation that "excludes all particularities in favor of a general equivalence" (Kittler, 265). We could apply Friedrich Kittler's description of "high literature circa 1900" to the Harkers' typewritten opus and say that it is "a despotic, indeed murderous command to limit data to what the medium of script could exhaust" (267). This reduction converts seemingly horrifying information into factual "evidence" to be studied and utilized. It brings individual existential experiences of time within the strictures of world standard time. The final typescript that the Harkers produce carefully includes all references to the date and time of individual entries, so that in some cases the reader is able to account for every character's position at a given moment. While Wicke sees the text's combination of discrepant mass media as analogous to the act of vampirism, and thus revelatory of modernist anxieties over mass media's "vitiation" of time and space, these anxieties are greatly ameliorated by the text's careful arrangement of these discrepant elements into one uniform chronological text, with every place and time carefully noted. Were Stoker to have presented the various documents in random order, undated, and perhaps even typographically distinct from one another, the reader's response might indeed be estrangement or anxiety. The text Stoker gives us, however, meticulously dates and organizes every discrepant voice, standardizing what might otherwise be threatening nonsynchronous experiences and media.

Exotic space and foreign being are thus mediated through a rigidly controlled temporal apparatus. The detailed time records, a familiar device for establishing verisimilitude in the most fabulous fictions, take on a hyperactive character in Stoker's text, in which the ability to recall train timetables becomes integral to maintaining power. The first sentence of the novel introduces its exaggerated consciousness of time keeping: "3 May. Bistriz—Left Munich at 8.35 p.m. on 1st May, arriving at Vienna early next morning; should have arrived at 6.46, but train was an hour late" (9). The lack of railroad punctuality was, of course, the problem that the 1884 Prime Meridian Conference had ostensibly pledged to solve. For Harker, as for Kipling, train unpunctuality is a recognizable feature of the Orient. "It seems to me that the further East you go," he writes, "the more unpunctual are the trains. What ought they to be in China?" (11). Dracula himself shrewdly recognizes the association of Occidental power with railway synchronization. In preparation for his invasion of London he reclines on a sofa and reads the Bradshaw guide to train timetables as if it were a novel, studying the departures and arrivals at Victoria station as his fourteenth-century incarnation would have studied the designs of the castle he planned to breach.[4] Standard time, born with the English train, is both the stronghold and the weakness of empire. Turning technology against its makers Dracula attaches like a disease to the very ships sent out to ensure commercial dominance. The best defense against the monster is to have faith in and command of temporal precision. Mina is able to reproduce train departure times at will, to the amazement of the male hunters:

> "When does the next train start for Galatz?" said Van Helsing to us generally.
> "At 6.30 tomorrow morning!" We all stared, for the answer came from Mrs. Harker.
> "How on earth do you know?" said Art.
> "You forget—or perhaps you do not know, though Jonathan does and so does Dr. Van Helsing—that I am the train fiend. At home in Exeter I

always used to make up the timetables, so as to be helpful to my husband. I found it so useful sometimes, that I always make a study of the timetables now." (293)

Power depends on one's ready familiarity with the Bradshaw guide, a fact that Dracula himself recognizes in his preparations for invasion. Van Helsing and crew's battle plans in preparation for their pursuit of the vampire back to his country manifest an obsession over the careful calculation of time schedules:

> The *Czarina Catherine* left the Thames yesterday morning. It will take her at the quickest speed she has ever made *at least three weeks* to reach Varna; but we can travel overland to the same place *in three days*. Now, if we *allow for two days less* for the ship's voyage, owing to such weather influences as we know that the Count can bring to bear; and if we *allow a whole day and night* for any delays which may occur to us, then we have *a margin of nearly two weeks*. Thus, in order to be quite safe, we must leave here *on the 17th* or later. Then we shall at any rate be in Varna *a day before* the ship arrives, and be able to make such preparations as may be necessary. Of course, we shall all go armed—armed against evil things, spiritual as well as physical. (282; italics added)

More important than conventional weapons—garlic, stakes, pistols—is the great weapon of the timetable and the knowledge it endows of the speed with which space is traversed.

Dracula is to be fixed in *time* by a synchronized narrative apparatus, in the same way, and with the same violence, that he is to be fixed in *space* by a stake through the heart. Temporal uncertainty and indeterminacy are erased with the transformation of the Count into a textual figure. The two projects of the text, the destruction of Dracula and the production of a definitive text that narrates that destruction, are intimately linked. In fact the produced text replaces Dracula after his destruction. It becomes the only remaining cultural artifact pointing to the former existence of a timeless being. At death Dracula's body dissolves into dust, his teeth marks vanish from Mina's neck, and a later visit to Transylvania confirms that "every trace of all that had been was blotted out" (486). The text has become the relic and the killers a select band of antiquarians, whose construction of narrative is, in Susan Stewart's words, "an attempt to erase the actual past in order to create an imagined past which is available for consumption" (143). In the original manuscript, Stoker included at Dracula's death a kind of spatial apocalypse in Transylvania, where a "convulsion of the earth" like a "fierce volcano" swallows Dracula's castle and the "structure of the hill" on which it stood. It was as if this process, Stoker wrote, "had satisfied the need of nature" (325 n. 5). Nature here is that space which can be temporally located and unified with its surroundings. Stoker thus enlists global standard time both as a tool at the level of plot (with Mina's and the Count's competing mastery of timetables) and also as a principle of narrative structure (with discrepant time lines from various media synchronized into a uniform typewritten narrative). For Stoker standard time serves a double function: it preserves England's ontological purity by excising the temporally untranslatable and provides a model for a total narrative, able to assimilate various classes, nations, dialects (spoken by the multinational vampire hunters) and media. The ideal standard narrative has no temporal outside, no voices unassimilated to its seamless manipulation of space and time. *Dracula* narrates the violent struggle of the last vestige of an "outside" to standard time's grid. The ultimate elimination of that vestige, or more accurately, its transformation into a temporally synchronized narrative, provides the fin de siècle foundation myth for an empire of temporal uniformity.

As rigidly structured and generically codified a form as the late Victorian adventure novel was, it nevertheless manifested signs of deep instability in its enforcement of temporal exactitude on exotic populations. Haggard's heroes thrive outside the limits of Greenwich time, and their quests are often driven by a desire for some form of biological or archaeological continuity with lost tribes rather than a stark discontinuity.[5] Indeed the white queen Ayesha, as many commentators have noted, is as much a manifestation of the acutely domestic threat of the rise of the New Woman as she is a symbol of the colonial exotic. "For all its florid exoticism," Nina Auerbach writes, "*She* is a parable of female typicality" (38). Jennifer Wicke's insight that Dracula is an exotic mirror of a uniquely metropolitan problem of fragmented mass cultural forms similarly suggests that the late Victorian adventure novels were as concerned with internal as with external enemies. These authors find manifestations in the spatially exotic of inherent tensions in the progress of modernization itself, tensions they attempt to ameliorate through the temporal structure of narrative. Yet the pressures on conventional chronological narrative to contain the uneven and incommensurable temporalities of modernity are ultimately unsustainable. For Sara Suleri the "temporal derangements" brought about by what she calls "imperial time" would be more adequately captured by a journalistic language in the perpetual present tense than by narratives driven by chronology and historical continuity: "Even as empire seeks to occupy a monolithic historic space, its temporality is more accurately characterized as a disruptive sequence of a present tense perpetually surprised, allowing for neither the precedent of the past nor the anticipation of a future. Instead, its grim montage of autonomous moments implies a certain threadbare dynamism in which surface is the only space that legitimizes signification" (113). Among the "temporal extinctions" accompanying imperial narration, Suleri argues, are its abdication of historical continuity, chronology, and memory in favor of a boundless, open-ended, "perpetually surprised" present. Unable or unwilling to organize experience according to the logic of historical unfolding, imperial time relies on the arrangement or montage of spatial surfaces, dealing "one at a time" with those fragments, in the absence of any historical memory.

In recent essays on Olive Schreiner and Virginia Woolf Jed Esty has explored another "temporal extinction" driven by colonial temporality in the collapse of the Bildungsroman. Focusing on a tendency in late nineteenth- and early twentieth-century narrative for youthful protagonists to refuse or resist adulthood, Esty suggests that characters such as Dorian Gray, whose stunted adolescence "thwart[s] the realist proportions of biographical time," reveal transformations in the uneasy union between capitalism and the nation-state. While the insular nation provided the Bildungsroman with a "language of historical stability" in its limitation of and reconciliation with market forces, the late nineteenth century finds the nation threatened by the "imperial state," which Esty calls "a culture-diluting unit whose spatiotemporal coordinates violate 'national-historical' time" ("The Colonial Bildungsroman," 414). No longer able to tether itself to the nation-state's comforting logic of bounded adulthood, the perpetually adolescent modernist subject exposes imperial capitalism's "unending narrativity of modernization," a process with "no national boundaries and few political limits" (410). Esty and Suleri both usefully identify temporality as a zone of instability for the logic of global imperialism. Cut off from past and future, from limits and limitations, empire creates only the possibility for endless change, uncurtailed by the borders of maturity, growth, and completion. Chronometry becomes cartography, and any temporal experience outside of the perpetual present tense of modernization becomes primitive, anachronistic, and retrogressive. Though unexplored by Suleri or Esty, the exportation of Greenwich Mean Time as the cosmic time of empire certainly plays a key role in these temporal dynamics of modernity. What the delegates General Evans and Rustem Effendi objected to at the 1884 Prime Meridian Conference was precisely the new global map's too easy equivalence of time and space and its rampant disregard for the extent to which social temporality is informed and determined by national and cultural pressures. Global standard time demands that every experience of temporality be mapped according to precise coordinates dictated and regulated by imperial technology. Greenwich Mean Time provided the overarching rationale and transnational justification for the elimination of nonaligned temporality, undergirding the kinds of temporal "extinctions" charted by Suleri and Esty.

Haggard and Stoker attempted to eliminate the sources of temporal incommensurability by literally killing off exotic temporal others in their fiction. Yet anxiety over the efficacy of temporal technologies and of the chronological narrative itself as killing tools can be detected in the very structure of their narratives, which threaten always to dissolve into the temporal anarchy of the other and to embrace the horrors of the event time of the "primitive" rather than the bureaucratic rationalism of the clock. As Suleri's and Esty's readings of "imperial time" suggest, this anxiety might reflect the radical unsuitability of the traditional chronological narrative for narrating the fundamentally ahistorical cartography of the new global empire. A more apt narrative structure for the era of global standard time would embrace the transformation from chronometry to cartography at its core, avoiding the battle between temporal exactitude (vampire hunters) and incertitude (vampire) by subsuming all temporality within one benevolent and capacious system of cartography. The model for such a narrative is arguably Kipling's *Kim*, which, as Edward Said notes, stridently avoids any presentation of "two worlds in conflict" by giving us "only one" (*Culture and Imperialism*, 148). Contrasting the "loose structure" of *Kim*, "based as it is on a luxurious geographical and spatial expansiveness," with the "tight, relentlessly unforgiving temporal structure" of Thomas Hardy's *Jude the Obscure*, Said suggests that Kipling's unwavering belief in the natural fitness of India as a British colonial possession allows him to ignore, in his story of young Kim O'Hara, the typically devastating pressures of time on European protagonists. India is a place where "time is on your side" because the landscape is so thoroughly controlled and contained (159–60). Governing the progression of his eternally adolescent protagonist according to spatial rather than temporal processes, Kipling more effectively embraces the logic of the Prime Meridian Conference and global standard time than do Haggard and Stoker, his contemporaries. Whereas the latter see contesting temporality as a battleground for the possession of global space, Kipling's text accepts all temporality, no matter how exotic, as eminently assimilable to the overarching cartography of the imperial map.

This is by no means to suggest that Kipling denies the existence of radically distinct, culturally determined, local experiences of time and temporality. Temporal otherness is asserted repeatedly throughout *Kim* in editorial asides and constitutes part of Kipling's Orientalist presentation of a fixed and immutable Oriental character, as Said and others have noted.[6] The brunt of all of these representations of Oriental time is that Indians do not appreciate the value of punctuality nor the necessity of demarcating abstract units of time for the purposes of synchronized efficiency: "Even an Oriental, with an Oriental's views of the value of time, could see that the sooner it was in proper hands, the better" (22); "All hours of the 24 are alike to Orientals, and their passenger traffic is regulated accordingly" (26); "Swiftly—as Orientals understand speed—with long explanations, with abuse and windy talk, carelessly" (121); "The easy, uncounted Eastern minutes slid by" (158). These stereotypes are certainly intended as humorous and curmudgeonly truisms on Kipling's part, yet his goal hardly seems to be to erase this cultural oddity or to confront Oriental inefficiency with a valorized English punctuality. Oriental temporality is not threatening, as it is in Haggard and Stoker. Rather it contributes to the piquancy and charm of the colonized. More than that it is what endows Kim with his cultural authenticity and power when he is on his long, happy, "Asiatic" holidays with the lama. While fully capable of racing against the clock when on imperial duty, as he does when he disguises E23 on the train, Kim is also capable of giving himself over to the "happy Asiatic disorder which, if you only allow time, will bring you everything that a simple man needs" (57). During the most grueling periods of his education at St. Xavier's Kim "fell back, Oriental fashion, on time and chance" (91). Able to embrace the abundance and pleasure of slow and inefficient Indian temporality, Kim and the lama embrace natural rhythms whereby their "stomachs told them the time" (179).

Given the stark opposition these Orientalist truisms stake out between Western punctuality and Eastern inexactitude, one might anticipate the railways constructed by the East India Company to be sites of cultural confusion and conflict in Kipling's text, or to be battlegrounds over the proper management of social temporality, as the railways are in Stoker's novel. This is far from the case, though. Although the lama expresses occasional fear and distaste for the train and railway station, calling the *te-rain* "cramped" (12) and exclaiming that the railway station with its "sheeted dead" of sleeping passenger cargo is "the work of devils" (25), his naïveté-bred rejection of the wonders of train travel is not shared by the other characters in the text, who marvel, sometimes begrudgingly, on the extent to which the train has created a unified community in India, cutting across ancient caste and religious prejudices. "There is not one rule of right living," a moneylender asserts early on in the text, "which these *te-rains* do not cause us to break. We sit, for example, side by side with all castes and peoples" (27). If the moneylender resists the train's dissolution of social hierarchies, others celebrate it for its unifying powers. The Jat whose son Kim has healed calls the *te-rain* the "one good thing" the government has given in exchange for its many taxes. "A wonderful matter," he says of the train; it "joins friends and unites the anxious" (166). Even the lama acknowledges to the curator of the Wonder House that his quest for the River of the Arrow, that elusive metaphysical site unlisted on any map, foreign or indigenous, will be aided by the "written paper of the hours of the trains that go south" (13). The train is a symbol of English technology's capacity to hold multiple, divergent populations comfortably within its compartments, assimilating loose-limbed Asiatic temporal inexactitude within its overarching temporal precision. In this sense it even mirrors the goal of the lama's mystical "Middle Way," which he declares to be free of racial and caste hierarchies (20). Indeed the train lines themselves are only the more modern manifestation of that engineering marvel of the Suri dynasty, the Grand Trunk Road, famously celebrated in *Kim* for its manifestation of an array of local colors, sights, smells, and sounds. Despite the daunting obstacle facing the lama and his *chela* in their quest for an unmapped mystical river, the Grand Trunk Road promises an exhaustive cartographic survey of all the rivers the lama could care to see. The Grand Trunk Road, the lama learns, "crosses all streams on this side of Hind," allowing him the ease to "test each stream that it overpasses" (41). If the River of the Arrow resembles other mystical sites in the imperial Gothic, such as Haggard's diamond mines or Temple of Truth, in that it represents a source of "Eastern power" and strength unmapped by imperial cartography, it importantly differs from those sites because it exists within the comfortable limits of the Great Game of imperial ethnography and espionage. The lama finds his river in the end, not because of Kim's rejection of his racial and imperial destiny, but in tandem with Kim's embrace of that destiny. Whereas Ayesha's lost temple threatens English sovereignty, with its suggestion of queen-making powers that might eclipse Victoria's, the lama's river threatens nothing because its location is so easily mapped by the narrative as part of the resolution of Kim's racial heritage and Creighton's political success.

In part Kipling achieves this happy assimilation of exotic temporality with British punctuality by refusing to entirely segregate the foreign from the indigenous. In Stoker's novel there is a hard and fast ontological distinction between the living and the undead. The one obeys the dictates of human temporality while the other defies them. This Manichaean divide between good and evil marks all aspects of Stoker's moral universe, including his attitude toward time. Foreign, unpunctual, unlimited time is evil, whereas the bordered, measured, and instrumental time of the English is valorized. The former must die at the hands of the latter. For Kipling, though, such stark oppositions between Occidental and Oriental versions of temporality are unnecessary, given a framework comprehensive enough to comfortably hybridize the two. Hybridity can function as a tool to assimilate and anaesthetize the danger of unregulated, unmeasured colonial time. Hurree Babu is a fine example of this hybridized version of cultural temporality. Able to rob, trick, and mock the Russian agents to Kim's great admiration, while still making it back punctually to "catch the 4.25 p.m. to Umballa" (233), Hurree also embraces his stereotypical role as the lackadaisical Asiatic, repeating twice the European pun on his name, "No hurry for Hurree" (188). If the foreign agents despise this aspect of Hurree, calling him a representation of "India in transition" in his "monstrous hybridism of East and West" (199), their claim to know better than the English how to "deal with Orientals," presumably by spatiotemporally segregating them, is belied by their comically ineffective ending, in which they are roundly trumped by the very monstrous hybrid they have been mocking. Clearly Kipling celebrates as politically expedient the English method of colonial hybridism. Kim himself is of course the great hybrid: Irish by blood, Indian by birth, and British by occupation, he resists cultural or racial profiling. "What am I?" he asks Mahbub. "Mussulman, Hindu, Jain, or Buddhist? That is a hard knot" (121). Able to borrow "right- and left-handedly from all the customs of the country he knew and loved" (65), Kim is the ideal future colonial administrator, not shocked into Gothic horror by the "great, grey, formless India" (82), but intoxicated by, comfortable with, and proficient at manipulating that unmapped space. By simply being who he is, a mixture of sahib and Indian, Kim is able to both enjoy the exotic pleasures of event-based Indian temporality and conform rigidly to the punctual dictates of Creighton's secret service machinations. The success of the Great Game, Kim realizes with awe, simply happens of its own, "through no craft of Hurree's or contrivance of Kim's, but simply, beautifully, and inevitably" (207).

In this sense Kim represents a development of Kipling's ideas about the proper leadership of India and the correct management of natives from earlier boy heroes like Wee Willie Winkie, who, as part of growing up in British India, must learn that the natives outside the cantonment are not "goblins" but only "bad men" who can and must be put in their place by a "child of the Dominant Race." A much more conventional Bildungsroman, in which the child becomes a man by his recognition of national and racial superiority to natives, "Wee Willie Winkie" is at a great extreme from Kim's anti-Bildung narrative, according to which there is no need to learn to struggle with one's racial and cultural identity, nor to fear or condemn the natives outside the cantonment or the Catholic school. Colonial space is so thoroughly managed, mapped, and timed that one can simply inhabit it luxuriously and with impunity. Time is not a problem for Kipling as it was for Haggard and Stoker, who alternately feared and were exhilarated by the dark spaces and the unmeasured times of the globe. Kipling's narrative casts such fears aside. There is no bright center or dark periphery in *Kim;* there is only one mass of hybridized gray. This can lead Kipling happily to affirm, along with the lama, that in the Middle Way there is no "Time and Space" (225). A map as capacious and uniform as Creigthon's ethnological survey eliminates the problems of incommensurable space and time which had produced the terrors of the imperial Gothic. If world standard time was effectively mapping the uneven temporalities of global space, Kipling's narrative assured readers that precision and imprecision were not irreconcilable opposites to be figured in terms of some Gothic contest between good and evil, but could be wholesomely and productively hybridized in the very body and rhythms of the ideal Anglo-Indian administrator, a precocious scamp able to delight readers, appease natives, celebrate mysticism, and perhaps most important carry out the work of empire.

It is not surprising, then, that when Kipling presents his version of the familiar nineteenth-century figure of the ageless immortal (his version of Ayesha, Dracula, or Dorian Gray) in one of the stories from *Plain Tales from the Hills* the character is not an exotic Other but an Anglo-Indian matriarch.[7] In "Venus Annodomini" Kipling represents the temporal idiosyncrasies of Anglo-Indian life in the Raj by lightheartedly playing with linguistic strategies of temporal standardization. In Kipling's empire confronting the ageless Other is a subject for comedy rather than Gothic horror. The comedy of the story derives from the protagonist's confusion over the age of his love interest, a middle-aged woman referred to simply as Venus Annodomini. In Kipling's Anglo-India the age of the Anglos appears to be deliberately indeterminate. Imperial control of native populations depends on a construction of the eternal youth of the white body—a deception designed to instill in the population a sense that the colonizing face is always at the height of its virility and strength.[8] In Kipling's story this is clearly illustrated by the name of the protagonist's father, "Young" Gayerson, a nickname that necessitates the awkward and unusual naming of his son, "Very Young" Gayerson. Aging in Kipling's Anglo-India is not standardized but is purely a question of relativity. The English must always remain young, and the indigenous population must be frozen in a state of petulant childhood. When the Bengali writers of the anti-imperial newspaper in the story target "Young" Gayerson as a "'Nero' and a 'Scylla' and a 'Charybdis,'" Gayerson's reaction to their political agitation is patronizing benevolence. He "rather liked Babus, they amused him" (250). If the natives are amusing children, the British are always at their peak in youth and virility. At the center of the story is the Venus herself, a fountain of youth who sends generations of young colonial soldiers off to do the work of empire. Like Wilde's Dorian Gray, Venus retains her youth while those around her show signs of decay: "Men rode up to Simla, and stayed, and went away and made their name and did their life's work, and returned again to find the Venus Annodomini exactly as they had left her. She was as immutable as the Hills" (247). Venus is representative of the "everlasting order" of the Annodominis. Her family name, the temporal designation itself of the Christian era, renders Venus the benevolent and idyllic exemplar of Christian rule in India, the installation on the "Babu's" land of a figure from the Vatican itself. Men who worship her produce offspring who similarly flock to her shrine. Her compulsive lure lies in the temporal indeterminacy she provokes and embodies: "Six years in her eyes were no more than six months to ordinary women, and ten made less visible impression on her than does a week's fever on an ordinary woman" (248).

The humor of the story lies in the mutual confusion regarding the respective ages of the characters, a phenomenon taken to be a characteristic of Anglo-Indian life, where the familiar temporal signposts of

English social life are absent or altered. The Anglo-Indians are, in a temporal sense, *unreadable*. Their ages are all relative to one another, and no one commits the gaucherie of disclosing anyone else's actual age. This temporal indeterminacy stimulates rather than hinders colonial productivity. The Venus's legions of male admirers leave her shrine to do "their life's work" in India, leaving a new generation to draw sustenance from the same shrine. Kipling's narrative, however, works to interrogate the productivity stimulated by this temporal vagueness. His narrator fixes the ageless characters with more or less precise temporal referents. Like a socially inept guest at a dinner party he calls out the ages of the respective diners. In the story Very Young, who has pined after Venus for months, thinking her a young woman, is shocked to learn that she is the mother of a nineteen-year-old daughter. Very Young, himself only twenty-two, learns not only that Venus is old enough to be his mother, but also that she carried on a relationship in her youth with his own father, Young Gayerson, an intimacy that promises to rekindle at the end of the story, much to Very Young's further humiliation and embarrassment. The narrative itself defuses the legend of the ageless Venus with a series of time referents: "He reminded her of a lad, who, *three-and-twenty-years ago*, had professed a boundless devotion for her" (249); "'Young' Gayerson—he was about *five and forty*" (250); "'Very Young' Gayerson, who was a short *twenty-two years old*" (250). These referents provide enough of a temporal framework for the reader to expose the age of the Venus Annodomini and thus call the bluff of her divinity. (If we do the math we learn that she is roughly forty-five.) The conflict in the story begins when Venus herself gives away the age of her daughter: "She is nineteen and a very sensible nice girl I believe" (250). It is this momentary lapse in the pretense of agelessness that facilitates Gayerson Senior's rekindled romance with her. He no longer has to pretend that he is older than she. In the last lines of the story the two make plans for their assignation with sober practicality:

> "At five tomorrow, then," said the Venus Annodomini. "And mind you are punctual"
> "At five punctually," said "Young" Gayerson. (252)

Young Gayerson is no longer burdened with having to live up to his nickname, and in the last sentence Venus says his name for the first time in the story: "'Good-bye, Tom,' whispered the Venus Annodomini" (252). The utterance is a whisper, and Venus's real name remains undisclosed. The veils of mystification are too powerfully productive to be publicly shed. Tom Gayerson will presumably remain Young Gayerson to the Babus and Venus will continue to launch her thousand ships into battle. The reader, though, along with Very Young Gayerson, has caught a glimpse of the true face behind the timeless mask of empire. The satire is gentle and affectionate, not biting, and the empress unclothed is contained and softened within the general geniality of the *Plain Tales* collection.[9]

As in *Kim* temporal variance and indeterminacy are bound up with colonial power, forming a hybrid of sober British punctuality and mystical timelessness. Timelessness is not a threat to power but a pillar of Anglo-Indian control. Kipling's affectionate satire goes only so far as to show the humor behind the supposed majesty of the rulers, who are not gods but mortals. Eternally young Young Gayerson is not the timeless shepherd of amusing Babus but simply Tom, a forty-five-year-old civil servant. British time humanizes and naturalizes the Anglo-Indians, revealing their simplicity and humility, their humanity and humor. Not only an effective tool of national defense, British time is also a mark of ontological authenticity. Kipling's work, as I have suggested, naturalizes standardized Greenwich time as a unifying and humane medium, capable of hybridization with a host of local and seemingly incommensurable temporalities. His faith in the power of imperial time to continue limitlessly into the future was not necessarily shared by all fin de siècle writers, however, particularly those less sanguine than he about the benevolence of empire. H. G. Wells, who called Kipling's style "turgid" and "degenerate," fit only for praising "a modest button on the complacent stomach of empire" (*Tono-Bungay*, 389), interrogates the power of spatiotemporal precision to assimilate and manage foreign space and time in his 1895 novella, *The Time Machine*. Wells's Time Traveler presents his own version of an instrument capable of synthesizing and unifying wildly discrepant temporalities. The time machine itself is founded on the premise that "Time is only a kind of Space" and can thus be traversed with ease (5). Disavowing the power of time to radically disrupt continuity or to resist the most careful predictions and calculations, the logic of the time machine depends on a conception of temporality as a fixed, stable, and unvarying dimension that one can map, manipulate, and traverse. Demystifying the ephemeral power of time, the time traveler insists that time is "a fixed and unalterable thing" and thus capable of manipulation and management. Just as Stoker uses technological methods of standardization (the precisely synchronized London trains) to neutralize and contain a spatially distant being, Wells's Time Traveler employs a technological invention to spatially map an exotic and threatening foreign time.[10] When the Time Traveler confronts the exotic Eloi in the London of A.D. 802,701 his instinct is to assimilate them comfortably within his own vision of uniform, historical progression. He sees salutary social developments in the late nineteenth century comfortably reflected in Eloi society, claiming that their disavowal of the "efficient family" and "specialization of the sexes" is simply the culmination of developments begun in his own time (28). The future, for all its initial exoticism, is read by the Time Traveler as a logical "completion" of the present. Clinging to a dependable theory of social development and implicitly trusting that the state's "benevolence" regulates human reproduction, the Time Traveler mentally establishes a seamless continuity of temporal development throughout the "Time-Dimension."

When the Morlocks are introduced, however, the Traveler's comfort in a continuous human development is disrupted, and his revulsion at the physical touch of the future working class suggests a violent disjunction between his own time and that of A.D. 802,701 The time machine's promise of a comfortable standardization of human temporal experience has proven a disabling hoax. As John S. Partington argues, the time machine's very existence is the result of a leisured gentleman-scientist's abundant labor time and thus embodies a denial of the structured inequalities that will eventually produce the Morlocks and the Eloi. Complicit in the production of future social ills, the time machine is a purely technological innovation with no inherent social value.[11] The machine is compared twice to a bullet. When its prototype is sent forward in time the Psychologist notes that we can no more apprehend its presence than we can "a bullet flying through the air" (11). Before his first use of the machine, the Time Traveler compares his anticipation to that of "a suicide who holds a pistol to his head" (20). The Traveler has to forcibly recall his scientific goals when he experiences the "hysterical exhilaration" of temporal acceleration (19). Turned nihilist by the vision of a futuristic apocalyptic landscape, he becomes, as the narrator speculates in the last paragraph, unstuck in time, a temporal flaneur only viewing horrors with none of the interventionary agency of many of his later twentieth-century film manifestations. As a tool that treats time as a form of manipulable space the time machine is revealed to have no meaningful social applicability. In the end, the narrator argues, we must live as if we did not know the future that the time machine has shown us, as if the future were "still black and blank" (114). In *The Time Machine* we see a critique of the technological use of temporality to measure and control foreign space. World standard time, like the Time Traveler, treats time as a manipulated spatial quantum for ostensibly the same benevolent social ends. Wells represents the power of British science to read and manipulate human temporality as inefficacious and irresponsible.

The effect of the time machine on the Traveler is to destabilize his comfortable assumptions about time and timekeeping. Thrown immeasurably far into the future, unable to anchor his perceptions to a dependable theory of social progress, and left with only the alternate exhilaration and horror of the temporal flaneur, the Time Traveler experiences the same shock and defamiliarization in regard to temporality that would later become characteristic of a new modernist aesthetic. Paul A. Cantor and Peter Hufnagel have argued that Wells's novel can be read as a "central text of both modernist and imperialist literature" in that the kinds of temporal disjunctions provoked at the "imperial frontier" of the Morlock caves are analogous to the temporal shifts characteristic of modernist literature. The cultural disorientation that accompanies colonial confrontation leads to inevitable temporal difficulties in orientation and narration. The "distinctive techniques of modernist fiction—delayed decoding and abrupt shifts in narrative frameworks," Cantor and Hufnagel claim, are "analogous to the distinctive experience of the imperial frontier" (49). Michael Valdez Moses has similarly argued that the temporal dimension of Joseph Conrad's modernist aesthetic was driven by his own experience of unevenly developed and anachronistic communication systems at the "fringes of empire." In contrast to metropolitan life, with its efficiently synchronized transportation and communication networks, life on the imperial periphery involved negotiating an "unevenly developed and distributed system of communication" which rendered the distribution of information an "arduous, imperfect, slow, and technically difficult task." The linguistic struggles of Conrad's narrators are thus concrete manifestations of the anachronistic "systems of social organization and communication that prevail at the peripheries of empire" (62). Moses and Cantor and Hufnagel provocatively suggest how a confrontation with the temporal dynamics of empire drove modernist style. In both of these readings it is the "unevenness" of temporality outside of the synchronized and insular nation that confronts literary aesthetics with the demand to rethink narrative temporality in order to accommodate a more "worldly" temporal vision. As I have suggested in this chapter, however, the late nineteenth-century fiction of empire embraced numerous strategies of containment and management in its attempts to deny or forestall those more troubling implications of nonsynchronous global temporality. Domesticating the time of the Other involved compartmentalizing it within carefully plotted coordinates. Ontological or metaphysical distinctions between a valorized British time and a demonized time of the Other served as a bulwark against the existential contamination threatened by vampiric, Asiatic, or otherwise exotic temporalities. This is how the fiction of Haggard and Robert Louis Stevenson, for example, managed to confront the "fringes of empire" without compromising the formal integrity of the conventional adventure narrative. Experimental modernist fiction, however, confronts uneven imperial temporality without either the existential imperatives or the narrative constraints of adventure fiction. Encyclopedic in their narrative scope and eschatological in their worldview, modernist fictions confront the heterogeneity of spaces and times without a Bradshaw to orient them. In fact the power of Bradshaw to tersely enforce synchronized imperial networks is derided by the modernists as rigidly authoritarian, as we see most memorably in *Mrs. Dalloway* in the character of Dr. Bradshaw, who maintains the imperial values of Proportion and Conversion even as he exorcises England of its mental and physical degenerates. Attacking the fin de siècle compulsion to eliminate temporal barbarians at the gates, modernism instead creates and perpetuates its own nonsynchronicities while reimagining alternative temporal networks outside of empire's latitudes and longitudes.

CHAPTER 4

"The Shortcomings of Timetables"
Greenwich, Modernism, and the Limits of Modernity

In chapter 3 I described how Bram Stoker's *Dracula* enlisted global standard time both at the level of plot, with Mina Harker's and the Count's competing mastery of timetables, and also as a principle of narrative structure, with discrepant time lines from various media synchronized into a uniform typewritten narrative. For Stoker standard time served a double function: it preserved England's ontological purity by excising the temporally untranslatable, and it provided a model for a total narrative, able to assimilate various classes, nations, and dialects (spoken by the multinational vampire hunters) as well as various media. Modernist texts attack standard time's authority at both levels. In the modernist novel Greenwich Standard Time is not a powerful weapon for eliminating or assimilating temporal Others. The London of Conrad's *The Secret Agent,* for example, is shot through with "holes" in time, spaces of temporal uncertainty, and abysses in which clocks became unreliable or even dangerous. While the empire's system of electrically coordinated clocks promises a seamless coordination of action and a preservation of social stability, the modernist landscape seems to enjoy none of that uniformity or stability. Standard time's unification is shallow and tenuous, and reliance on its power leads only to greater confusion. If, at the level of plot, standard time is no longer an effective tool of social organization, it similarly fails, at the level of narrative, to provide a principle of temporal organization. Although people and events can still be coordinated in relation to the time of the clock, this no longer proves to be the central stimulus for narrative organization. At crucial moments in Mrs. *Dalloway* Woolf may tell us where each character is in relation to the chiming of Big Ben, but the principle of temporal connection suggested by the clock ultimately only hints at more meaningful organizations of social time. In an empire in which the Greenwich Observatory can no longer effectively unify its subjects, discrete narrative voices can no longer be stitched together chronologically, as they are in Stoker's text. The modernist narrative, in the absence of Greenwich's authority, must produce its own principles of temporal organization. The burden on the modernist narrative is thus not simply to register the absence of standard time's power, but also to explore new configurations of social temporality within the spaces opened up by that absence.

In this chapter I discuss the representation of Greenwich time at key moments in three canonical modernist texts: Conrad's *The Secret Agent* (1907), Joyce's *Ulysses* (1922), and Woolf's *Mrs. Dalloway* (1925). In these texts Greenwich time is situated within its larger political, commercial, and imperial contexts, bearing evidence of the extent to which Greenwich by the early twentieth century had entered modernist consciousness as a powerful symbol of authoritarian control from a distance and of the management of diverse populations. The association between standardized time and manipulative forms of imperial control constitutes a problem for modernist writers, as they attempt to formally and thematically mediate between a host of competing temporal demands, negotiating (without ever necessarily resolving) a complex array of temporal models, alternately centered in the body, the mind, the state, the empire, and the globe. These narrative negotiations of competing temporalities are uniformly frustrated by the injunction to fit all human time into a single standardized system of measurement explicitly designed for the maintenance of global commerce. Exposing what Conrad's character Comrade Ossipon calls "the shortcomings of timetables," these modernists sought to dislocate human temporality from its enlistment in the standard time system by resituating temporal processes within more meaningful, contextually determined, and variable social patterns. These three texts are particularly useful for a study of standard time and modernism because, in making direct reference to Greenwich Mean Time, Greenwich-coordinated clocks, or the Greenwich Observatory itself, they bring to the surface latent tensions over temporality within a larger body of modernist fiction not as explicitly or obviously concerned with Greenwich. Fraught mediation between multiple or competing temporalities characterizes a dominant strain within a range of modernist literatures.[1] The references to Greenwich in these three texts help to clarify the extent to which this modernist preoccupation with multiple temporalities was a product of its historical period, when politicians, astronomers, philosophers, and artists wrestled with contesting definitions of temporality in the light of a legislative campaign to install Greenwich Mean Time as the one, true, "cosmopolitan" time of modernity.

In *The Secret Agent* Conrad dramatizes an alleged bombing attempt on the Greenwich Observatory by a French anarchist named Martial Bourdin in 1894. Readers confronting Conrad's text for the first time and hoping to find in it a coherent motive behind Bourdin's attack on standard time will be frustrated by the extreme lengths to which Conrad goes, both in the novel itself and in his 1920 authorial preface, to *empty out* the Greenwich Observatory of any meaningful political significance. A reading of the Observatory as a politically charged symbol is immediately complicated by the text's surface rejection of the politics of astronomy, expressed in no uncertain terms by Mr. Vladimir early in the novel.[2] Vladimir goes to some lengths to convince Mr. Verloc that the Greenwich Observatory is the ultimate *apolitical* site, associated as it is with the "sacrosanct fetish" of science. "It would be really telling," Vladimir declares, "if one could throw a bomb into pure mathematics" (31). The greatest incitement to irrational fear and repressive backlash, he argues, would be stimulated by an attack with no conceivable economic or political motivations. "I defy the ingenuity of journalists to persuade the public that any given member of the proletariat can have a personal grievance against astronomy," Vladimir sneers. Conrad, driving the point home in his 1921 dramatic adaptation of the novel, includes a new bit of dialogue between two women at the home of Michaelis's patroness:

> *Third Woman's Voice:* Astronomy is so difficult, so remote from one's other interests.
>
> *First Woman's Voice:* Isn't it? I can't see how it can have any connexion with politics. Those anarchists must be simply mad. (*Three Plays*, 134)

This language is perfectly straightforward, as are Conrad's prefatory remarks about the alleged bombing itself: "[It was a] blood-stained inanity of so fatuous a kind that it was impossible to fathom its origin by any reasonable or even unreasonable process of thought. For perverse unreason has its own logical processes. But that outrage could not be laid hold of mentally in any sort of way, so that one remained faced by the fact of a man blown to bits for nothing even remotely resembling an idea, anarchistic or other" (5). Conrad's insistence on the "inanity" of choosing Greenwich as a political target is a serious challenge to any critical attempt to read *The Secret Agent* as an attack on standard time's authority.

Yet Conrad's denial of any logical motive behind the bombing is not reflective of the general tenor of the coverage in the London *Times* of Scotland Yard's inquest into the Bourdin incident in 1894. Randall Stevenson has insisted that the *Times* was as bewildered as Conrad over the incident, but the original coverage reveals a fairly consistent attitude that the Observatory was necessarily a symbolically rich target for attack.[3] The special correspondent for the *Times* claimed to have "consistently" held to the view of a French bias against the building: "Colonel Majendie [head of the inquest] could come to no other conclusion than that [Martial Bourdin's] intention was to attack the Observatory. This view has been held consistently in The Times. . . . The fact that the reputation of the Greenwich Observatory is world-wide, and that Frenchmen have rather an objection to its pre-eminence, may have been influential in the mind of a Frenchman who was clearly, by his brother's testimony, fairly educated."[4] The reporter offers this statement not only as a likely hypothesis, but also as the guiding conviction behind the coverage of the incident to that date, and indeed the *Times* never wavered in its presentation of the bombing as a deliberate attempt on the Observatory.[5] The critical commonplace that the Bourdin incident was represented as an inscrutable mystery by the popular press thus reveals the extent to which Conrad's authorial comments have dictated our understanding of the event. The political role of the Observatory in the history of standard time was presumed to be common knowledge for the average London reader of 1894. Conrad relied on the *Times* as a source, and we can reasonably assume that he had read its declaration of likely motive.[6] Mr. Vladimir, the embassy official in *The Secret Agent*, echoes the *Times* correspondent's claim that the Greenwich Observatory's reputation was "world-wide." The "whole civilized world," down to the "very boot black," had indeed heard of Greenwich, as Vladimir claims (32). What he does not say, though, is what every reader in 1894 would presumably have known: that its worldwide reputation was bound up, at least in the 1880s and 1890s, with its involvement in political struggles for commercial power. The politically charged debates between France and England at the Prime Meridian Conference ten years earlier had after all been well documented in the *Times,* which regularly published accounts throughout the month of October 1884 detailing French attempts to capsize the proceedings.⁷

Despite his insistence on the fundamental inanity of bombing an Observatory, Conrad seems very much aware that to attack Greenwich is to attack the British authorities' ability to manage and manipulate the threatening rhythms of a foreign-based population of anarchists in London. He sees the challenge to standard time as coming from a larger foreign threat to British national autonomy. This interpretation of the bomb outrage largely derives from the London *Times*'s 1894 news coverage, on which Conrad clearly relied. The *Times* suggested that a worldwide terrorist conspiracy was daily spreading throughout all of Europe. In the days and weeks following Bourdin's death the paper devoted nearly half of its world coverage to descriptions of anarchist arrests, trials, police raids, seizures of underground newspapers, attempted and successful bombings, and bomb threats. What invariably made these events newsworthy was that they all occurred on foreign soil or, in the case of the London-based Autonomie Club, were committed by immigrants to England.⁸ The Sunday after the explosion the *Times* ran an inflammatory three columns on the "haunts and objects" of the members of an "international dynamite plot." Describing the results of the police raid on the Autonomie Club, of which Bourdin was a member, the reporter reveals the national origins of the detainees: "There are about eighty in all, including French, Italians, Bohemians, Poles, Austrians, Scandinavians, Danes, Belgians, and Spaniards. Not a single English name is to be found amongst them."⁹ These reports suggest that the challenge to Greenwich standard time comes, as it did in *Dracula,* from a shadowy yet endlessly proliferating foreign presence, against which England had to take staunch retributive action. If the Greenwich Royal Observatory, as the symbol of imperial power, was analogous to the Twin Towers and the Pentagon, as ʻSven Lütticken has recently argued (100), the fallout of the Bourdin incident was England's late nineteenth-century war on terror, a war that would be fought against spatiotemporal others outside the borders of a barricaded England.¹⁰

Conrad's ironic commentary on Home Secretary Henry Asquith's war on terror, however, is to localize the foreign provocateur by making him an embassy official in London. Embassies, the narrator reminds us in chapter 10, are "part and parcel of the country to which they belong." When Vladimir asks the Assistant Commissioner if the outrage was planned abroad, the latter responds, "Theoretically only, on foreign territory; abroad only by a fiction" (172). Europe here is only "theoretically" or "fictionally" distinct from London. In matters of praxis or "fact," the Assistant Commissioner implies, Europe is as local as is Scotland Yard. The transformation of Europe into a merely theoretical modification of England proper is highlighted in the marvelous scene in which the Assistant Commissioner, prior to his interrogation of Verloc, dines at an Italian restaurant. It is in the "immoral atmosphere" of this restaurant that the Assistant Commissioner feels himself, with a sense of "evil freedom," losing his own identity. His reflections on the experience are worth quoting at length:

> On going out the Assistant Commissioner made to himself the observation that the patrons of the place had lost in the frequentation of fraudulent cookery all their national and private characteristics. And this was strange, since the Italian restaurant is such a peculiarly British institution. But these people were as denationalized as the dishes set before them with every circumstance of unstamped respectability. Neither was their personality stamped in any way, professionally, socially, or racially. They seemed created for the Italian restaurant, unless the Italian restaurant had been perchance created for them. But that last hypothesis was unthinkable, since one could not place them anywhere outside these specific establishments. One never met these enigmatical persons elsewhere. It was impossible to form a precise idea what occupations they followed by day and where they went to bed at night. And he himself was becoming unplaced. It would have been impossible for anybody to guess his occupation. (115)

In a world commercially globalized by standard time, in which theoretically the inhabitants of Casablanca, Dakar, and Reykjavik were to share the same time as London, Conrad suggests an equally disorienting and liberating sense in which the incorporation of cultures as they are devoured by London disables the identities and histories of devoured and devourer alike. That this is figured by a scene in a foreign restaurant, in which the devouring of food represents the literal consumption of fraudulent cultural products, is highly prescient of Conrad. The benignity of the global market is, after all, so frequently evidenced in contemporary globalization debates by the proliferation of foreign restaurants available for the delectation of the global diner in New York or London. Conrad perfectly captures both the perversion of national and racial culture in the "foreign" restaurant that is "peculiarly British" and also the resultant illusory intoxication of placelessness induced in the diner. Once the immigrant has been "denationalized" and divested of profession, class, and race it becomes impossible to narrate any legible account of his or her national past. The effect of this on the Assistant Commissioner is that he is allowed to fantasize himself as placeless, a global traveler with no visible origin or conceivable destination. While the Italian is fixed within the confining parameters of the restaurant, outside which he is "never found," the English citizen imagines himself liberated from all local contexts. While the Italian patron trades his culture for a disabling fraudulence, the British diner devours, along with his pasta, all cultures and contexts, replacing his nationality with a cosmopolitan "feeling of independence." Conrad's narrator, though, undercuts this pleasure immediately in his description of the London street that the Assistant Commissioner confronts upon leaving the restaurant: "He advanced at once into an immensity of greasy slime and damp plaster interspersed with lamps, and enveloped, oppressed, penetrated, choked and suffocated by the blackness of a wet London night, which is composed of soot and drops of water" (116). With Chekovian irony Conrad slaps the Assistant Commissioner in the face with a concretely local London night. Despite his illusory sense of liberation in the face of denationalized immigrants, the Assistant Commissioner is environmentally localized and enmeshed with not one but five verbs in wonderful succession: "enveloped, oppressed, penetrated, choked and suffocated." A London that is both local and global, both city and universe, Conrad suggests, is something of a hoax, a delusion of global placelessness derived from its confrontation with a foreignness that is at best a theoretical fiction.

London's subsumption of all foreignness within its overarching context becomes even less convincing as the novel draws to a close. After Winnie kills her husband she, like the Assistant Commissioner, emerges into a London night that is more a confining prison than a great global vista of possibilities. London to Winnie is "sunk in a hopeless night" and rests "at the bottom of a black abyss" (203). Comrade Ossipon, suddenly aware of "the insular nature of Great Britain," recognizes the difficulty of escape from a London that resembles a well-structured cell. "Might just as well be put under the lock and key every night," he thinks (212). So long as they agree not to escape from it, London provides its inhabitants with the illusion of global freedom. Why ever leave, after all, when London is all the world? Trying to get out, though, Ossipon feels like a man with a "wall to scale," and London is suddenly small and bordered, swimming in a dark and terrifying abyss that is the real world beyond its borders, an abyss into which Winnie ultimately plunges: "Spain or California. Mere names.

The vast world created for the glory of man was only a vast blank to Mrs. Verloc" (203). The attempt on the Royal Observatory in the novel fails to provoke the backlash that Vladimir desires, but it does set in motion a narrative apparatus that interrogates the ability of the building to perform the function it had only recently been assigned. The Royal Observatory, ostensibly setting the temporal standard for the rest of the world, is situated in a text that is radically suspicious of England's ability to even acknowledge that another world exists outside of its concretely oppressive locale. The Observatory sends out its signals into a "black abyss"—into a Europe imagined as already "peculiarly British."

What distinguishes Conrad's treatment of standard time from Stoker's is that in Conrad's metropolis, Greenwich time no longer appears to be working. The Bradshaw guide, so crucial in navigating and appropriating the flows of imperial power in Stoker's text, would be utterly ineffective in Conrad's universe. The Assistant Commissioner and Chief Inspector Heat preserve the fiction that they can monitor any given anarchist "hour by hour," "inch by inch and minute by minute," but their bitter knowledge of inevitable gaps in that narrative, of "unexpected solutions of continuity, sudden holes in space and time" (69), undercuts their surface confidence. Conrad's anarchists, with their belief in a carefully synchronized explosive revolution, are equally as unsuccessful as the British authorities at managing precise intervals of time. The anarchist Professor attempts to devise the "perfect detonator" that will "adjust itself to all conditions of action, and even to unexpected changes of conditions," a "variable and yet perfectly precise mechanism" with a less than 20-second deviation of error (56). Yet despite his temporal fanaticism his explosive still blows up poor Stevie in the park, meters from his destination. For Conrad London itself is as temporally unstable and fraught with nonsynchronicities as is any colony. His Londoners ambivalently navigate among a range of temporal demands, none of which can be easily synchronized to conform to the dictates of imperial policy. Mechanistic clock time is juxtaposed against organic temporal markers of the sun and the heavens, while private, bodily experiences of temporal rhythm are differentiated from social or communal rhythms. Temporal anarchy and revolutionary uncertainty sit uncomfortably alongside temporal precision and bureaucratic certitudes.[11] In part a Londoner's relationship to metropolitan time is class-determined. The London elite are contemptuous of the "vulgarity" of time, as is Michaelis's patroness, of whom Conrad writes, "She had that sort of exceptional temperament which defies time with scornful disregard, as if it were a rather vulgar convention submitted to by the mass of inferior mankind" (83). Inspector Heat similarly thinks of the reliable progress of time as a "vulgar conception" as he imagines Stevie experiencing "ages of atrocious pain and mental torture" in the "instantaneous" moment of death (71).

Standard time was a powerful fiction of global uniformity supported by a massive material infrastructure of telecommunications and transport technology. To remove oneself from the empire's grid is to court an anarchical, terrifying chaos of temporal indeterminacy. In *The Secret Agent* Verloc's disconnection from reliable clock time hardly feels liberating to the character or to the reader. Unlike Proust's *memoire involuntaire,* temporal disjunction in Conrad is frightening and disabling. Whereas Proust's involuntary memories are synthetic and constructive, uniting discrete spatial and temporal events through a sensual synthesis (of, for example, a bedchamber at Combray and at Balbec), in Conrad space and time are not creatively synthesized but frighteningly dispersed, like the adolescent Stevie's body, beyond recall. Moments of temporal contraction or expansion in the novel are often stimulated by tragic jolts or encounters with authority, as when Verloc leaves the embassy after his demeaning encounter with Mr. Vladimir: "Though the mortal envelope of Mr. Verloc had not hesitated unduly along the streets, that part of him to which it would be unwarrantably rude to refuse immortality, found itself at the shop door all at once, as if borne from west to east on the wings of a great wind" (33). If Proust's involuntary memories are empowering, Verloc's loss of volition frighteningly corrupts his ability to control the rhythm of his own stride.

For Conrad one potential escape from this disorienting temporal multiplicity was in the idealized natural processes of the sun and stars, processes that the urban wastelands were obscuring but not entirely eliminating. His narrative project in part attempts to resurrect temporal models based on social labor: time dictated by the sun, stars, and the work at hand. In "Joseph Conrad and the Metaphysics of Time" J. M. Kertzer has convincingly illustrated that throughout his works Conrad valorizes a temporality of regularity and rhythmic labor. In the absence of "civilizing" influence his mariners create their own assuring rhythms and conventional patterns of dependable time, wherein the connection between social labor (the community of seamen) and the movement of the sun and stars is intimate and inviolate. At the close of the second chapter of *Lord Jim,* for example, Jim observes the sun's regularity with a pleasure reflected by the cadence of the prose: "Every morning the sun, as if keeping pace in his revolutions with the progress of the pilgrimage, emerged with a silent burst of light exactly at the same distance astern of the ship, caught up with her at noon, pouring the concentrated fire of his rays on the pious purposes of the men, glided past on his descent, and sank mysteriously into the sea evening after evening, preserving the same distance ahead of her advancing bows" (16). Time at sea is not irregular or disjunctive, but is intimately tied to solar rhythm.[12] While modernist time is often characterized as private, subjective, and detached from shared or communal standards,[13] Conrad's idealized treatment of often inaccessible organic rhythms suggests the extent to which some modern writers sought social or collective alternatives to the temporal rigidity and abstraction of industrial modernity. It was in the context of this idealization of solar rhythm that popular early twentieth-century theories of irreversible solar decay were so terrifying and apocalyptic to the modernist sensibility, as Michael Whitworth has demonstrated in *Einstein's Wake*. Whitworth argues that the popular discourse on entropy was frequently translated into terms of social and biological "dissipation," particularly of the sun's energy, which, before the discovery of radium, was assumed to be entropically losing energy and irreversibly cooling.[14]

The London sun of *The Secret Agent* bears not even a family resemblance to the celestial body in *Lord Jim*. Conrad's London is a black hole, a "cruel devourer of the world's light" in which there is "darkness enough to bury five millions of lives."[15] The city, cut off from the sun, is a kind of vampiric, shadowless entity, as we learn in the opening of chapter 2, when Verloc walks to his meeting at the embassy:

> A peculiarly London sun—against which nothing could be said except that it looked bloodshot—glorified all this by its stare. It hung at a moderate elevation above Hyde Park Corner with an air of punctual and benign vigilance. The very pavement under Mr. Verloc's feet had an old-gold tinge in that diffused light, *in which neither wall, nor tree, nor beast, nor man cast a shadow. Mr. Verloc was going westward through a town without shadows* in an atmosphere of powdered old gold. There were red, coppery gleams on the roofs of houses, on the corners of walls, on the panels of carriages, on the very coats of the horses, and on the broad back of Mr. Verloc's overcoat, where they produced a dull effect of rustiness. (15; italics added)

The "bloodshot" sun over London is divested of its power to produce the shadows of walls, trees, beasts, and men. It has taken on instead the properties of clockwork machinery. It is "punctual," yet the only light it casts, on roofs, walls, carriages, beasts, and Verloc himself, is "red, coppery gleams" with a "dull effect of rustiness." The sun is rusting like machinery and spreads its corrosion like a dead copper-cell battery left to decay. The transformation of the sun into a rusting machine signals Conrad's critique of the Observatory, which replaces the sun's authority with mechanical precision. If the Londoners of *The Secret Agent* are, as Stephen Bernstein notes, gothic ghosts, it is largely because, for all their massive corpulence, their bodies have been divorced from any meaningful link to solar activity. Their life in a "town without shadows" is a kind of victimization, a point clearly made when Winnie's shock over Stevie's death is equated with that of populations in the Southern Hemisphere deprived of the light of the sun by an eclipse: "Mrs. Verloc remained immovably seated. She kept still as the population of half the globe would keep still in astonishment were the sun suddenly put out in the summer sky by the perfidy of a trusted providence" (185).[16] The passage resonates with echoes of the famous episode in Haggard's *King Solomon's Mines* when Quartermain and company terrify the Kukuana tribe by using their almanac, which predicts a total eclipse at "11.15 Greenwich time," to "put out" the sun (172). Greenwich precision is used to deny the Kukuana natives their own power to predict or control solar activities, just as, in Conrad's novel, it challenges the power of Londoners to regulate their own quotidian rhythms. The ultimate fate of Comrade Ossipon reveals the degenerating impact of standard time on the daily rhythms and routines of Londoners. The penultimate chapter ends with Ossipon, immediately after his abandonment of Winnie, walking the streets by night and sleeping by day: "When the late sun sent its rays into the room he unclasped his hands, and fell back on the pillow. His eyes stared at the ceiling. And suddenly they closed. Comrade Ossipon slept in the sunlight" (224). Comrade Ossipon has become a kind of vampire, in that his temporal rhythm has been completely reversed. As Claire Rosenfield notes, Ossipon's actions "reverse the normal bodily functions with which we greet the natural order of day and night. He sleeps 'in the sunlight'" (86). Significantly he suffers his temporal disorientation immediately after his attempts to use the English standard time system for his own dastardly purposes. Hatching his plan to escape with the Verlocs' savings he reflects in despair on "the shortcomings of timetables" (212). Realizing that a train leaves at 10:30 from Waterloo Station to Southampton, Ossipon begins a synchronized computation of the minutes required to carry out his plan of dispatching Winnie. He instructs her to wait in the ladies' waiting room "till ten minutes before the train starts" (210). After drinking in the station bar for "seven minutes" he raises "his eyes to the clock." Winnie, "punctual" in following Ossipon's directions, enters the train. Ossipon, looking out from the train to the station clock, counts "eight minutes more" and also counts the "three of these" that Winnie spends in tears. As she weeps Ossipon evaluates her like a clinician specializing in degeneracy, even temporally standardizing her "symptoms": "He watched the symptoms with a sort of medical air, as if counting seconds" (223). He uses British standard rail time to expel from England a woman who has begun to embody, in his eyes, biological degeneracy. Standard time seems beautifully suited for this purpose, yet Ossipon pays a heavy price for his temporal manipulations.

In an essay on cartography written late in his career Conrad lambastes his early geography teachers for their advocacy of a kind of soulless cartography that respects lines and angles over terrain and exploration: "Unfortunately, the marks awarded for that subject were almost as few as the hours apportioned to it in the school curriculum by persons of no romantic sense for the real, ignorant of the great possibilities of active life; with no desire for struggle, no notion of the wide spaces of the world—mere bored professors, in fact, who were not only middle-aged but looked to me as if they had never been young. And their geography was very much like themselves, a bloodless thing with a dry skin covering a repulsive armature of uninteresting bones" (*Last Essays*, 12).[17] The very skin of the geographers reflects deficiencies in their conceptions of global space, just as Ossipon and his anarchist cohort suffer death or disfigurement for their embrace of a similarly soulless standard time. Conrad may parrot the rhetoric of astronomy's neutrality in the political sphere, but in fleshing out the skeleton of the Bourdin incident and in attempting to inhabit the skin of the revolutionary the fiction itself belies its author's rhetorical position. Conrad's narrative counterproject is to reinvest the too rational modern world with fear, uncertainty, stumbling, indeterminacy, or "horror." The torturous struggles of his narrator Marlow to tell even the simplest tale are symptoms of a hyperactive attempt to recreate the mysteries of global space and time, which have became too rigidly and easily graphable. The emotional extremities of early modernism's affect can be understood in part as an attempt to give flesh and substance to the wraithlike bodies of the geometers and their correspondingly skeletal creation: the standardized world map. The salvation of modernity is not in a Bergsonian disavowal of spatial conception, but in a recuperation of a deliberately imprecise geography in which the numbers will not always add up, a project for which Conrad's and Ford Madox Ford's literary impressionism is thus finely suited. Conrad's entire narrative project could be understood as an elaboration on the eternal mystery and inscrutability concealed and obscured by each tick of the cosmopolitan clock. Linguistically investing every moment with a hyperbolic indeterminacy, he and his narrators hint at the temporal incommensurability between an action and its narrative representation in temporal terms. Jim's leap from the *Patna,* Karain's story, and Winnie's murder of Verloc would all be inaccurately represented according to standard time's grid. They all gesture to emotional investments within time that can only be circled around narratively, alternately sped up and slowed down, as in the killing of Verloc, when Verloc has the temporal leisure to contemplate his wife's mental state and a plan of defense even after the knife has been "planted in his breast." In the moment of the murder Winnie is described as having invested in the act "all the inheritance of her immemorial and obscure descent, the simple ferocity of the age of caverns" (197). Conrad's narrative strategy is encapsulated in this scene, in which each instant "between the successive winks of an eye" gestures toward vistas of time and complex social relationships unable to be represented in the instant of time on the clock. Edward Said suggests in *Culture and Imperialism* that Conrad's work opens the gateway for a colonial agency that Conrad himself was never able to recognize.[18] The temporal incommensurability between Conrad's narrative time and standardized time that I have been tracing here is one such opening through which occluded stories and experiences can find habitation.

If Greenwich time is unreliable in the heart of Conrad's darkest London, it is even more deceptive in Joyce's Dublin, where a negotiation of competing metropolitan temporal demands is substantially frustrated by the overarching imposition of an imperial Greenwich standard onto local Dublin time. In the "Lestrygonians" episode of *Ulysses* Leopold Bloom becomes abruptly aware of this time discrepancy between Greenwich and Dublin. Joyce uses the episode to challenge the complicity of Greenwich standard time with imperial designs to restructure and redirect the spaces and rhythms of a colonized Ireland. Setting his urban opus in a Dublin still (in 1904) twenty-five minutes deviant from Greenwich Mean Time Joyce challenges the political power inherent in astronomical knowledge, as Bloom attempts to reclaim from an expert class of astronomers his power to use the sun to mark his temporal progress through the city. Postcolonial readings of Joyce have demonstrated the extent to which his texts engage the discourses of imperialism and colonial resistance. Vincent J. Cheng argues that imperial history is "written all over the face" of Joyce's Ireland, forming the "hour-by-hour subtext and context" of his characters' thoughts and experiences (169). For Enda Duffy Bloom's wanderings through his city differ substantially from those of other European flaneurs in that he witnesses "explicit evidence of exploitation" rather than merely the city's commercial and imperial wares (69).[19] Among the evidence of exploitation that Bloom observes is certainly the Greenwich time ball's distortion and deception of his "hour-by-hour" time consciousness. When he becomes aware of the disjunction between Greenwich and Dunsink time he loses faith in his own ability to meaningfully orient himself in space and time without the mediation of an elite class of experts. This inability to integrate oneself into a "coherent, constructive" world is one of the many damaging effects of colonization, as Frantz Fanon has written.[20] It is entirely appropriate that Joyce should situate a critique of Greenwich time within the "Lestrygonians" episode of *Ulysses*. Bloom meditates in that episode on the interrelationship of time with capitalism, social organization, natural phenomena, the body, language, and colonialism.[21] Joyce's understanding of the complicities of time with these diverse regimes of knowledge and power militates against any schematic reading of the text as an expression of interior, psychic, or private modernist temporality.[22] What is at stake for Joyce, as for Conrad, is the relationship of the individual both to the movement of the sun and also to quotidian rhythms of life and labor. Joyce does not, as Stephen Kern's reading would have it, disavow clock time altogether in favor of a placeless "cosmic" time (17), but rather attempts to reassert the power of the individual to reclaim access to reliable temporality. Joyce juxtaposes safe and comfortable verities of timekeeping (six o'clock is simply six o'clock; the time ball keeps the local time; time can be made profitable) against more unsettling temporal systems, in which time is linked to betrayal (personal and global), commerce, food consumption, and linguistic productivity. Far from embracing a temporal evasion into the "cosmic," this high canonical modernist text trenchantly investigates the impact of manipulations of cosmic temporal phenomena on every aspect of daily life, ranging from the intimate, through the local, to global relations of production and consumption.[23]

Bloom is instinctively a clock watcher, if only because he is obsessed with knowing the exact moment he will be cuckolded by Blazes Boylan.

He waits for six o'clock to come, knowing that it will be "safe" for him to return to a house without Boylan. Without the threat of the sexual rendezvous Bloom's time consciousness effectively ends: "Just a bite or two. Then about six o'clock I can. Six, six. Time will be gone then. She . . ." (174). Tellingly confusing Boylan for time itself (not "Boylan will be gone" but "Time will be gone"), Bloom reveals his intensely personal investment in the time registered on the clock dial, which appears to transparently register his domestic shame. Throughout the day, though, Bloom is continually faced with conflicting information registered on various timepieces, as when he realizes that the "bilious clock" in the pub is "five minutes fast" (173). His clock watching is observed by his pub mates, who note that he cannot "imbibe" anything without first looking at his watch (178). This anecdote links him with Mina Purefoy's husband, whom Bloom criticizes earlier in the episode for "eating with a stopwatch, thirtytwo chews to the minute" (161). Time is thus linked to consumption, which is later linked to war, as when Bloom speculates that "peace and war depend on some fellow's digestion." Nosy Flynn tells an anecdote about a woman who "hid herself in a clock" to spy on the rituals of the Freemasons (177). The linkage of power relations with food, with money, and ultimately with time reveals the vast terrain of cultural activity that depends on the correct calculation and control of time. Bloom imagines a social welfare program in which "every child born" receives "five quid at compound interest up to twentyone," a calculation that requires a stable and dependable temporality for the accrual of capital (161). The comfortable notion of profiting on time's passage though favorable interest rates, though, is juxtaposed with Bloom's equation of time with water, a substance that, by its very nature, cannot be owned. Bloom reflects on the capital investment in water as he watches a rowboat on the Liffey with a billboard advertising trousers: "Good idea that. Wonder if he pays rent to the corporation. How can you own water really? It's always floating in a stream, never the same, which in the stream of life we trace" (153). The questionable ownership of water in this passage forecasts Bloom's later comparison of time with water: "Can't bring back time. Like holding water in your hand" (188). Time's evanescence, along with its complex interactions with personal history and domestic tragedy, make it resistant to ownership. Within this narrative landscape, in which time is linked to betrayal, commerce, food consumption, and linguistic productivity (as when Molly quips that Ben Dollard is "big Ben" [154]), Leopold Bloom is initially unaware that his rambling thoughts on time might have any

The Limits of Modernity | 115

implications for the dependability of his watch, which he trusts for its ability to orient him in spatial and social relationships.

The seed of Bloom's doubt in the reliability of timepieces is planted, however, when he passes the Ballast Office time ball, which he mistakenly believes to have dropped at 1:00 P.M. Dunsink Time:

> After one. Timeball on the ballast office is down. Dunsink time. Fascinating little book that is of sir Robert Ball's. Parallax. I never exactly understood. There's a priest. Could ask him. Par it's Greek: parallel, parallax. Met him pikehoses she called it till I told her about the transmigration. O rocks!
>
> Mr. Bloom smiled O rocks at two windows of the ballast office. She's right after all. Only big words for ordinary things on account of the sound. (154)

Time balls indeed drop at 1:00 P.M. every day, but, as Bloom only recalls some thirteen pages later, the Dublin time ball dropped at 1:00 P.M. *Greenwich* time, which would still, in 1904, have been only 12:35 *Dublin* time, according to the observatory at Dunsink. Ireland would not legally adopt Greenwich time on all its clocks until 1916.[24] Bloom knows that there is a discrepancy between the Dunsink controlled clocks and the Greenwich controlled time ball, but he temporarily suppresses the knowledge. Instead he recalls from the astronomer Robert Ball's book the term *parallax,* which refers to the "apparent displacement of an object brought about by a change in the position of the observer," an effect Ball illustrates by instructing the reader to note the optical illusion produced by focusing on a near object first with one eye closed, then the other. Robert Ball was himself an opponent to the Irish adoption of Greenwich time, and his term *parallax,* associated in this episode with the sight of a Greenwich-controlled time ball, arguably gestures toward what was at the time a fraught national issue of privileged access to accurate interpretations of solar phenomena.[25] While the clocks operating on Dunsink time mark noon as the moment the sun crosses the local meridian, the time ball continues to register a British-controlled interpretation of astronomical phenomena.

For Bloom this discrepancy in time is first written off as the mere effects of optical illusion (as in Ball's eye-closing experiment) or else of inaccessible jargon ("big words for ordinary things"). It is a battle beyond the ken of the ordinary civilian, requiring the mediation of an expert class, such as the priest to whom Bloom imagines himself posing the question of parallax. Bloom's initial instinct is to empty out astronomy of all its potential political content. The Greenwich time ball keeps Irish time, he imagines, and any suggestion of division or discrepancy hinted at in the word *parallax* is either illusory or pedantic. The individual, he believes, can read the time of the clock transparently and regulate his personal affairs to it accordingly. At this point Bloom, who needs to know what time it is for very personal reasons, feels confident that he has access to the correct time. The problem occurs thirteen pages later, when he attempts to read a timepiece on the roof of a bank and is unable to see it because of the weakness of his glasses. Turning away from the bank he turns his eyes to the sun, which he blocks out with his fingers:

> There's a little watch up there on the roof of the bank to test those glasses by.
> His lids came down on the lower rims of his irides. Can't see it. If you imagine it's there you can almost see it. Can't see it.
> He faced about and, standing between the awnings, held out his right hand at arm's length towards the sun. Wanted to try that often. Yes: completely. The tip of his little finger blotted out the sun's disk. Must be the focus where the rays cross. If I had black glasses. Interesting. There was a lot of talk about those sunspots when we were in Lombard Street west. Terrific explosions they are. There will be a total eclipse this year: autumn some time. (166)

Joyce contrasts Bloom's relationship with two different timepieces: the watch on the bank and the sun itself. The bank's timepiece, signifying and regulating commerce and trade, is invisible to Bloom; he has no visual access to it and has to place his faith in its existence. To the sun, though, Bloom has direct access, controlling the extent to which he allows its rays to pass through his fingers. His bodily relationship to the sun leads to a train of thought about solar activity (sunspots and eclipses) with which he is very comfortable. The "explosions" of sunspots remind him of his social connections, and he remembers conversations in Lombard Street about solar phenomena.

In his experiment with the sun Bloom feels himself in a very graphic way the master of his surroundings, but a sudden recollection brings on a wave of helplessness. It is at this point that he remembers that the time ball, giving him Greenwich rather than local time, had been lying to him:

> Now that I come to think of it, that ball falls at Greenwich time. It's the clock is worked by an electric wire from Dunsink. Must go out there some first Saturday of the month. If I could get an introduction to Professor Joly or learn up something about his family. That would do: man always feels complimented, flattery where least expected. Nobleman proud to be descended from some king's mistress. His foremother. Lay it on with a trowel. Cap in

hand goes through the land. Not go in and blurt out what you're not to: what's parallax? Show this gentleman the door
Ah.
His hand fell again to his side.
Never know anything about it. Waste of time. Gasballs spinning about, crossing each other, passing. Same old dingdong always. Gas, then solid, then world, then cold, then dead shell drifting around, frozen rock like that pineapple rock. (167)

In his imagined confrontation with the astronomer Charles Joly Bloom recognizes that the observatory, with its control of social time, is a site of power. He imagines himself having to placate the royal astronomer's ego as he would a nobleman and being thrown out of the observatory for simply saying the word *parallax,* with its suggestion that the role of the observer has some meaningful relationship to what happens in the heavens. Thinking of his inability to understand or access forces beyond his control Bloom abruptly stops his experiment with the sun. His hand drops to his side, and the cosmos, which ten pages ago had been a comfortable place for him, is now a dead, cold world, more immutable than he can imagine, with laws he cannot shape. Bloom's role in the construction of his own social time is torn from him and cast onto an incomprehensible astronomical canvas. At this point the image of "pineapple rock" recurs as a fitting symbol for the dead and frozen cosmology that Greenwich time offers the colonized. In the first lines of "Lestrygonians" Bloom had seen an act of imperial betrayal in the fairly innocuous sight of children eating "Pineapple Rock" flavored ices from a street vendor acting as "Lozenge and comfit manufacturer to His Majesty the King." While the vampiric monarch is pictured on his throne "sucking red jujubes white," the children shovel down flavored ice that is "bad for their tummies" (151). Joyce equates Greenwich's temporal order both with the dead rock of a cooled earth (a common fear for the modernists) and metaphorically with pineapple rock, a sugar-sticky confection sold to Irish children by the blood-sucking English. The construction of time as something beyond humanity's control, making, or understanding is packaged here for Bloom with the same effects and for the same ends as the pineapple rock, an imperial tool designed to make the Irish forget their hunger but leaving them with no real nourishment in its place.

If Conrad's strategy is to open standard time up to gaps and holes in its grid, Joyce's approach is to linguistically overwhelm it with an abundance of information that cannot be easily mapped. The word *parallax,* which I have discussed in relation to Robert Ball's critique of Greenwich time, becomes a linguistic talisman in *Ulysses* as it is placed in constellation with other words, sounds, and images in a verbal stew. As a case in point, the word unexpectedly recurs in "The Oxen of the Sun" episode, in an apocalyptic context. Wrested away from its initial use in "Lestrygonians" as an example of technical jargon *parallax* here takes on the character of a mythological beast: "The voices blend and fuse in clouded silence: silence that is the infinite of space: and swiftly, silently, the soul is wafted over regions of cycles of cycles of generations that have lived. . . . And on the highway of the clouds they come, muttering thunder of rebellion, the ghosts of beasts. Huuh! Hark! Huuh! Parallax stalks behind and goads them, the lancinating lightnings of whose brow are scorpions. . . . Ominous, revengeful, zodiacal host! They moan, passing upon the clouds . . . all their moving moaning multitude, murderers of the sun" (414). In this image the infinite expanse of cosmological space, with its steady, regular unfolding of cyclic time, is violently interrupted by the word *parallax,* which goads the astrological zodiac into cataclysm, disrupting the stable hierarchy of the heavens. It is entirely appropriate that the word should be performing the role of executioner of a stable cosmological space, given that its initial function in the text was to goad Bloom into recalling Greenwich's manipulation of Dublin clocks. More important than this thematic link for the present argument is that Joyce uses a word like *parallax* as a device to provoke surprising linguistic associations, to set in motion alliterative connections, and to call attention to the social constructedness of language, which can be disassociated from its stable meaning and situated in new contexts. Joyce's focus is often on the sound rather than the meaning of *parallax,* as Bloom searches for the etymological root and geographical origin of the word: "Par it's Greek: parallel, parallax." Unable to locate the word's origins Bloom appropriates the word to his own purposes, and his appropriation yields surprising insights into the imperial manipulations of time and their interactions with a stable view of an infinite cosmos. Joyce's linguistic experimentations presuppose an orientation to time that is incommensurable with standard time's reliance on a stable, unchanging connection between spatial and temporal orientations. The word is not localized to its textbook definition and etymological source; it is not temporally fixed, but is adaptable to the changing needs of the writer. Joyce's attitude toward language, regardless of any specific content, is thus intrinsically opposed to the temporal coordination of the standard time system. If Conrad opens a gateway to temporal gaps that he can register only as a verbal lack, Joyce provides a linguistic model for inhabiting those gaps with an abundance of endlessly transformative language.

While Joyce associates Greenwich's foreign standard with disenchanted and inert astronomical matter, Virginia Woolf equates it with the crass manipulation of bourgeois commerce in a key image at the midpoint of *Mrs. Dalloway*. The image occurs when Hugh Whitbread is strolling down Oxford Street and sees a "commercial clock, suspended above a shop," announcing Greenwich time. In the paragraph immediately preceding this image Woolf has described the action of the clocks of Harley Street as "shredding," "slicing," and "nibbling" away at the "mound of time" in an attempt to "counsel submission and uphold authority." In comparison to these clocks the commercial clock that Whitbread sees is comparatively friendly:

> [It] announced, genially and fraternally, as if it were a pleasure to Messrs. Rigby and Lowndes to give the information gratis, that it was half-past one.
> Looking up, it appeared that each letter of their names stood for one of the hours; subconsciously one was grateful to Rigby and Lowndes for giving one time ratified by Greenwich; and this gratitude (so Hugh Whitbread ruminated, dallying there in front of the shop window), naturally took the form later of buying off Rigby and Lowndes socks or shoes. (102)

Whitbread's "gratitude" for having been given the precise English time leads "simultaneously" to a rumination on the necessity of buying the store's wares. Greenwich time's imperial significance is marvelously deflated by Woolf here, reduced to a sales device for advertising socks. Woolf's "commercial clock" of Messrs. Rigby and Lowndes (who conveniently share between them twelve letters of the alphabet, one for each space on the clock) is an ironic counter to the radical clock dials proposed by the French and Canadian standard time proponents, Jules Janssen and Sandford Fleming. Janssen and Fleming were key antagonists at the Prime Meridian Conference who both advocated clock-face reform (a decimal clock with ten numbers, in Janssen's case, and a twenty-four-hour clock with the letters of the alphabet, excluding J and Z, in Fleming's).[26] In *Mrs. Dalloway* Janssen's decimal clock and Fleming's twenty-four-hour clock have yielded inevitably to the Rigby-Lowndes clock (figures 3, 4, and 5). Woolf's image is a brilliant encapsulation of the latent ambitions of the Prime Meridian Conference as well as a biting satire of its imperial hubris. The names of petty merchants are inscribed on the clock face as if they were the embodiment of the universal time over which Janssen and Fleming fought.

FIGURES 3, 4, and 5. Illustrations of three radical clock-dial reforms. Figure 3 shows the decimal clock of the French Revolution, designed in Year II of the Revolution and advocated by the French delegate Jules Janssen in his bid for metric time at the 1884 International Prime Meridian Conference. Figure 4 is Sandford Fleming's twenty-four-hour clock, designed to conform to his early attempts to designate a letter for each hour of the day (omitting J and Z). Figure 5 is my recreation of Virginia Woolf's image from *Mrs. Dalloway* of the commercial clock of Messrs. Rigby and Lowndes hanging above a shop in Oxford Street. Figure 3 source: http://www.antiquehorology .org/_Editorial/RepublicanCalendar/default.htm, retrieved February 17, 2009. Figure 4 source: Fleming, Sandford. "Uniform Non-local Time (Terrestrial Time)."

Woolf's interest in the dangers of temporal standardization is not confined to *Mrs. Dalloway*, but is an extension of themes and images she had worked through earlier, in her 1919 novel, *Night and Day*. The strange and novel presence of telephony in that novel has attracted some critical comment, but Woolf's critique of standard time in the text has been unexplored.[27] Rigidly maintained temporality in *Night and Day* is closely associated with the character of Mary Datchet and her work at a suffrage office, where synchronized machinery coordinates human activity. Mr. Clacton has "perfected and controlled" the "machinery" that produces a committee meeting, during which "the door kept opening as the clock struck the hour, in obedience to a few strokes of his pen on a piece of paper" (171). Mary's personal life is precisely timed and her thoughts synchronized with her actions. Her favorite moments of the day, we learn, are "the minutes between nine-twenty-five and nine-thirty in the morning" (74). On her march to work she imagines herself engaged along with the morning commuters in "the serious business of winding up the world to tick for another four-and-twenty hours" (75). During the commute Mary's thoughts follow a predictable mental "groove" in which she is capable of "thinking the same thoughts every morning at the same hour, so that the chestnut-colored brick of the Russell Square houses had some curious connection with her thoughts about office economy" (76). Mary inherits her respect for temporal precision from her father, who has become clumsily antisocial from a lifetime of watching clocks and counting train cars. Reverend Datchet "would pace up and down at the same hour every morning, with a sundial to measure the time for him" (186). Mary's attempt at a conversation with her father about the garden prompts an idiosyncratic ramble about train departure times: "The traffic's very much increased, you know. More rolling-stock needed already. Forty trucks went down yesterday by the 12.15. Counted them myself. They've taken off the 9.30 and given us an 8.30 instead—suits the business men, you know. You come by the old 3.10 yesterday, I suppose?" (189). Reverend Datchet duplicates Mina Harker's encyclopedic knowledge of the Bradshaw guide in *Dracula,* with the crucial difference that Datchet's knowledge, far from a powerful tool of empire, merely evidences his doddering inefficacy. In contrast to the Datchets' lives of hollow precision, the upper-class Hilberys remain insensible to standard time. Mrs. Hilbery insists to Katharine at the end of the novel that life "consists in missing trains" (525), and indeed Katharine's life of "solitary wandering" according to "a plan in her mind which required Bradshaws" (461) is transformed by the efforts of her mother and Ralph into the life, for better or worse, of a wife who lets her husband act as her guide (as we see in the expedition to Greenwich, which Katharine significantly mistakes for Dulwich [484]).

The command center of the temporally precise suffrage office is figured in a series of metaphors as existing at the heart or center of a network of connecting lines. Mary feels, as she works, "that she was the centre ganglion of a very fine network of nerves which fell over England" (78). Mrs. Seal believes that the office is the "exact spot on the surface of the globe" where "all the subterranean wires of thought and progress come together" (279), a sentiment echoed by Mr. Clacton, who describes the office as "the centre of an enormous system of wires, connecting us up with every district of the country" (269). Katherine, however, compares Mary and her coworkers to "enchanted people in a bewitched tower ... so aloof and unreal and apart from the normal world did they seem to her, in the house of innumerable typewriters, murmuring their incantations and concocting their drugs, and flinging their frail spiders' webs over the torrent of life which rushed down the streets outside" (92). The suffrage office attempts to unite, but fails to meaningfully impact, the rush of life in "the normal world." As

Mary's relationship with Ralph disintegrates she becomes aware that the network of lines radiating from the suffrage office fails to connect with human life in any meaningful sense. The machine, like Mrs. Seal, does not acknowledge the "terrible side of life which is concerned with the emotions, the private lives, of the sexes" (276). Mary recognizes that Mr. Clacton and Mrs. Seal are "undeveloped human beings, from whose substance some essential part had been cut away" (279). Intoxicating absorption into the crowd later seems to Mary only a defense against a recognition of emptiness: "One could keep step with the crowd and never be found out for the hollow machine, lacking the essential thing, that one was conscious of being" (272). Woolf's critique of Mary and the suffrage office is that they presume to predict, control, and maintain human activity according to a system of spatial mapping and temporal precision. The maintenance of such an efficient machine requires stunted human beings, eccentric at best and completely asocial at worst.

The localized political activity of the suffrage office in *Night and Day* becomes in *Mrs. Dalloway* the god of Proportion, whose throne is in London but whose power extends across the globe. The high priests of the god of Proportion are the Bradshaws, whose family name, as critics have noted,[28] is significantly that of England's railway timetable guide. Sir William Bradshaw and his wife live rigidly synchronized lives. Bradshaw gives "three-quarters of an hour" to his patients, and Lady Bradshaw spends "four nights out of seven" at home with her son (99). The Bradshaws use standard time to compartmentalize the sick from the healthy, the profitable from the unprofitable. Proportion works by seclusion and segregation; it "secluded . . . lunatics, forbade childbirth, penalized despair, made it impossible for the unfit to propagate their views" (99). The Bradshaws' temporal Proportion is further linked to the "sister goddess" Conversion, which is "even now" engaged in "dashing down shrines, smashing idols, and setting up in their place her own stern countenance" (100).

As a counter to the Bradshaws' authoritarian approach to time Woolf offers a series of alternative metaphorical patterns of temporal relationships. *Mrs. Dalloway* has been read in terms of a dichotomy between the body and authoritarian time, with Clarissa's fluid temporal reminiscences starkly challenged by the demands of Big Ben.[29] Yet Woolf's critique is not of any and all forms of temporal organization, but rather of standard time's particular enlistment of that organization to serve the imperial demands of what she terms the "twin gods" of Proportion and Conversion. The standardized clocks of Harley Street point out "in chorus the supreme advantages of a sense of proportion" (102). Woolf thus explicitly links synchronized clocks and their Proportion with the imperialist processes of Conversion, a goddess who imposes "her own features" on the colonized both abroad and at home ("the heat and sands of India, the mud and swamp of Africa, the purlieus of London" [100]). Perhaps more explicitly than either Conrad or Joyce, Woolf directly challenges the role of temporal synchronization in imperialism. Her work, once emblematic of a politically untainted aestheticism, has increasingly been placed in a more meaningful constellation of political struggles over imperial policy as well as over women's rights. Kathy Phillips, offering in *Virginia Woolf against Empire* the most sustained reading of Woolf's engagement with imperialism to date, reads *Mrs. Dalloway,* with its references to the empire's hold on Africa and India and Lady Bruton's munificent expatriation of undesirables to Canada, as a key text in Woolf's anti-imperial canon.[30] With her provocative exploration of the interrelationship between standardized temporal technology, commercial manipulation, and overseas abuses Woolf challenges the manipulation of a desirable ideal of universal temporal connection to serve the interests of imperial control and commercial profit. Hardly anarchical Woolf's prose explores alternative metaphorical systems in order to represent human connectivity within a local milieu, cutting across class and gender barriers through an imaginative transformation (rather than a rejection) of clock time.

Woolf's counter to standard time's organization of space is embodied in her suggestive association of people and events according to contextually determined social factors rather than according to standard time's coordinated clocks. For Woolf standard time's synchronization of people and events can unify only at the level of imperial power and commercial manipulation. Nevertheless its unification gestures toward the possibility of more meaningful social connections which Woolf will try to forge through narrative.[31] The synchronized coordination of standard time with empire and commerce in *Mrs. Dalloway* is perhaps most evident in the early scene where a mass crowd is unified in its thoughts and gaze, first by a motor car and then by a sky writer. The fact that "every one looked at the motor car" is terrifying to Septimus Smith, who sees oppression and violence in such a mass fixity of gaze. Imagining the queen or prime minister in the car, the crowd is synchronized in its gaze for a precisely demarcated space of time: "For thirty seconds all heads were inclined the same way" (17). Their fixed gaze coincides with microcosmic enactments of imperial oppression in the colonies, as "a colonial" insults "the House of Windsor" in a public house, leading to "words, broken beer glasses, and a general shindy" (18). The car produces thoughts of sacrifice for empire and aristocracy, as men watching the car "seemed ready to attend the Sovereign, if need be, to the cannon's mouth," and their thoughts turn to "flowing corn and the manor houses of England" (18). If the car suggests empire, the sky writer clearly signals commerce, as it spells out an advertisement for toffee. Here again the crowd is synchronized in its gaze: "Everyone looked up"; "All down the Mall people were standing and looking up into the sky" (20). The motor car may be a spectacle signaling the power of empire and property to produce a single-minded fixity of gaze, yet Woolf wants us to understand that it nevertheless touches a profound desire for a more meaningful organization of urban space. "The swift agitation of the passing car," she writes, "grazed something profound" (18). The question is not *whether* a unification of people in time is desirable, but *how* one unifies people meaningfully rather than according to surface spectacles and jingoism.

Woolf offers a number of metaphors for the linkages of bodies in space, from webs and threads to the aural linkage of chiming clocks. Recognizing standard time as a crass, commercial device aimed at division and control she imagines alternative linkages of human time and spatial organization. Early in the novel Clarissa imagines all of London in June as existing above the surface of the Earth "wrapped in the soft mesh of the grey-blue morning air." In one of the book's great images the mesh unwinds and drops everyone and everything down to the surface in midstride, like the ponies "whose forefeet just struck the ground and up they sprung" (5). This "mesh" in the air is later figured as a web that connects Londoners by invisible strings and later as a surface of water on which all of London floats. The image of floating on the surface is juxtaposed with another metaphor, of Whitehall being "skated over by spiders" (164). The spider's web connects bodies, as when Lady Bruton is described as being connected to Richard Dalloway and Whitbread by a "thin thread" that becomes "hazy with the sound of bells . . . as a single spider's thread is blotted with rain-drops, burdened, sags down" (112). The mesh in the air, the skating of spiders on threads, and the floating boats on London's streets suggest together an invisible surface whose coordinates are felt but not seen. In the British Museum manuscript the delicate fragility of the web is even more apparent. Following a paragraph that begins by asking whether Harley

Street was "founded on the truth," Woolf continues her web imagery: "Spinning its . . . lovely web over the inner hollows, shop tossed, the glittering skein from [?]to shop across the street; or hats, clothes, & diamonds; brittle as glass the filaments stretched, upon which the & the race balanced" (*Virginia Woolf's "The Hours"*, 147). The human race "balances" on a "brittle" thread of filaments across a street, like spiders skating across a web. *Mrs. Dalloway's* space is a surface woven by a fragile and tenuous thread of connections concealing a core that cannot be reached except by sudden and transitory illuminations. Clarissa has one such "sudden revelation" of "something central which permeated; something warm which broke up surfaces" (31). Like a blush the "thin skin" of the world "splits" and gushes "alleviation over the cracks and sores" (32).[32] These glimpses of a center are momentary, though, as Clarissa, meditating on Septimus's death, recognizes "people feeling the impossibility of reaching the centre which, mystically, evaded them" (184). The inaccessibility of the center accounts for Clarissa's ignorance of the location of the equator, a global blindness that leads her to "muddle Armenians and Turks" (122).

Woolf's exploration of bodily depth offers a resistance to a standardized grid that links hollow bodies only for the purposes of manipulation and profit. Peter Walsh, walking the streets after his meeting with Clarissa, sees a frightening symbol of standardized uniformity and compulsion in the spectacle of "weedy" boys in uniform, marching with a wreath. Walsh reads "on their faces an expression like the letters of a legend written round the base of a statue praising duty, gratitude, fidelity, love of England" (51): "On they marched, past him, past every one, in their steady way, as if one will worked legs and arms uniformly, and life, with its varieties, its irreticences, had been laid under a pavement of monuments and wreaths and drugged into a stiff yet staring corpse by discipline" (51). If London's motor cars are the "pulse irregularly drumming" through the "body" of the city (15), the "weedy soldiers" are the body's extremities—the fingers and toes of empire, turned corpse-like as if through some error in the circulatory system. For Woolf a standardized sense of Proportion was equivalent to a kind of physical deformity, as the corpse of "weedy boys" suggests. In an oft-cited passage from *Orlando* (1928) Woolf's narrator argues that functioning human beings ("successful practitioners of the art of life") embody a microcosm of the global standardization of time. These "unknown" people "somehow contrive to synchronise the sixty or seventy different times which beat simultaneously in every normal human system so that when eleven strikes, all the rest chime in unison, and the present is neither a violent disruption nor completely forgotten in the past. Of them, we can justly say that they live precisely the sixty-eight or seventy-two years allotted them on the tombstone. Of the rest, some we know to be dead, though they walk among us; some are not yet born, though they go through the forms of life; others are hundreds of years old though they call themselves thirty-six" (305). The mediocrities whose lives consist only of submission to standard time are contrasted with an assortment of temporal oddities, among whom the heroine of the novel can certainly be counted. Even the undead appear in this litany of beings, a clearer indication than any of modernism's reversal of position on the potential threat of temporal Others in London. Orlando herself is a kind of Dracula, whose temporally immeasurable life is the embodiment of a time beyond the control of standard time's grid. The narrator later reflects that the "difficult business" of "time-keeping" is completely "disturbed" by "contact with any of the arts" (306). To be in "contact with the arts" is to radically frustrate official timekeeping and to bring up against its compartmentalization of human life the "two thousand and fifty-two" people "all having lodgement at one time or another in the human spirit" (308). Modernist art for Woolf consists in the wresting away of time keeping from the guardians of empire and commerce and in reclaiming the diverse experiences of time in a single body or in a community of bodies. Her decision to change the title of her work from *The Hours* to *Mrs. Dalloway* itself signals this project.

To bring out the interior "blush," as Clarissa Dalloway attempts, is to suggest the possibility of more meaningful social linkages that resist the precision, proportion, and conversion of imperial time. For Woolf it is the role of the artist to generate more meaningful, contextually determined temporal linkages. This is not achieved conclusively in *Mrs. Dalloway*, nor is there necessarily meant to be a conclusive system of temporal linkage. The goal of articulating and rearticulating such linkages drives Woolf's formal experimentation. Clarissa speculates that death is one conclusive linkage, and earlier that "the mist between people she knew best" is another, but these are only two among many such metaphorical connecting devices in Woolf's texts. Clarissa's party is a metaphor for Woolf's narrative project in that it attempts to create linkages between people across space and time that are not "superficial" and "fragmentary": "But to go deeper, beneath what people said (and their judgments, how superficial, how fragmentary they are!) in her own mind now, what did it mean to her, this thing she called life?

Oh, it was very queer. Here was So-and-so in South Kensington; some one up in Bayswater; and somebody else, say, in Mayfair. And she felt quite continually a sense of their existence; and she felt what a waste; and she felt what a pity; and she felt if only they could be brought together; so she did it. And it was an offering; to combine, to create" (122). Clarissa's social project to "combine" and "create" meaningful patterns of temporal organization across social divides arguably mirrors modernism's larger narrative project of forging alternative networks of temporal connection. These variable and nonsynchronous networks evade or short-circuit the imperial grid of standard time, which unifies technological infrastructures for the purposes of commercial mobility, profiting the dominant power elite while disenfranchising and co-opting all other forms of localized, contextually determined temporal organization.

For Conrad, Joyce, and Woolf the connections between people and nations by standard time's uniform grid is a hollow linkage forged for the interests of empire and commerce, while more meaningful social linkages and manipulations of time remain disenfranchised and degraded. The global totality of standard time represents empire's pretension (and failure) to represent global space as merely a network of coordinates. Yet it is important to state that these accumulated critiques of standard time are not necessarily motivated by, and do not even imply, a politics of anti-imperialism on the part of the individual authors. The impetus for critiques of standard time vary from author to author, depending on biographical factors, value systems, and class positions. Woolf's critique of standard time in *Night and Day*, for example, reads much more as contempt for the working-class drone than as a critique of British overseas policy, while Conrad's anti-Greenwich stance lambastes landlocked bureaucrats of one political stripe or another while valorizing the seamen who do the business of empire in more "organic" settings. Thus it seems less that imperialism is intrinsically at stake in the formation of these modernist interrogations of standard time, and more that a certain form of centralized control of space and time is being weighed against the narrative demands of spatiotemporal representation and found lacking.

This does not necessarily translate into a political platform on the part of modernist artists, but its potential anti-imperial implications should not go unacknowledged. As a system of global representation that facilitates capital penetration and military dominance, standard time demands recognition of its foundational principles of time and space as abstract, unchanging, and uniform. Alternative representations of time and space that contest these principles must necessarily call into question the constructedness and contestability of the system. If, as Stuart Hall has written, "time and space are the basic coordinates of all systems of representation" (301), or in Paul Ricoeur's more dramatic formulation, narrative is the only means whereby human time can be expressed (88), then the modernist project of radically reconfiguring narrative time necessarily opens a gateway to a condemnation of the imperial policies that support, enforce, and make evanescent the manipulations of GMT (or its twenty-first-century analogue, GPS). Although modernism's stylistic codes have been accused of complicity in imperial strategies of representation (most notably by Ian Adam and Helen Tiffin),[33] the subversive potential of modernism's project of spatiotemporal representation may indeed extend beyond the individual British modernists' own ability to explicitly identify with anti-imperial positions. This is not to suggest that modernist style created or spread anti-imperialism, but rather that it provided aesthetic models for alternative representations of social time within the parameters of modernization and modernity.[34]

The aesthetic developments I have traced in British modernism do not, however, tell the whole story of standard time's relationship to twentieth-century literary forms. Standard time was necessarily a global phenomenon, experienced variably by diverse populations already producing their own aesthetic representations of space and time. In the next chapter I turn to literature produced in English by subcontinental Indian writers in the fifty years after India's 1906 legal adoption of Greenwich-based standard time. These writers are rarely considered alongside Joyce and Woolf in an often balkanized literary field, yet their texts contribute to the same aesthetic project of examining and reshaping the limits of spatiotemporal representation. If the mapping strategies of standard time were ineffective tools at the heart of empire, where the clocks ran with cold precision, what function did they serve for writers in a colony that, as Rushdie claimed in *Midnight's Children,* was "usually a few hours wrong"?

CHAPTER 5

"A Few Hours Wrong"

Standard Time and Indian Literature in English

> Time, in my experience, has been as variable and inconstant as Bombay's electric power supply. Just telephone the speaking clock if you don't believe me—tied to electricity, it's usually a few hours wrong. Unless we're the ones who are wrong. . . . No people whose word for 'yesterday' is the same as their word for 'tomorrow' can be said to have a firm grip on time.
>
> —Salman Rushdie, *Midnight's Children*

Saleem Sinai's observation on time in India, near the beginning of Salman Rushdie's *Midnight's Children* (1981), provocatively links cross-cultural temporal difference with uneven modernization and linguistic variance. Saleem cannot decide whether the difference between Indian and English time is simply a technical glitch in the Bombay power supply, correctible by a more even and equitable distribution of electric current, or whether it rests on a more fundamental cultural distance written into the very vocabulary and syntax of Hindi. His indecision is emblematic of a central crisis in the treatment of time in the Indian novel in English. Is there an "Indian time" which is either resistant to or else adaptable with British standard time? Or is the notion of cross-cultural temporal variance (spiritual, behavioral, or linguistic) merely a mirage that vanishes with a more streamlined system of standardized rail and telegraphy? If there is an Indian time, how and by whom might it be invoked, and for what political ends?

Saleem's dilemma is by no means confined to the English-language Indian novel. Rushdie's offhand narrative observation about the Bombay speaking clock gestures toward the fraught and ambivalent signification of time itself in postcolonial narrative and theory. If there has been a noticeable absence of significant theoretical analyses of time in contemporary critical theory it is perhaps only in postcolonial theory that time, as a privileged locus in investigations of identity and oppositional politics, has found a home. Yet the time that is so often celebrated in postcolonial discourse remains generally opaque and ephemeral. In fact it is time's very opacity and ephemerality that render it so malleable in the hands of theorists determined to wrest postcolonial experience and agency away from the master narratives of historicism, teleology, and subjectivity.[1] If spatial categories remain rigidly stable, time (figured as delay, lag, speed, in-betweenness, process, or performance) is protean in its ability to frustrate the colonizer's attempts to affix all heterogeneous temporalities onto a standard graph or grid. An obvious, if unacknowledged neo-Bergsonism marks the discourse of postcolonial time. Yet whereas Bergson conceived of the durée as a universal human characteristic, postcolonial theorists insist on a durée that is uniquely situated within the migrant or exilic conditions of postcoloniality. If Europe and the West succumbed to a mechanized, standardized, and spatialized telos, the postcolonial keeps the Bergsonian flame alight, performing in its very being the temporality that has been excised from all Western conceptions of humanism and history. Time, wrested from historicism in postcolonial theory, is mobilized as a bulwark against assimilation into universal schemas or spatial categories. Ineffable, incommensurable, and heterogeneous, time becomes an ontological essence divorced from the telos-driven epistemologies of the West.[2]

When Saleem Sinai in *Midnight's Children* ponders whether the time discrepancy between India and Greenwich is caused by an unequal distribution of electrical current or by some more fundamental condition of temporal "otherness," his indecision thus trenchantly exposes fault lines within the postcolonial discourse on time. To attack the uneven distribution of and access to electricity in the subcontinent is a substantially different battle than to affirm a cultural-linguistic countertemporality outside the power grids of modernity. Does the postcolonial demand access to material resources, or deny the validity of those resources on ontological principle? In this chapter I examine the representation of time and standardized technologies in three early English-language Indian texts, S.K. Ghosh's *The Prince of Destiny* (1909), K.S. Venkataramani's *Murugan, the Tiller* (1927), and Kushwant Singh's *Train to Pakistan* (1956), all of which are situated at the crux of Saleem's dilemma, unsure whether to embrace a uniform technological modernity or to entrench themselves in linguistic and philosophical notions of the temporally untranslatable. The viability of a uniquely postcolonial politics of time rests on the resolution of this dilemma. The accelerated implementation of temporally standardized technology (railway and telegraphy) in the colonies, coupled with cultural disjunctions in temporal management between colonizer and colonized, potentially renders the colonial situation a unique locus for the formation of an oppositional temporal politics.

The novels under consideration were published within fifty years of the 1906 legal adoption of Greenwich Standard Time in the subcontinent, and all of them place the time of the British railways in direct contrast with an "Indian" temporality. My argument is that early English-language Indian writers no more disavowed the material dimensions of temporality than did their English modernist contemporaries. Whereas modernist time has often been construed as isolationist, antinational, and antimaterial, postcolonial time is often articulated in terms of brash contrariety: contra modernity, contra history, contra nationality. This construal of postcolonial time as a mystically ineffable zone of anarchical rhythm forecloses a host of important questions about the mechanics of temporal imperialism, specifically the legislative attempt to align all global timekeeping to that of British science, industry, and commerce, an alignment in the face of which anarchic, "performative" time seems inadequate and ineffectual. The early fiction of Ghosh and Venkataramani was uniquely situated to explore clearsightedly the impact of standard time on the subcontinent. The connection between time and empire, which must be teased out of British twentieth-century fiction (as I have done in previous chapters) is in fact thematically central in the Indian texts I consider here, where the train and its synchronized timetables are clearly represented as tools of disenfranchisement rather than symbols of a unified vision of national development. My goal in this chapter, then, is not to claim that early Indian writers staunchly opposed the imposition of Greenwich time, or even that they were directly aware of the battles begun in the 1890s by standard time advocates like R.D. Oldham in the Asiatic Society of Bengal and elsewhere to align the subcontinent with Greenwich precision.[3] Such a claim might be possible but would necessitate its own book-length study, involving an exhaustive analysis of literature, media coverage, and political movements in early twentieth-century India. The present chapter is intended merely as prolegomena to that larger project, laying the critical and theoretical groundwork for the contours of a more specifically postcolonial study of standard time and literature. In part my contribution is to suggest the relevance of a body of texts often ignored in contemporary scholarship. While works by Raja Rao and Kushwant Singh are justly part of the canon of Indian literature in English, pre-1930s writers like Sarath Kumar Ghosh, Kaneripatna Sidhanatha Venkataramani, Siddha Mohana Mitra, Cornelia Sorabji, and others are often little read and analyzed outside of a small subset of scholars. Yet their work, situated during a period of increasing regimentation of temporality through the tentacular growth of British-controlled railways, offers unique insight into a confrontation between competing regimes of temporal control before railway time became fully naturalized and domesticated in the subcontinent. Ghosh and Venkataramani, writing in the first three decades of the twentieth century, could imagine and articulate alternatives to railway time based on social and economic reorganization strategies; by the time of Partition, however, railway time had become so deeply ingrained within the patterns of village life as to be inseparable from other networks of social economy, as Kushwant Singh's 1956 novel so vividly suggests. A tension between British railway time's coercive organization of experience and alternative systems of temporal organization is uniquely characteristic of this body of fiction.

Meenakshi Mukherjee, however, has argued that early Indian English-language fiction was in fact ill equipped to wrestle cogently with the material dimensions of modern temporality. In her important study of Indian fiction in English, *The Twice-Born Fiction,* Mukherjee argues that the first Indian authors writing in English operated with a philosophical orientation toward time and space that prevented them from meaningfully representing contemporary historical tensions. Romanticizing a timeless time and a spaceless space, Indian fiction's metaphysical bent was ill suited to the Western novel form. Whereas Western fiction shows the effects of time and space on man, early Indian fiction (in Mukherjee's terms, anything written before the emergence in the 1930s of the triad of Raja Rao, Mulk Raj Anand, and R. K. Narayan) was preoccupied with "unchanging moral verities and their presentation in a timeless setting" (18). In order for Indian writers to "mature" they would have to acquire a "historical and geographical awareness of the Indian situation" (18). Ghosh's *The Prince of Destiny* romanticized "past history" (Mukherjee writes that its history is "entirely romantic with no basis in actual facts" [20]), whereas Venkataramani's social reform novel *Murugan, the Tiller* romanticized "the history of the present" (22). In both cases, Mukherjee charges, the impulse to romanticize frustrated the ability to produce narrative because it is "impossible to write a good novel today that remains suspended out of time and space" without a "definite location in temporal and spatial reality" (18). Indian writers had to accept the Western orientation, Mukherjee suggests, according to which life is portrayed "by time" rather than "by values" (27). I disagree with Mukherjee's assertions that the novels in question are not good (a judgment serving only the interests of canon formation) and that Ghosh and Venkataramani romanticize and essentialize timelessness without any attentiveness to the historical contradictions of their age. I read their novels quite differently. The timelessness that Mukherjee identifies in them is not romanticized; it is instead placed in acute tension with competing temporal systems, a tension rooted in the texts' anxieties over the socioeconomic transformations accompanying standardized transportation and communication networks.[4] These novelists interrogated England's temporal ascendancy, not by denying material temporality on romantic or spiritual grounds, but by wrestling with the temporal dimensions of nationalism, divinity, social service, and the idea of struggle itself. As Josna E. Rege explains in *Colonial Karma,* the very notion that the Hindu religion was "world-denying" in its timelessness and passivity was itself an Orientalist construct, "conveniently" allowing the English colonizer to assert Western culture as contrastingly active, forward-looking, and dynamic (2–3). In fact Rege reads early Indian fiction as a vehicle for "social reform and political action" (4). If its narrative and philosophical roots can be located in the *Bhagavad-Gita,* this is not evidence of a romantic timelessness, but rather of a dialectical engagement with questions of action and passivity, mental and physical struggle, detachment and engagement.

My exclusive focus on English-language novels is a conscious one. I take seriously Aijaz Ahmad's warnings about the Western use of English-language texts as exclusively representative of India,[5] and these three English-language texts are not meant to represent even a partial range of cultural practices, attitudes, beliefs, or political stances in early twentieth-century India. The political conservatism of Ghosh, for example, is arguably symptomatic of a larger, predictable conservatism in the form itself, since the ability to write in English presupposes a socioeconomic position more likely to produce a reactionary attitude toward Indian resistance. One has to turn, for instance, to a Bengali-language text such as Sarat Chandra Chatterjee's *Pather Dabi* (1926), a novel centering on an underground resistance group, for a political position threatening enough to incite a British ban. The reason I have focused on English-language fiction is that its authors, precisely because they are already linguistically translating Indian life into English expression, are necessarily predisposed toward an examination of the problems of cultural translation. The East-West encounter forms a key component in the texts of authors who all lived and studied for a period in England.[6] Already wrestling with a linguistic standardization of narrative method, their insights into temporal standardization are given a more central role than in the indigenous-language fictions. This can be illustrated by looking at Raja Rao's famous preface to *Kanthapura* (1938), in which he articulates the problems of translating Indian life and speech into the English language: "One has to convey in a language that is not one's own the spirit that is one's own. One has to convey the various shades and omissions of a certain thought-movement that looks maltreated in an alien language. I use the word 'alien,' yet English is not really an alien language to us. It is the language of our intellectual make-up—like Sanskrit and Persian was before—but not of our emotional make-up" (vii). The dialectic between intellect and emotion for Rao has a distinctly temporal dimension that complicates any easy bilingual translation. Rao begins by suggesting an immediacy of puranic lore in the present day. The Indian village's very makeup bears the traces of past heroes ("Rama might have rested under this pipal tree, Sita might have dried her clothes, after her bath, on this yellow stone" [vii]). In addition to the indelible trace of the past in the present, the tempo of Indian life and speech produces tensions in English expression: "We, in India, think quickly, we talk quickly, and when we move, we move quickly. There must be something in the sun of India that makes us rush and tumble and run on. And our paths are paths interminable. . . . We have neither punctuation nor the treacherous 'ats' and 'ons' to bother us—we tell one interminable tale" (viii). For Rao cultural temporal variance becomes a key problematic in the very act of English expression. The struggle to harness "interminable" tales into a syntax of full stops and innumerable prepositions leads directly to a speculation on nonlinguistic differences, such as "emotional makeup" or the unique character of the sun in Indian life and labor. In the body of *Kanthapura* Rao uses the present tense with little punctuation to convey a sense of a time rushing onward without being framed, contained, or analyzed in retrospect. Evading standardization, such set pieces as the riots at the coffee estate are sheer surges of words and actions, in which it is difficult to pinpoint characters in space or time. Rao seems at first to have little difficulty in translating village rhythms into the English narrative form. Gandhian ideology throughout the novel is translated into puranic terms, with the Mahatma an avatar of Krishna—an embodiment in the present of the heroic past. However, Rao's text does not in the end easily translate the past into the present. The village of Kanthapura is *destroyed* in the riots following the strike at the coffee plantation and the ensuing police retributions. The "interminable" history of Kanthapura is in fact terminated at the end of the novel, the village decimated and its homeless inhabitants irretrievably launched into the temporally "modern" struggles against imperialism. The attempt to convey Indian temporality in English expression is here inextricably bound up with the dialectic between village traditions and Western modernization. The only means for the Kanthapurans to protect the village as the site of solidarity and communal struggle is to engage in coordinated civil resistance, an act that ultimately brings about the village's destruction and a loss of communalism. That Moorthy, the Gandhian acolyte, is moving at the end of the novel toward a European-style communism (via Nehru) and away from *satyagraha* and a uniquely Indian communalism signals the dissolution of his conviction that the ideals of Indian village life can be sustained in the inevitable conflict with imperialism. Rao's benchmark summation of the problems of linguistic translation thus also captures the interrelated perils of larger sociocultural translations: from communalism to industrial capitalism, from imperial dependence to political sovereignty.

In the work of Sarath Kumar Ghosh a clear and often polemical distinction is made between British standard time and a national, spiritual, or communal time understood as Indian. Ghosh sees the problems of British rule in India as directly stemming from British ignorance of the existence of deeply entrenched cultural differences, which are too often written off by the British as intractable nuisances hindering extensive technological modernization or uniform penal regulation. Published in 1909, Ghosh's *The Prince of Destiny* is self-consciously a product of the nationalist and anticolonial agitations in Bengal attendant upon the partition of that province by Lord Curzon from 1905 to 1911. The *swadeshi* agitations, provoked by this spectacle of a transparent divide-and-rule tactic on the part of the British, were crucial in the radicalization of many moderates within the Indian National Congress. As Bart Moore-Gilbert asserts, Ghosh's novel is also clearly situated within the context of Japan's defeat of Russia in 1905, a nationalist victory that suggested the possibility of a distinctly Asiatic coalition that might prove effective at repulsing British rule in the subcontinent. Crucial for the success of such an Asiatic unity was "access to the kind of technical education which had underpinned the successful emergence of Japan's military-industrial complex" (128). By the turn of the twentieth century India's railway was the fifth largest in the world, and railway production in other British colonies, particularly on the East African coast, contributed to a burgeoning Indian diaspora through the employment of indentured Indian workers in the construction of those railway lines.[7] The railways, despite clearly being structured to advantage British exports and to disadvantage internal travel, nevertheless remained a powerful symbol of industrial modernity that, with the proper training and discipline, might be appropriated by the Bengali anticolonial movement in the service of the kind of Asiatic nationalism that Japan had ostensibly pioneered. Such an appropriation drives the central political conflict of *The Prince of Destiny,* yet Ghosh ultimately challenges the viability of a Japanese-style industrial nationalism by juxtaposing it against a less militant version of cosmopolitanism which he represents as uniquely Indian. In the preface to the novel Ghosh directly addresses English readers, alerting them to their role in inciting the "unrest" on the subcontinent and "educating" them as to the uniqueness and viability of Indian "character" and "culture." His construction of the East inevitably carries with it an accompanying stance toward British imperialism. Forging philosophical connections between East and West that are based on such diverse sources as Hindu mythology, algebraic proofs, and Darwinian evolution, Ghosh demonstrates two potential approaches to the temporal unification of the East: one militantly anti-imperialist and the other philosophically ameliorative. Whether the East will follow the militant rather than the pacifist route is, Ghosh asserts, entirely up to the way the British continue to handle the exercise of their power in India.

The plot of *The Prince of Destiny* centers on Barath, future rajah of the fictional principality of Barathpur and incarnation of Lord Krishna. Anticipating the trope of the "simultaneous birth" that Rushdie will exploit so powerfully in *Midnight's Children,* Barath is born on the very day in 1877 that Queen Victoria is crowned imperial empress of India. The crowning of Victoria as empress was, Ghosh writes, "A magnificent scheme by which the last memories of the Mutiny would be buried for ever, and India would be bound to Great Britain not only by the ties of loyalty, but by the greater bonds of affection and patriotism; for India would be made to feel that she had a stake in the

British Empire and was to share alike in its perils and its triumphs" (138). The compact of the empress with her subjects, which Ghosh treats with utter reverence, is broken by the successive viceroys of India. The enthusiasm engendered by the scheme is converted in a short space of time to "sedition" by "the most culpable negligence" on the part of the English. Not only is the vision of Victoria "forgotten," but "the unhappy opinion began to spread in India that the very terms of Queen Victoria's first proclamation after the Mutiny had not been kept by her ministers, were never intended to be kept. A political agitation was begun, primarily in Bengal, afterwards elsewhere, for the restoration of those terms" (139). The British, assuming that independent principalities like Barathpur will most likely be the breeding grounds for sedition, pressure those regions in two ways: first by providing for the English education of future rajahs in order to indoctrinate them into English culture, and second by the creation of the official advisory position of a British resident in each principality. In the early twentieth-century the resident, previously a silent figure, became a more active presence not only as ambassador for England, but also as consul for the "mining, railway, and other industrial concessions . . . obtained on behalf of British capitalists" (145). For the high priest Vashishta, Barath's key advisor, the expansion of the duties of the resident is "the thin end of the wedge" toward a complete disavowal of Barathpur's sovereignty.

Meenakshi Mukherjee's judgment that the novel's romantic "history" is not based in any "actual facts" certainly seems unfair in light of the text's sober appraisal of the interrelation between foreign private investment, semi-autonomous princely states, and railway concessions. As Tara Sethia explains, the expanding railway network in the subcontinent demanded that the British assert increasing political control over the princely states whose territories the railway would traverse, compelling those states to "cede rights and jurisdictions" in addition to providing "free land, materials, and facilities to the railway lines" (106). The new Gladstone government in the early 1880s had attempted to resolve the Indian budgetary debt by openly encouraging the mobilization of British speculative capital on Indian public works (112–13). The management of these investments required intensive collaboration from indigenous officials well placed within the hierarchies of the princely states and capable of negotiating favorable railway concessions. As a case study Sethia describes the operations of Abdul Huk in the princely state of Hyderabad. Huk had been groomed by the British authorities, from his status as an army trooper to his receipt of the badge of Companion of the Indian Empire, to serve the demands of British capitalists. Deputed to England in 1883 he concluded railway negotiations "against the interests of his own government" to the tune of 4.5 million pounds capital (115). In Hyderabad, Sethia writes, "collaboration with local elites played a significant role in the working of imperialism" (116). Ghosh's appreciation of the British resident's interest in the personal destiny and political philosophy of the prince of the state of Barathpur demonstrates the author's acute engagement with the material and political dimensions of late nineteenth- and early twentieth-century imperialism in India.

Prince Barath is clearly being groomed in England to become a collaborator with the resident's plans for conceding the state's resources to British capitalists. His birth and subsequent education at Oxford take place in an atmosphere of increasing political crisis. Born precisely at the crux of what Ghosh views as the last chance for a semi-independent Indian federation with Britain, Barath's destiny is understood to be parallel to that of the subcontinent. *What* he is supposed to learn at Oxford and *why* are, in this context, subjects of contention. While his British "adoptive parents" hope simply to convince him of Britain's noble culture and history so that he will be an effective agent for empire in Barathpur, the high priest of the princely state, Vashishta, covertly enlists him in a larger project to bring back to Barathpur the knowledge of empire in preparation for revolution. Given capital's incursion into Barathpur and the inevitable industrialization attending that incursion, Vashishta recognizes the value of educating Barathpur's youth in the construction and control of industrial processes: "The young men of Barathpur were to receive a technical training, how to make and use the instruments that had built up the material greatness of Europe. One youth in particular was to speculate in the use of iron, the substance upon which a nation depends for its greatness—in peace or war. He was to learn how to make pins and needles, scythes and ploughshares—or the great big things of iron used for purposes other than those of peace" (147). Barath's Oxford education, intended for purposes of political amelioration by those who have paid for it, has an entirely different meaning for the band of Barathpur youths who plan revolution under Vashishta's guidance. Barath's destiny is complicated by the fact that he is not only a prince, but also the recognized avatar of Lord Krishna, a spiritual heritage that seems to manifest itself primarily through Barath's possession of otherworldly powers of mathematical abstraction. He is a mathematics savant, who astonishes his English tutors and is encouraged to study under Henri Poincaré in Paris, who normally "takes no pupils" (275). In several passages Barath algorithmically "proves" the existence of Hindu reincarnation and Darwinian evolution alike, intellectual examples of the kind of cross-cultural assimilation that Barath will eventually advocate at the political level.

The cultural disconnect between Barath's life in India and his time at Oxford is rendered in temporal terms. Time moves more quickly in England, and the six years during which tremendous changes alter the landscape of Barathpur are to him "but six days" (372). His unconsciousness of the passage of time and its effects on his homeland are in part a function of his otherworldliness, the evolutionary vestiges of his holy spirit. When he meets the English poet Francis Thompson the two are immediately recognized as soul mates. For Thompson, as for Barath, the earthly passage of time is irrelevant and unmarked. Thompson, Barath's adoptive father explains, "has to be so preoccupied mentally as to be unaware of the flight of time; hours and days mean nothing to him. Why should they to him whose vision is limited to eternity itself?" (188). Thompson conducts Barath's tour of the London slums, where Barath envisions the emergence of a "new Haroun al-Raschid" bringing to "this Bagdad" of London "a knowledge of Eastern methods of instant action, instant justice, instant retribution, instant reward; perchance one who had walked at night with a single escort through the streets of Delhi and Lahore and Benares" (252). In one sense Ghosh is invoking "Eastern methods" of jurisprudence in solving the problems of the world, but in another sense he is temporally collapsing discrete social problems. Barath, like Thompson a mystic with his eye on eternity, sees no distinction between the Baghdad of the Arabian nights and late nineteenth-century London. In his vision all time and space are the same, and the problems of London can be solved with the techniques of Haroun.

The disavowal of any socioeconomic distance between East and West is not simply a means of invoking a transnational solidarity of the oppressed, as it is more importantly a philosophical stance earned at the expense of the kind of material creation of infrastructures and bases for anti-imperial resistance with which Vashishta is occupied back in India. Barath's world outlook centers on "the art of dying," a position that, in the context of *The Prince of Destiny*, makes a mysticism of the concession of colonial power and life to the colonizer. Barath, to put it bluntly, is on the side of failure and death, regardless of that side's political or national affiliations.[8] In a striking scene early in the novel the ship that bears Barath to Europe passes a convoy of Italian troops being sent to fight the colonial uprising at Adowah in Abyssinia. As the terrified youths sail by on their way to certain death Barath is moved to cry, "Evviva l'Italia," a cry that is then taken up by the soldiers. The "thirteen thousand Italian boys" go to their deaths "at the call of this Hindu boy" (134). Moved to support not the side of colonial resistance but the dying individual imperialists, Barath glorifies individual failure over collective victory, however politically desirable that victory may be. Better to cheer the dying dictator than to support the thousands who victoriously take up arms against him. It is a strange position, and it continues to mark Barath's English career. In a masterfully written sequence Ghosh takes us through the week-long Oxford mathematics examinations, during which Barath deliberately decides to concede victory to an English classmate whose "need is greater" (270). The mercilessly timed examination nearly ruins the health of the English boy, who fills one examination book after another. Barath, practicing the "art of dying" in the classroom, retreats to a mystical timeless state in which he is elevated above the struggles of the earth:

> What was earth to him and all its triumphs? A shadow of a shadow. Its richest prize might be thrust into his hand: if he closed his fingers he would find but emptiness. . . . In that hour, as he gazed at the paper, he seemed to have a vision of all the elements of man's existence in a single picture. Thus he saw a complete mosaic of the world's joys and pains, triumphs and failures. . . . He continued to gaze at the paper. The pen dropped from his hand. He heard it fall, but heeded it not. There he sat motionless while the clock crept on with thievish hand stealing the precious time: he heeded it not. (271–72)

Turning his back on the clock and the timed contest with its earthly rewards, Barath turns his back on historical progression and change. His vision of the world is quite literally a snapshot—a static picture of the essential elements of existence—frozen and eternal across all regions and times.

For Barath, caught in the no-man's-land of elite cultural translation, time has no meaning, yet Vashishta and his band of English-educated engineers must keep their eyes resolutely on the clock. During the six years of Barath's absence they have laid the groundwork for a synchronized revolution against the English, achieved by a coordinated attack on the railway and telegraph lines connecting Barathpur to the outside world. Unable to afford Barath's mystic position of timelessness and spacelessness, the Barathpur revolutionaries have taken control of the railway and telegraph lines, a material appropriation of the tools the English have used to measure and control time and space. When the British resident is confronted by Vashishta's angry mob, he argues that British retaliation will be swift. Vashishta counters:

> I have seen to it that the Imperial Government does not hear of it for a week.... Do you know what has happened throughout northern India this morning? I shall tell you. There is a railway strike and a telegraph strike. The telegraph wires have been cut at intervals, and the railway lines destroyed in parts, and the bridge blown up with bombs. The Imperial Government will be too busy restoring its own communications to wonder why it does not get the usual casual news from remote parts. Barathpur is completely isolated, and its own internal communications are in our control. Even when the Imperial Government gets the news, it will be unable to move till the strikes are over. (591)

This genuinely threatening revolutionary situation is dangerous precisely because of its carefully synchronized control of time and space. The revolutionaries gain leverage by regulating the speed with which bodies and information can spread. Not disavowing English temporal precision, but manipulating it, Vashishta's revolution is diametrically opposed to Barath's vision of a conciliatory Haroun lifted from the confines of time and space, healing East and West alike. The masses of Barathpur, however, will not revolt without the approval of their new Krishna, and Barath, predictably by this point in the novel, sides with the British resident and sends the armed populace home with a lesson of eternal forgiveness, an intentionally unsatisfying narrative resolution to the cultural and political tensions of the subcontinent as Ghosh has described them.

Ghosh thus sketches two extreme responses to standard time in the colonies. While Vashishta's revolutionaries respect and manipulate standard time for the purpose of resistance, the educated, "spiritual" Barath turns his back on time and space for a static, abstract conception of humanity as it dies a martyr's death. "Verily," his intended Indian bride tells him, "thou art the one true Cosmopolitan. Thou alone hast combined all earth East and West, in thy own person. Thou alone hast lived four thousand years—in the ancient wisdom of the East—and the modern knowledge of the West. Thou alone may stand upon Gaurisankar and embrace all earth in thy vision" (499). If Barath is the representative of cosmopolitanism, then he teaches an instructive lesson about the role of time and space in cosmopolitan vision; the illusion of lofty height, of floating above territories and time zones, inevitably bears with it a reactionary stance toward notions of collective struggle and even human character.⁹ The god's-eye view of the cosmopolitan freezes all earthly activity into a static picture of eternal struggle and eternal dying. For all his professed fusion of East and West, the practical application of Barath's philosophy is that the East should gracefully die while the West lays its grid of railway and telegraph lines for the benefit of Western capital. Barath's advocacy of timelessness, however, is not asserted dogmatically by Ghosh, but is the product of a fraught struggle with the material, temporally standardized demands of the revolutionary nationalists. Timelessness is thematized and historicized in *The Prince of Destiny,* rather than unquestioningly affirmed. Barath may romanticize the heroic past, but by placing him in direct conflict with a coordinated, violent, revolutionary mass, Ghosh demonstrates an acute awareness of the cultural and political tensions accompanying standard time's incursion into the subcontinent.

The success of a Barathpur revolution, Ghosh suggests, would lead to nothing more than a complete disavowal of what makes Eastern life, culture, and thought distinct from England, or the West. To embrace the railway and telecommunications grid is to place oneself on it and to stake one's physical and spiritual well-being to an English definition of spatiotemporal organization. In order for the railway to serve the purposes of a colonial revolution it would need to function as a symbolic locus for solidarity, as the village square does in so much early Indian fiction. Instead the railway in that fiction serves overwhelmingly as an ominous, divisive symbol. The railway imposes a regimented dissection of local times into standardized units, without any regard for variability in labor practices or social organization. The railway clock bypasses other organizations of daily time, just as the train itself often bypasses entire village communities without contributing at all to their mobility or general economic welfare. The negative imagery associated with the train in these novels is by no means reflective of a naïve prejudice in the face of modernity, but rather reflects a clear recognition on the part of writers of deeply ingrained structural imbalances in the very design and maintenance of the Indian railways themselves, the history of which clearly illustrates that the synchronization of colonial railways benefited expropriation rather than internal development.[10] Lord Dalhousie's scheme of grand trunk lines in India allowed for maximal connection between internal centers and ports, with minimal connection between interior centers themselves. D. R. Gadgil describes the "peculiar" characteristic of Dalhousie's lines:

Attention was not directed to connecting contiguous trade points, and to exploring thoroughly the trade of each district through which the railway passed by a systematic construction of feeder lines. Instead, the scheme followed was to construct grand trunk lines traversing the length and breadth of the country and connecting the big cities of the interior with the big ports—Calcutta, Bombay, and Madras. By 1875 most of the big centres were so connected. The construction of these trunk lines was mostly the work of guaranteed companies. The routes from the ports were generally sketched with the intention of traversing the important agricultural tracts of the interior, so as to facilitate the export of agricultural produce. (147)

The export of Indian cotton during the American Civil War was a crucial factor in the subcontinent's commercial viability for the empire, and without Dalhousie's grand trunk lines such massive expropriation from Ahmedabad through Bombay, for example, would have been unthinkable. At issue with the rails, however, and implicit in their very design was the question of who would benefit from their modernizing impact. From its construction until 1925 the Great Indian Peninsula Railway, which spanned the Lower Peninsula from Bombay over the Ghats to Madras and featured the first railway car in India in 1853, was entirely managed by private British companies. Indian public opinion was so patently opposed to private management of the railways that the secretary of state for India in 1920, William Acworth, was pressured to issue recommendations that a transfer be made from private to state ownership. As Aruna Awasthi writes, Acworth based the recommendations in his report on three crucial complaints: "The Committee, highlighting the importance of Indian public opinion in favour of State Management, stated that the Company management did not encourage the development of indigenous industries as they should have, it gave preferential treatment to import and export of goods in the favour of British interests, and the Indians were not employed to higher offices and with very little training facilities available to them" (190). The higher ranks of the railway service in India were marked, as Gopal Krishna Gokhale argued in 1910, by "practical exclusion of Indians" (Awasthi, 193). Meanwhile unfavorable rates for the carriage of raw materials for manufacture crippled the development of indigenous industry, and export rates were markedly low, making port cities like Bombay thrive while interior regions suffered serious decline. Although much was made of the Indian railway's philanthropic role in providing famine relief in Poona, Gujarat, and Hyderabad in the 1860s and 1870s, it is equally true, as a number of historians have pointed out, that the railways with their bulk transportation of food grains to

England created the very famine conditions they purportedly alleviated. Awasthi quotes R. C. Dutt, who argues that the "homes and villages of a cultivating nation" were "denuded of their food to a fatal extent" in order to pay their exorbitant revenue and rents (132).

These were the rails that the apostles of standard time began a concerted effort to temporally unify for greater efficiency in 1899. In part that struggle over temporal standardization represented only the most recent phase in a long history of the suppression of Indian sciences and social practices in the face of assumed Western superiority. Astronomy was valued highly in Islamic as well as Hindu societies in the eighteenth and nineteenth centuries, with astronomer pandits, for instance, producing complex computations of astral phases in published almanacs, which were then widely consulted for political and ritual events in Hindu life. As C. A. Bayly notes in *Empire and Information,* skilled Indian astronomers, "who were contemptuous of the slow mental arithmetic of the Europeans, could compute eclipses and other heavenly events with extraordinary speed using cowrie shells" (249). Like Macauley's famous dismissal of all of Sanskrit for one shelf of European literature, British astronomers represented Indian astronomy as either "tyrannous" or mere "humbugging," while Western astronomy brought, in one Calcutta editorialist's words, "the authority of the very God of Truth" (Bayly, 256). The Indian railways, bypassing networks of social, economic, and political connectivity in the interests of an economically exploitive regime, bore the symbolic weight of cultural superiority and the suppression of alternative systems of knowledge.

Mohandas Gandhi's critique of the railways in *Hind Swaraj,* published in the same year as *The Prince of Destiny,* hinged on his belief in the corrupting influence of speed itself. "Good travels at a snail's pace," Gandhi's "editor" famously argues, but "evil has wings" (48–49). Gandhi's imaginary interlocutor suggests that railways can also serve as a tool for nationalist unification, but Gandhi's "editor" suggests that the unification they forge is rushed, shallow, and divisive. "It was after the advent of the railways that we began to believe in distinctions," he argues (49). A truly meaningful nationalism will be forged only through a painstakingly slow and careful process, which the railways circumvent. "To build a house takes time," Gandhi argues. The influence of Gandhi's ideas, particularly after the Amritsar massacre of 1919, can be traced in the disavowal of speed and the celebration of slowness that markedly characterize the Gandhian social reform novels of the 1920s and 1930s.[11] In K. S. Venkataramani's *Murugan, the Tiller* (1927), one of the most accomplished of the novels of this period, the railway is inextricably associated with Western values and British education. The novel concerns two childhood friends, Ramachandran (Ramu) and Kedari, who have incurred enormous debts at the Law College at Madras, which have crippled their village estates. While Kedari's fortunes as a lawyer rise, Ramu's inability to pass his B.A. examination leads him into humiliation and degradation. As the novel progresses, though, Kedari's debts and expenses escalate out of control, until his involvement in a local election scandal brings about his disbarment and financial ruin. Ramu, on the other hand, inspired by the tireless manual labor of his servant Murugan, engages in agricultural engineering projects modeled after Gandhian ideals of communalism and economic independence. Winning over the British officials for whom he clerks tirelessly, Ramu is placed by the British in a position to create an ideal, self-sufficient agricultural community, to which Kedari, broken by his ambition, debt, and enslavement to Western ideals, comes for sanctuary.

Venkataramani's idealized colonial administration is ready and willing to see Indian communities economically self-sufficient and politically self-governing. The author envisions an unlikely frictionless Gandhian revolution whereby the good-natured English simply step aside and even provide monetary support for the evolution of economically independent communes. What is of interest to the present study is Venkataramani's use of the railway lines as symbols of Western linearity, division, and distance incompatible with the Eastern ideals of tradition and the recurrence of the seasons. Kedari's rooms at the Law College look out on the railway lines; in an early scene with Ramu, Kedari delivers a speech, "not facing his audience but gazing out upon the wide meadow in the front and irregularly fixing his eyes upon the smooth and shining rails that ran in parallel lines to the infinity of Rameshwar. Kedari's mind roamed along these lines of destiny like a light engine uncurbed by tender or load" (25–26). The effect of the railroad on Kedari is to turn him away from human contact. Ramu notices Kedari's distraction and thinks bitterly that the "flush of success" has swept away "years of [Ramu's] intimacy and sacrifice" (25). Kedari, ever comparing himself to the train, notices his own rudeness and apologizes by saying, "Words are sometimes rogues, derail us and send us on the wrong track to collide blindly with friends and foes" (27). His identification with Western technology is so great that his very speech and thought are envisioned in railway metaphors, his words "derailed" and his mind "a light engine." The distance of the train from the communities it bypasses is figured here in the description of Kedari's mind as "uncurbed by tender or load." Later Kedari anticipates a complete break with Ramu and justifies it in terms of "geometrical exactitude." Invoking rail metaphors again, Kedari thinks, "When the terminus was different how long could two moving objects try to run on parallel lines?" (45). The parallel lines of the smooth and shining rails have here become a geometrical problem. Ramu, however, ultimately operates in terms of non-Euclidean geometry. His and Kedari's parallel paths do in fact intersect at the end of the novel, as they sit in a wide meadow in Ramu's agricultural community, untouched by the divisive geometry of railway lines.

In their final conversation Kedari, though financially ruined, still argues for unencumbered mobility as an inalienable human right, while Ramu urges him to understand "the price of locomotion":

> "Man wants to be more, a good deal more. He wants to think and act and move about. The glory of motion has swept him from all primitive conditions of ease and peace into a higher world of joy. What is wrong then?"
>
> "But look at the price he has paid for it! The price of locomotion is the loss of the gift to nourish yourself even as you should with a morsel of innocent food from earth, air, and water, which is the glory of all plant life. One gift of Nature takes away another." (262–63)

Ramu understands that Western technological imperialism is a zero-sum game, that it is impossible to benefit one community without impoverishing another. Motion, speed, and "progress" exact heavy tolls. Instead Ramu advocates a cyclical understanding of time, in which the regularity of the seasons is observed and human material wants never exceed a government-sanctioned three acres of land. Government's only role, he argues, is to "enforce the common good against greedy individuals" (287). Given a system that curbs disparities in wealth, Ramu argues that the only "real forces" in life will be "the tradition, the atmosphere, and the season" (285). As does Ghosh, Venkataramani understands the East as offering a model of temporality distinct from British standard time. Urging communal agriculture with no vestiges of Western innovation, from trains to books, Venkataramani envisions an Eastern time measured purely by atmospheric conditions and the character of communal labor. The synchronized train's division of communities, entrenchment of privilege, and imposition of Euclidean logic onto the "wide meadows" of agricultural life have no place in Venkataramani's construction of "Indian time." The faith that rail and communications technology will provide a locus for solidarity in India comes up against deeply entrenched cultural differences based not only on philosophical or religious grounds, but also on the structure of social life and labor practices. The train, rather than signifying unification and progress, is a symbol of division and segregation.

Yet Venkataramani's creed of rural reconstruction divorced from the exploitive regimes of British industry and transportation was not wholeheartedly embraced by all Indian nationalists. In Mulk Raj Anand's *Untouchable* (1935), Iqbal Nath Sarshar ("the Poet") articulates in an impassioned speech an alternative vision of national reconstruction which begrudgingly embraces "the machine" while promising to beat the "enslavers" at "their own game" (152). Possessed of a "race-consciousness" allowing them to "steer clear of the pitfalls" of Western greed and idiocy, independent Indian nationals, the Poet declares, will be able to accept the machine's restructuring of their modes of awareness and knowledge without losing their ontological core. This core of race-consciousness, anticipating Leopold Sedar Senghor's manifestos of Negritude, is expressed by the Poet in temporal terms, as rhythmic and eternal. While learning to "feel new feelings" and "be aware with a new awareness," Indian nationals will avoid pure mimicry of industrialized, imperial England because of their alternative possession of a uniquely Indian time-consciousness: "We know life. We know its secret flow. We have danced to its rhythms. We have loved it, not sentimentally through personal feelings, but pervasively, stretching ourselves from our hearts outwards so far, oh, so far, that life seemed to have no limits" (153). The Poet's language of flow, rhythm, and limitless existence suggests that the salvation of Third World industrialization lies in its adoption of patterns of time distinct from the regimented, bordered, and arhythmical time of the colonizer. The contest for Anand's Poet is not between the linear machine and the cyclical pattern of the seasons, as it was for Venkataramani's Ramu, but rather between culturally distinct internal metrical rhythms. The Poet (arguably speaking for Anand) suggests that machines can be harnessed to alternative rhythms and mobilized in national projects for which they were not originally intended. If Kipling in *Kim* represented the train's power to benevolently accommodate and unify a range of culturally distinct temporal rhythms within its capacious compartments, Anand's oppositional politics finds fault with the "enslaver's" use of technology, but not with the machine itself, infinitely malleable as it is to culturally and nationally nonsynchronous demands.

Anand's faith in a culturally distinct appropriation of Western industrialism is less evident in Kushwant Singh's postindependence Partition novel, *Train to Pakistan* (1956). Singh depicts the nightmarish collapse of national unity in 1947 as in part a breakdown in the ability of Indian time consciousness to retain a distinct ontological core uncorrupted by the rhythms and demands of railway modernity, here depicted as conduits of mass violence rather than as vehicles of unity and limitless growth. Singh's novel dramatizes the violent disruption of a fictional Kashmiri village, Mano Majra, in the summer of 1947. When a trainload of the bodies of massacred Hindus and Sikhs pulls into the Mano Majra station the train becomes no longer an empty marker of communal time, but an efficient means for mass slaughter. The passage or blockage of another train through the Mano Majra station ultimately becomes the climactic contest of the plot, as young Sikhs plan to stop the train bearing Mano Majra's Muslim population, while the protagonist, Juggut, makes his heroic stand by single-handedly stopping the blockade. As we learn at the opening of the novel, Mano Majra has not been untouched by modernization. Rather its rhythms and tempos have been crucially restructured by the integration of synchronized rail technology. Only a limited number of passengers use the Mano Majra station; its primary function is as a thoroughfare for industrial transport. "Not many trains stop at Mano Majra," Singh writes. "Of the many slow passenger trains, only two, one from Delhi to Lahore in the mornings and the other from Lahore to Delhi in the evenings are scheduled to stop for a few minutes. The others stop only when they are held up. The only regular customers are the goods trains. Although Mano Majra seldom has any goods to send or receive, its station sidings are usually occupied by long rows of wagons. Each passing goods train spends hours shedding wagons and collecting others" (12). Significantly Mano Majra itself, with no goods to send or receive, derives no economic benefit from the trains bearing raw goods for export. Other than the "small colony" of shopkeepers who "grow up" around the station to cater to its few passengers, there is little evidence that the station in its midst has brought about any substantial increase in the village's economic resources or general quality of life. Nevertheless the station has changed them. Mano Majra, Singh writes, is "very conscious of trains." The temporal rhythm of the day's activities is marked or stimulated by the periodic passing of trains:

> Before daybreak, the mail train rushes through on its way to Lahore, and as it approaches the bridge, the driver invariably blows two long blasts of the whistle. In an instant, all Mano Majra comes awake. Crows begin to caw in the keekar trees. Bats fly back in long silent relays and begin to quarrel for

their perches in the peepul. The mullah of the mosque knows that it is time for the morning prayer. . . . By the time the 10.30 morning passenger train from Delhi comes in, life in Mano Majra has settled down to its dull daily routine. . . . As the midday express goes by, Mano Majra stops to rest. . . . When the evening passenger from Lahore comes in, everyone gets to work again. . . . When the goods train steams in, they say to each other, "There is the goods train." It is like saying goodnight. . . . The goods train takes a long time at the station, with the engine running up and down the sidings exchanging wagons. By the time it leaves, the children are asleep. The older people wait for its rumble over the bridge to lull them to slumber. Then life in Mano Majra is stilled, save for the dogs barking at the trains that pass in the night. (12–14)

All activities, from religious rituals to communal labor, are stimulated by or integrated into the predictable passage of trains. The linguistic corruption that transforms "Goodnight" into "There is the goods train" importantly signals a shift from neighborly sentiment to a statement of fact, an observation directed not to one's repose but to the machine lumbering by. While the integration of standardized rail time into communal life appears to have had no adverse effects on the villagers in this opening passage, its effect on the animal population is perhaps an indication of the impending railway carnage to come. The bats "quarrel" after the train whistle blows, and the dogs are agitated throughout the night.

In a village of only "three brick buildings" knowledge of the outside world is scarce and irregular. The subinspector claims, "No one in Mano Majra even knows that the British have left and the country is divided into Pakistan and Hindustan. Some of them know about Gandhi but I doubt if anyone has ever heard of Jinnah" (22). The trains, despite their regular transport of goods across Mano Majra's borders, have not served the purposes of modernization and unification. The villagers are hyperconscious of the train, yet the recognition is not reciprocated by the train owners and operators, for whom the villagers remain irrelevant. News of Partition and its accompanying violence is signaled to the villagers not by word of mouth or newspaper, but by disruption in the time service of the railway:

> Early in September the time schedule in Mano Majra started going wrong. Trains became less punctual than ever before and many more started to run through at night. Some days it seemed as though the alarm clock had been set for the wrong hour. On others, it was as if no one had remembered to wind it. Imam Baksh waited for Meet Singh to make the first start. Meet Singh waited for the mullah's call to prayer before getting up. People stayed

in bed late without realizing that times had changed and the mail train might not run through at all. Children did not know when to be hungry, and clamored for food all the time. In the evenings, everyone was indoors before sunset and in bed before the express came by—if it did come by. Goods trains had stopped running altogether, so there was no lullaby to lull them to sleep. (77)

The first signal of the violence of Partition is the disruption of temporal routine. Significantly, though, the routine that Partition disrupts is the one imposed by the British trains, which have encouraged such dependence on their regularity that preexisting social codes for activity and behavior have been supplanted. Children's hunger is no longer dependent on biological need, but on train schedules. The train's dominance in Mano Majra is symptomatic of the power of the British Raj in the subcontinent as a whole, which created indelible linkages of power and dependency not easily erased.

Claims of national identity and distinct ontological essence have little purchase on Singh's villagers, who recognize that their economic disadvantages will persist regardless of any change in leadership. Thus Meet Singh argues to the communist agent, Iqbal, "Freedom must be a good thing. But what do we get out of it? Educated people like you, Babu Sahib, will get the jobs the English had. . . . We were slaves of the English, now we will be slaves of the Educated Indians—or the Pakistanis" (62). Here class realities outweigh ideological claims that the key contest between Britain and India is staged at the level of identity. The division that concerns Meet Singh is not between two forms and philosophies of temporal existence, but between the economically advantaged and disadvantaged. The problem is not that Indian life is culturally untranslatable into terms of English temporal precision, as Rao, Ghosh, or Venkataramani had suggested. As the opening paragraphs of *Train to Pakistan* illustrate, the two can be agreeably synthesized, but only if the power relations between them remain starkly uneven. Increased technological modernization in the form of trains or electric power stations does nothing to challenge entrenched social problems of the inequitable distribution of economic and political power, something Singh's outspoken villagers clear-sightedly perceive. Meet Singh's casual indifference to British rule also suggests, however, just how unsuccessful the British rails have been as an ideological tool for inculcating a uniform sense of colonial or national participation. As in the British modernist texts I considered earlier, synchronized timetables here serve only a shallow kind of unification during periods of relative economic and political stability. When the timetable becomes unreliable Mano Majra's thinly veiled economic and cultural tensions explode, and its population finds itself open to manipulation by outsiders bent on enlisting the villagers in power struggles they scarcely understand. The final contest, in the last pages of the book, is staged over the actual train itself, with murderous vigilantes planning to halt the train in its tracks and Juggut Singh sacrificing himself in order to permit the train to continue on its way. The British, conspicuously absent, no longer control the machine nor the schedule by which it runs. That task has been appropriated by the villagers themselves, who will ultimately decide whether the train can serve as an instrument of liberation or annihilation.

Here we might return to Saleem Sinai's dilemma in *Midnight's Children* over the nature of time discrepancy in India's clocks. Is it simply the result of an inefficient technocracy, or must it always be discrepant because of the unique character of Indian time it represents and controls? For Ghosh true Indian time turned its back on standard time and its synchronized grid of trains and telegraphs, for the purposes either of exploitation or of resistance. Embodying a pure Eastern time, Prince Barath's refusal to sanction the synchronized anticolonial uprising of his people is a clear statement of the incorruptible essence of Indian ontology and the intransigence of British forms of power and technology. Venkataramani draws not on a spiritualized version of Indian time, but on alternative models of economic independence based on an antitechnological communalism, rejecting the British train not for its corruption of Indian time, but for the dependent relationship with British industry it enforces and in fact renders inevitable. Singh's novel, written after World War II and decolonization, is situated in a world in which the rejection or acceptance of synchronized technology is no longer a pertinent question. The train has come to stay, altering even the most intimate forms of behavior and address. For Singh ontological essentialism is not a form of resistance, but simply the motivation for communal violence. The question is whether the train and its rhythms can be meaningfully appropriated in a postcolonial context to redress the needs of the disenfranchised, or whether the train will continue to be a tool of division, segregation, and death.

This brief survey of the role of time in early twentieth-century Indian fiction suggests the complexity of essentializing a unique Indian temporality that might prove linguistically or narratively incommensurable with standard time's grid or Western narrative's conventions. The narrative strategies of the Indian novel in English were developed in the context of India's temporal alignment with world standard time. Navigating the same terrain as their British modernist contemporaries, writers like Ghosh and Venkataramani enacted alternative forms of social temporality within the interstices of standard time's global grid. In this sense their strategies mirror those described by the Caribbean novelist and critic Wilson Harris, who proposed his own negotiation of the divide between uniform history and incommensurable temporal otherness. Arguing that narratives of colonial victimization are themselves a kind of world standard time, Harris writes that "catalogues of injustices" promoting "irreconcilable differences—irreconcilable frontiers—irreconcilable ghettos" obey "a static clock that crushes all into the time of conquest" (28). Dichotomous schemas, in which the white colonizer represents standard time and the native represents liberated time, obscure common global linkages of oppression and resistance. Harris writes, "When the horrors of slavery were being mounted in the Caribbean, press-gangs roved England in search of able-bodied men for the Navy—the appalling deprivations such men suffered in the age of Nelson, the great Admiral, would make for a catalogue of almost unbelievable horrors. Surely this is a related aspect of a civilisation which saw man as bundles of labouring, fighting time, time-fodder to fertilise the fields of industry or to fence the high seas" (28). Conscripted British sailors and Caribbean slaves were equally rendered "time-fodder" for the needs of industry, all victims of world standard time's system of abstraction. For Harris the more interesting and productive forms of temporal resistance were staged within the times and spaces of that common oppression, as in the case of the limbo dance, born from the constricted spaces of the slave ships of the Middle Passage. Harris calls limbo a "gateway" that, rather than recall the past, produces a "new corpus of sensibility that could translate and accommodate African and other languages within a new architecture of cultures" (10). Limbo, Harris argues, was a new cultural configuration of space and time forged from within, but not assimilated to, the spaces and times of imperial abstraction: "The limbo dance becomes the human gateway which dislocates (and therefore begins to free itself from) a uniform chain of miles across the Atlantic. This dislocation of interior space serves therefore as a corrective to a uniform cloak or documentary stasis of imperialism" (11). Limbo emerges within the spaces of imperial violence, a cultural product neither enclosed in the ghetto of temporal isolationism nor lost in the cosmopolitan ether of temporal transnationalism. My study of early Indian fiction in English has similarly traced the fraught emergence of temporal gateways neither assimilated to standard time's imperial grid nor entrenched in a romanticized past. The struggle to narrate a path through that gateway aligns the project of these early writers in India with the canonical modernists in England, all of them bound up within the same uniform temporal standard of Greenwich Mean Time, and all variously engaged in the modernist project of working out viable temporal alternatives to that imperial standard.

CONCLUSION

A Postmodern Politics of Time?

Negri's "Global Phenomenological Fabric" and Amis's Backward Arrow

What is the value of resuscitating a temporal politics of modernism, as this book has attempted to do? If, as I have suggested, modernism represented a crucial stage in the history of the suppression of temporal politics because it alternately engaged in that suppression and resisted it, what can we learn from modernism about the political constitution of time in the age of GPS and instantaneity? My argument has been that we can draw from modernist temporality a model for a politicized time that is neither subsumed under global standard time's uniformity nor retracted into a psychical, fluid interiority. Somewhere between conformity and isolationism is the modernist temporal subjectivity. Modernism raised a problem in temporal politics that was evaded or suppressed rather than resolved in the postmodern or antimodern aesthetics after World War II.[1]

To assert that the modernist engagement with time remains vital in the contemporary period and is not merely the expression of a historical oddity or a fleeting fashion necessitates an engagement with key historical representations of the modern-postmodern divide. David Harvey's convincing presentation in *The Condition of Postmodernity* of the transition from Fordism to flexible accumulation as the dominant mode of capitalist production suggests that the temporal struggles of Joyce and Conrad belong definitively to an earlier era rather than to our age of economic globalization. Harvey, like Lefebvre, insists that spatial and temporal practices and conceptions are never neutral; rather that they are infused with and express "some kind of class or other social content, and are more often than not the focus of intense social struggle" (239). Any meaningful analysis of time and space, Harvey recognizes, must always begin with the materialist assumption that it is human practices that shape and construct our conceptions of space and time and resist capital's insistence that such conceptions are merely unsavory deviations from the "single, objective yardstick of time's ineluctable arrow of motion" (203). According to Harvey, a key tension throughout the history of Western thought has been between social theory's privileging of time or temporal processes and aesthetic theory's necessarily spatializing tendencies to freeze discrete moments, rescuing them from "time's tyranny" (206). Modernism's particular negotiation of this tension is reflected in the rise of geopolitics in the early twentieth century, Harvey avers. Geopolitical emphases and struggles suggest a shift away from historical change toward "national cultures and destinies" that aestheticize (and thus spatialize) a politics of place and a myth of origin. If the modern period was an age of geopolitical struggle, the postmodern condition is one of transnational placelessness, in which the past, the future, and indeed any sense of temporal continuity gives way to an overwhelming present tense of existential homelessness, a condition Harvey identifies in key postmodern films by Ridley Scott and Wim Wenders and diagnoses as the product of capitalist transformations since the 1970s.

Yet Harvey does not intend to collapse all of modernist cultural production within the overarching rubric of geopolitical, nationalist aestheticism. Modernism was engaged, he suggests, in a "perpetual dialogue with localism and nationalism" (276), a dialogue that appears to have been short-circuited in postmodern aesthetics, with its unmediated representation of a plurality of individuals, universes, and choices that mirror the capitalist mirage of unlimited consumer pleasures while evading the thorny problem of class relations. Harvey's narrative of increasing time-space compression since the Enlightenment, along with his schematic understanding of larger Western tendencies to dichotomize space and time, militate against any kind of stark periodization between modernity and postmodernity, at least when it comes to the politics of time. Temporal globalization, while it became more seamless from 1884 to 2011, never experienced as radical an ideological shift as capitalism did in the 1970s. There is a fundamental distance between the Keynesian model of the immediate postwar years and the free market neoliberalism of the present day, but no such ideological distance separates the standard time of 1884 and the instantaneity of 2011. To be sure the economic model of flexible accumulation has helped to achieve standard time's goal of temporal simultaneity and spatiotemporal seamlessness more effectively than could state-organized capitalist systems, but the dream of erasing time as a limit, a border, or a value has remained constant across those larger shifts in capitalist organization. The global penetration of capital has made the standard time advocates' dream a reality. As I argued in chapter 1, that penetration was in fact the motive force behind standard time from its inception. To argue for the continuing relevance of modernist expressions of time is thus not to disavow historicism tout court, but simply to recognize the seamless ideological link between modernist time and our own. It is to recover an earlier awareness of the radical novelty and provocative disjointedness of standard time before it became a largely invisible ideology.

In contemporary discourse, struggles over the conception, management, and ownership of time and rhythm have come to seem decidedly passé, products of a period before time's promise of radical disjointedness collapsed into the spatial logics of global capitalism. In most strains of postmodern theory time no longer seems to function as a discrete concept or experiential entity, having instead been compressed, distantiated, or shattered by an implacable spatiality. This conceptual shift away from the chronometric has motivated imaginative attempts to articulate conceptual paradigms or experiential practices within the capacious category of space, in the form of heterotopias or smooth spaces. Yet the old problem of time control and precise management of global rhythm is no less persistent in an age of global positioning and simultaneity. In fact the management, manipulation, and if necessary, elimination of territorial units of space today depends heavily on the kinds of nineteenth-century practices of temporal management made globally legitimate by the Prime Meridian Conference. This is especially clear in the history of the Global Positioning System, a powerful tool that not only defines and delimits the kinds of spaces we inhabit today, but also arguably defuses particularly suspect notions of the possibility of experiential freedom within theoretically constructed rhizomes or nomad spaces.

The ubiquity of GPS receivers in handheld devices and car dashboards has familiarized the notion of a global common coordinate frame in ways that would have been unimaginable less than a decade ago. Global positioning, dependent on the precision of carefully synchronized atomic clocks, is the direct ideological and technological descendent of the Prime Meridian Conference. It was designed in the 1970s by a joint naval and air force team in New Mexico for the express purpose of precision bombing. The first director of the joint program office, Colonel B. W. Parkinson, recalls the team's inspirational motto: "Drop 5 bombs in the same hole . . . and don't you forget it!" (Parkinson and Spiker, 9). GPS employs twenty-four satellites, each equipped with atomic clocks, configured in three orbiting rings around the earth, with eight satellites per ring. The space segment is now controlled by five centers,[2] each equipped with satellite signaling equipment and atomic clocks synchronized to Universal Coordinated Time (UTC), a measurement that retains the use of Greenwich as global time-zero without being dictated, as it was in the late nineteenth century and early twentieth, by the Royal Observatory in Greenwich. Instead UTC is coordinated against a number of participating national observatories, including the U.S. Naval Observatory and the Paris Observatory. To achieve effective precision bombing, the atomic clocks onboard the GPS satellites must be coordinated to within a fraction of a second. James Gleick, reporting on the leap second for the *New York Times* in 1995, observed the importance of precise temporal coordination for military operations: "It is no accident that the Directorate of Time belongs to the Department of Defense. Knowing the exact time is an essential aspect of delivering airborne explosives to exact locations—individual buildings or parts of buildings."[3] Although the leap second seems absurd to civilians, Gleick notes that for GPS "an error of a billionth of a second means an error of a foot—the distance light travels in that time." GPS demonstrates the inherently militaristic capacity of a hypersynchronization of time and space: to determine exact space with precise time is to have already eliminated threatening or uneasily assimilated spaces.

GPS poses a challenge to dominant trends in the intellectual discourse on global space. Poststructuralist theoretical celebrations of a global shift toward denationalized, deterritorialized spaces become less compelling when the role of GPS in manipulating global space and time is taken seriously.[4] That national borders are being eroded and threatened in the age of transnational capital is quite clear, but the *use* of space, even as a conceptual tool, has not been equally distributed. The world is becoming unified, but only the dominant power has the right map to read and manipulate that unified space.[5] This was quite clear in the first Gulf War of 1990–91, referred to by Colonel Parkinson (with characteristic sensitivity) as a "boutique war to demonstrate the effectiveness of

GPS." Tactical commanders in that war were, Parkinson writes, "finally able to experience the power that comes from precise knowledge of position in a common coordinate frame" (Parkinson and Spiker, 24). In their book *The Precision Revolution* Michael Russell Rip and James M. Hasik describe the integral role of GPS in the so-called Revolution in Military Affairs of the past two decades. The "glue" of that revolution, they argue, is GPS's "capability of accurately geo-referencing physical, social and cultural features of the earth's surface" (xiii). U.S. forces in the desert performed complex and efficient hook maneuvers around Iraqi soldiers that would have been absolutely unthinkable without the use of GPS receivers.

The greatest threat to the common coordinate system of GPS is the proposal of the European Union's Galileo system, a civilian-run version of GPS that would wrest from the U.S. military the exclusive power to locate people and objects in space. Galileo has been a recent subject of contention for the United States, whose hegemony over global positioning will not be yielded easily.[6] The U.S. military had previously granted the use of GPS to the civilian sphere only after the crash of Korean Air Lines Flight 007 in 1983, an international relations disaster that prompted the Reagan administration to give civilian aircraft the GPS access previously reserved exclusively for military aircraft and weaponry (Rip and Hasik, 9–10). Even then the military retained exclusive control over the more accurate positioning signal, with a civilian signal emitted at a degree of accuracy several magnitudes lower. Thus even with the best GPS receiver American dollars can buy a civilian's ability to determine location in global space will necessarily pale before the ability of an autonomous cruise missile equipped with a GPS receiver. The civilian can determine his or her position within the space of a city block; the cruise missile can determine it within the width of a street. Until May 2000 GPS had a fail-safe mechanism to be used in cases of national emergencies called "selective availability," which essentially scrambled the civilian signal. The fail-safe ensured that, because the U.S. military gave global positioning to the public, it could readily take it back. Colonel Parkinson declared quite clearly that selective availability and the dual-signal system were implemented to ensure that GPS "not be used against its builders, the U.S. military" (Parkinson and Spiker, 24). Yet the commercial potential of GPS, so demonstrable in the explosion of now ubiquitous GPS devices in cars, cell phones, and even children's toys, clearly outweighed the needs of the military. President Clinton ordered the discontinuation of selective availability on GPS satellites in 2000 in an attempt to "encourage private sector investment in and use of U.S. GPS technologies and services."[7] The advantages of precise positioning as a "global utility" are manifold, but the struggle for equal global access to those advantages will no doubt stratify along familiar class lines.[8]

The Global Positioning System, then, has been particularly successful at using nationally controlled temporal synchronicity to manipulate transnational spaces and populations, projecting itself as a democratizing tool while at the same time enforcing existing geopolitical imbalances. The very existence of national struggles over the management and control of a precisely measured "empty, homogenous time," whether through competing versions of satellite positioning systems or the national rivalries manifest at the 1884 Prime Meridian Conference, suggests that the age of geopolitical nationalism is by no means over. Transnational capitalism will perhaps inevitably always function alongside of and in tension with nationalist constructions of spatiotemporal management. Sandford Fleming's cosmopolitan time will likely never be able to entirely assimilate all rhythms, nations, and peoples to its rationality. National or geopolitical struggles to dictate and measure unique temporal constructions of pasts, presents, and futures suggest that a secular and placeless "empty, homogenous time" is perhaps not as crucially constitutive of nationalism as Benedict Anderson famously asserted in *Imagined Communities*. For Anderson empty, homogeneous time, measured by clock and calendar and reliant on the simultaneous and dependably steady actions of an anonymous collectivity, is what enables and produces the very idea of the nation as a (if not *the*) stable and infinitely reproducible political form. World standard time should be the one thing, given Anderson's thesis, on which every nation can agree, in that it constitutes the very conceptual framework and invisible horizon of nationalism itself, through the imaginative productions of print capitalism (newspapers and novels) and the global distribution of temporal measurement tools (clocks and watches). The readings in this book, suggesting that the dissemination of world standard time provoked temporal disjunctions and arrhythmias, implicitly challenge Anderson's arguably overstated assertion of the power of global capital to homogenize experiential everyday reality through material and conceptual tools. A number of critics have reflected on this aspect of Anderson's thesis, most notably in a special issue of the journal *diacritics* in 1999, dedicated to an analysis of the legacy of Anderson's landmark book in the wake of the publication of its belated sequel, *The*

Spectre of Comparisons. Marc Redfield, Partha Chatterjee, and Harry Harootunian each explore problems with Anderson's interpretation of Benjamin's empty, homogeneous time as monolithic and totalitarian. As Redfield suggests, Benjamin's own conception of empty, homogeneous time involved shock, rupture, and discontinuity alongside and intrinsic to homogeneity. Modernity is about "fracture and rupture," Redfield asserts, an aspect of Benjamin's thought that Anderson "elides" (64). Chatterjee similarly argues that Anderson's imagination of the time of capital as an "aspect of time itself" ignores the extent to which actual spaces and peoples (particularly in postcolonial spaces) necessarily resist the utopian vision of homogeneous capital. "People can only imagine themselves in empty, homogeneous time," Chatterjee writes, but "they do not live in it" (131). While Chatterjee seems to accept that capitalist temporality is as homogeneous and monolithic as Anderson's thesis would have it, Harootunian challenges even that assertion, arguing that capitalist modernity itself has depended on cultural unevenness and social interdependence as conditions of possibility. Elsewhere Harootunian has argued that attempts to find privileged sanctuaries outside of capitalist homogeneity (one necessarily thinks of Chatterjee's work) has simply transformed "older spatialized categories that shrilly announced the unity and universalism of the West over an incomplete East" ("Some Thoughts," 39). Rather than prop up postcolonial heterotopias as bulwarks against an imagined capitalist homogeneity, Harootunian suggests, we might more productively explore everydayness as a temporal rather than spatial category in order to determine how capitalism "reproduces its conditions of social existence." This is the "mystery of time's difference," he argues in particularly Woolfian language, manifest in "the repetitive routine and the unfolding of one day after another" (48).

A recuperation of temporally disjunctive everyday rhythms, however, is far more bound up with early twentieth-century modernist temporal projects than with the aesthetics of postmodernity. To illustrate this I conclude with a study of two postmodern attempts, in cultural theory and in literary aesthetics, to articulate a viable temporal politics. Antonio Negri's *The Constitution of Time,* written in 1981, characteristically reads "beyond Marx" to articulate a "communist subjectivity of time"; Martin Amis's inspired *Time's Arrow* (1991) borrows a conceit from Kurt Vonnegut to read the life of a Nazi doctor in reverse, from death to birth. Both writers attempt to liberate human time from a grim historical determinism by radically questioning the value of individual human time as it contests its appropriation into a larger unified system (represented by both Negri and Amis as fascism). In representing the fundamental opposition as the struggle between individual, bodily experience and nationalistic, authoritarian fascism, Negri and Amis both reveal the extent to which the complex ambiguities of the modernist temporal project have degenerated in the postmodern era into a dichotomy of the body against the state. Negri's "corporeal communism" and Amis's narrator entrapped on a backward-moving body both represent a more radically simplified view of the temporal interrelations between the individual, the state, and the globe than their modernist precursors would have accepted. Although both writers offer countless pleasures to their readers, they fail to register the global imperial tensions in temporality that were always implicit in modernism. If the antagonists in Joyce and Woolf were the narrative project and the imperial project, the antagonists for postmodernism have become the body and the state. Of the multiform tensions in modernist temporality, only the most isolationist version of Bergsonism appears to have survived, in which the individual's fluid time resists any kind of spatial organization or collective representation as inherently corrupting.

Negri's work is characteristic of much Marxist writing of the 1970s, which attempted to rework an orthodox party dogmatism in the context of an era of mass civil disobedience, decolonization, and reactionary state retrenchments, reworking Marx through the lenses of psychoanalysis and poststructuralism. Applying the principles of his *Marx beyond Marx* to the particular problem of relative and absolute surplus-value, Negri's *The Constitution of Time* lays the foundation for the larger project of articulating a communist subjectivity in Deleuzian terms that his wildly successful collaborations with Michael Hardt, *Empire* and *Multitude,* would later make surprisingly marketable. For Negri the problem with orthodox Marxism is that its seamless understanding of the mutually defining interaction between capital and labor leaves no room for a truly antagonistic or subversive zone of resistance to develop. The problem for Negri is that Marx's very understanding of working-class temporality is derived from the rigid temporal standards of measurement produced by capitalist power. Absolute surplus-value transforms people and their labor into inert things that can be abstractly circulated. Marx's relative surplus-value is a category describing the laborer's semi-autonomous reaction to the demands of absolute surplus-value through a limited variability of labor power over time. It is not, as Negri believes it should be, a reaction against *the very idea* of defining human value in terms of an abstract, standardized, temporal quantity. A worker is defined by inherent ontological properties, outside of the coercive demands of capitalist power, Negri believes. His project, then, is to provide a fundamental ontology of a communist subjectivity or community, defining itself outside of the terms of capitalist labor.

It is not difficult to understand Negri's frustration with what he sees as a base tautology in Marx. Marx's faith in a mass industrialization of India, despite the fundamental irreconcilability of industrial models with deep-seated cultural practices, has driven much of the postcolonial criticism of Marxist Eurocentrism. For Marx the machine (train, telegraph, factory) was not inherently disruptive. In fact its modernizing effects were desirable, if only its benefits could be wrested from a controlling minority. As we saw in the novels of Kushwant Singh and K. S. Venkataramani, though, the evils of industrialism in India did not lie solely in their minority control, but in their very method of manipulating nature and uprooting traditional practices, both social and spiritual. Marx's communist worker was necessarily an industrial worker, accepting and even celebrating the practices of streamlined, Taylorist, precision work that accompanied industrial productivity. Given the twentieth century's repeated demonstrations of the dehumanization and ecological devastation of industrialism and the inspiring models of small-scale projects of "green," ecologically friendly, agricultural communes of the 1960s and 1970s, it is not at all surprising that a new wave of Marxism would attempt to define a communist worker in nonindustrial terms. For Negri this meant elaborating a human ontology of time that did not take its modus vivendi from the factory-room clock, or even from labor practice at all. In fact, Negri argues, a "liberated" human temporality struggles "against work." Outside of the capitalist equation of "time-as-measure" a liberated time understands itself as a subjectivity actively constructing itself through "versatile, omnilateral, universal relations" within a collective community (120). Liberated time enacts itself through the body and in terms of "love" (121). Evoking a kind of orgiastic anarchy of the rhizome, Negri sees the spontaneous joining of bodies as the "temporal territory" of communism (103).

Negri's anarchism is acutely clear when he defines any form of nonspontaneous collectivity as inherently fascist. The state, *any state,* is necessarily antagonistic to truly liberated time. If liberated time is versatile, spontaneous, and fluid, any kind of unilateral collective organization must necessarily corrupt human temporality. The democratic ideals of the constitution or of representation are authoritarian because they take a limited segment of temporal movement and stratify it in a hierarchy of command: "Now the *constitution,* any constitution, is a *slice of time,* a segment, it is a block of temporality. This happens all the more in real subsumption. What definitively *undergoes crisis* is the fundamental concept of *representation:* it is in fact not reactionary here because—according to the classical critiques—it annuls the particular in the general, but fundamentally because it *annuls the being of time,* the reality of movement. Representation is the destruction of collective and productive time" (84; emphasis in original). Negri's bodily, subjective, liberated time is *"a before* and not *an after"* (35). It precedes and is immediately corrupted by the demands of any organization except the spontaneous and anarchical.

If Negri's great Satan is the state, his angel is the body—free, loving, and variable, responding only to its inherent, "ontological" instincts. How one feels about Negri ultimately depends on how viable one considers anarchy as a principle of human collectivity. At any rate it is not at all difficult to see that in temporal terms Negri's work establishes a simple dichotomy between the body and the state. The former is the domain of time, and the latter is the annulment of time. Time is the essential possession of the body, and any exterior demand is construed as a challenge to time itself. Even the most Bergsonian of modernist writers would have rejected as facile Negri's opposition of the temporal body against the atemporal state bureaucracy. While *Mrs. Dalloway* has been read in terms of a dichotomy between the body and authoritarian time, I argued in chapter 4 that Woolf challenges not the existence of the state itself, but rather the specific manipulation of a desirable ideal of universal temporal connection in the interests of social control and commercial profit. Hardly anarchical, Woolf's prose explores alternative metaphorical systems to represent human connectivity within a local milieu, cutting across class and gender barriers through an imaginative transformation (rather than a rejection) of clock time. Similarly Conrad's attack on temporal anarchy in *The Secret Agent* makes the body of the anarchist stand in for the governmental attempt to manipulate human time for imperial and commercial dominance. The demands of ship duty, always the idyll for Conrad, would little tolerate anarchical, fluid, bodily temporality, taking its dictates, as it does in *Lord Jim* and elsewhere in Conrad's oeuvre, from solar activity. The modernist "temporal territory," in other words, negotiated, without ever resolving, a much more complex array of temporal models, alternately centered in the body, the mind, the state, the empire, and the globe, demonstrating the modernist subject's fraught but necessary mediation of competing temporal demands.

What Negri loses in his total rejection of work is any higher principle on which to found collective consciousness and solidarity. If Marx's labor power necessitated an acceptance of the capitalist's rules of the game, it also provided a foundation for immediate identification. The worker is the one who *works,* who produces, who uses his or her hands, the fruit of whose labor is always and everywhere being appropriated. If the communist no longer works, as in Negri's ontology, who defines oneself as a communist, and more important, how does any necessary work get done? Who grows the vegetables and builds the shelters? Marx understood that work is a natural, spontaneous human activity that could be joyous rather than exploitive. If Marx's problem was that he accepted the capitalist's definition of work and time, surely the corrective is not to reject the unifying principle of work altogether, as does Negri, replacing it with terms like *love* and *bodily connections* (certainly terms the capitalist or bourgeoisie has no difficulty accepting).[9] Rather a globalizing, collective solidarity of work could be based on alternative, noncapitalist temporal models (the annual harvest, the weekly yield of produce, etc.). Negri wants to base global solidarity on what he calls "the global phenomenological fabric" of liberated time (29), but he rejects the very idea of social labor—the work that produces food and shelter—that might provide the stitches in his global fabric. Work precedes time and dictates its variable organization, one might reasonably counter. Conrad, hardly a Marxist, understood this quite clearly.

The project of modernism was to mediate the competing temporal demands of empire, state, commerce, family, and body through exploratory prose. If anything provided an escape from disorienting temporal multiplicity it was the idealized natural process of the sun and stars, processes that the urban wastelands were obscuring but not entirely eliminating. The sun at sea in Conrad, the "heat of the sun" in Woolf, and Joyce's stellar parallax held out a valorized realm of organic human rhythm always inaccessible to the modern subject, but ever desirable. Like Chaplin's tramp in *Modern Times,* leaving the factory and walking into the sunset of the countryside, modernist writers idealized a social rhythm based on unmediated contact with the sun or the heavens, and it was this that provided the glue for human collectivity, far more than a variable, schizophrenic, anarchic, and private human temporality. As in Bergson, though, whose disciple Negri ultimately is, Negri's ontology turns away from its own shadows, disavowing human social collectivity based on a "unilateral" solar rhythm, accepting instead a retreat from any social labor into the anarchy of the interior, rejecting as "fascist" any kind of unilateral organization.

If the body is the site for a postmodern liberation of time, then Martin Amis's *Time's Arrow* finds the greatest narrative position for that liberation in its "narrator as parasite," a kind of mental flea riding along with and unable to influence its host body, a Nazi doctor who experiences his life in reverse chronological order. *Time's Arrow* employs a reversal of time in the modernist spirit of a shock to the accepted verities of established narrative. In unhinging traditional chronology and toying with the clocks his characters live by, Amis's project is very much of a piece with Woolf's or Joyce's. In Amis, as in the earlier writers, there is an attempt to liberate time from its enlistment in a grim determinism. What constitutes the difference, then, in temporal expression between *The Secret Agent,* for instance, and *Time's Arrow?* To answer this question is to get at the heart of the division between modernist and postmodernist temporal aesthetics and politics. Amis's innovation is to reverse the process of entropy, with his narrator inhabiting a universe in which creation is easier than destruction and energy is accumulated rather than dissipated. In focusing on the irreversible arrow of entropy, Amis's interests are squarely with the modernist fixation on a fundamental physical law that had only begun to be popularly explored in fiction, despite its early articulation in the 1820s. As Michael Whitworth has demonstrated, the popular discourse on entropy was frequently translated into terms of social and biological "dissipation," particularly of the sun's energy, which, before the discovery of radium, was assumed to be entropically losing energy and irreversibly cooling (*Einstein's Wake,* 58–82). In the context of this grim physical determinism modernist authors, as I argued in chapter 4, attempted to dislocate time and narrative from its enlistment in a system of imperial and commercial dominance, resituating temporal processes instead within the realms of social labor (Conrad's seamen), colonial difference (Joyce's parallax), or patterns of social connection (Woolf's "webs").

To turn from the modernist project of recontextualizing temporality to Amis's reverse-chronology novel is to dramatically turn away from a horizon of possibility and back to determinism. The seeds of this determinism are planted in Amis's source text, Kurt Vonnegut's *Slaughterhouse Five* (1969), another great postmodern book on time. Combining metaphors of technological simultaneity and mental instability, Vonnegut characterizes his method on the title page as a "telegraphic schizophrenic manner." When Billy Pilgrim becomes "unstuck in time" his detachment from chronology is by no means a liberation. It is rather a nightmarish and futile enslavement to a series of life moments that have already been determined. Reliving his death, his wedding, his prison camp experience again and again, in random order, Billy feels a constant "stage fright" about what part of his life he will relive next (29). In this context the actions of the clock become meaningless, not because they are linked to a project of imperial Proportion, as in Woolf, but because their parceling of time is too microscopic and meaningless in the larger frame of reference within which Billy bounces around. When Billy and Montana Wildhack are kept in the alien Tralfamadorian zoo their captors seem to understand the meaningless human fixation on the movements of clock dials. "They're playing with the clocks again," Montana notices, as the aliens turn the hands back and forth in the interests of experimental research (266). The Tralfamadorian view of time is cosmological. They see temporality at a macro level, with all the parts of a life simultaneously available for view "just the way we can look at a stretch of the Rocky Mountains" (34). Tralfamadorian temporality has implications for political ideology and for narrative practice alike. The historicism that demands causal explanation is frustrated by this macrological view of life and history. To ask *Why?* is a human failing, Billy is told. "This moment simply is," the Tralfamadorians tell him. "Have you ever seen bugs trapped in amber?" (97). The implications for narrative are clear in the Tralfamadorians' description of their books as providing not sequential pleasures, but the beauty of "depths of many marvelous moments seen all at one time" (112). Given this description, Vonnegut's own book of course aspires to the Tralfamadorian aesthetic.

In the context of this schizophrenic rehearsal of predetermined moments the celebrated "certain paragraph" that Amis draws on for *Time's Arrow* is memorable for its uniqueness. As he waits for his alien abduction (which he has already experienced countless times) Billy watches a late-night movie about World War II. In this particular instance the unsticking process gets slightly skewed, so that Billy watches the movie "backwards, then forwards again" (93). It is in the backward viewing of the late show that Vonnegut's marvelous moment occurs, in which a temporary reprieve from the horrors of determinism is enacted. The corpses are resurrected, the bullets sucked from planes, the bombs dismantled, and the soldiers turned into babies. It is the only moment in the novel when Billy experiences something he has never experienced before. It is a surprise, a shock, a reversal. The result of a temporary cosmic glitch, it is memorable because it hints at a liberatory antiwar utopia that Billy, as soon as the glitch is corrected, will never experience again. The saucer comes, he is abducted, and he continues his schizophrenic rehearsal of random moments. Among postmodern texts, where the prodigious textual pleasures derive from the absurd grimness of determinism rather than from its resistance, these few paragraphs are uniquely modernist. As a glitch in the larger macro-level frame of time, however, the temporary liberation they offer is not sustainable.

What happens when they are made to sustain the framework of an entire novel? This is Amis's challenge, which he meets with characteristic inventiveness and intelligence. The immediate effect of reading Amis's book is that we experience a shock at seeing our expectations reversed. What would happen if everything went in reverse and a human had to adjust his or her worldview to that process? Everything, from micro to macro level, is ultimately naturalized by the narrator, who can view events only from inside the central character's body. Excrement is sucked into anuses from toilet bowls, dining is an act of regurgitation, hospitals inflict wounds and insert glass shards into foreheads. All of this is inordinately funny, provocative, and unsettling. The moment of supreme topsy-turveydom occurs in the Auschwitz sections of the book, in which the narrator watches his host body, a Nazi doctor, take ashes, smoke, and bones from crude ovens and build an entire population of Jews, whom he thinks of as his children.

What is ultimately distinctive about Amis's extension of Vonnegut's few paragraphs is that it quickly establishes its own grim fatalism, simply in reverse. In fact the fatalism is all the more acute because the reader always knows what the narrator never knows: how things "really" are, were, and will be. From Vonnegut's brief moment of liberated time in an otherwise deterministic text Amis has created an even tighter narrative of fatalism, enlisting the reader as a "correct" historian to the narrator's reverse view. The narrator's futility ultimately mirrors a larger worldview in which history is predetermined, like the Tralfamadorians' mountain range. Calling himself a "parasite or passenger" on his host body (63), the narrator is "hitched up" to this doctor's body, without the doctor ever knowing of the narrator's presence. The existential "loneliness" of the narrator, his inability to control the doctor—"This body I'm in won't take orders from this will of mine. Look around, I say. But his neck ignores me" (6)—typifies a larger worldview in which time, *regardless of direction,* is inseparably linked with a grim historicism over which we have no control. In this context the text's pleasures involve brief, isolated moments in which time seems suspended, and regular, ordinary routines are unassimilated into the larger historical regression back to Auschwitz, as when the narrator records blocks of time in which the doctor strolls around Washington Square Park and visits the superette: "Time passed. Time, the human dimension, which makes us everything we are" (68). At the end of the book, when the host body is three years old, the narrator explores the brief liberation of toddler time, a liberation achieved solely by the toddler's unawareness of a larger temporal progression: "He pauses for a moment, in the field. Only a moment. There are no larger units of his time" (165).

In modernist texts the attempt to dislocate time from its appropriation happens in the "moment" (of epiphany, connection, dramatic action). In the postmodern text the liberated "moment" is not a moment of action, connection, or resistance, but the opposite: inaction, routine, senility, senselessness. Time is not a social construct, able to be shaped to suit human activities and relationships, but rather an ontological possession, felt most "truly" by the senile and the infantile. This is Negri's ontology of time, wrested from historicism. In Amis its moments are brief, and historicism ultimately triumphant. The human ability to transform social time, pertinent and passionate in modernism, is an impossibility in the postmodern. The clock, any clock, is a manipulation of a historical progression over which our bodies and minds have no control. Any time but that of the body is inherently fascist time. The Nazis, like the Tralfamadorians, play games with the clocks, as the narrator of *Time's Arrow* sees when he visits Treblinka, where the Nazis have constructed a fake railway station to "reassure the Jews" en route to the camps. At the "prop" station, a painted clock forever reads 12:20:

> But we passed again, later, and the hands hadn't moved to an earlier time. How could they move? They were painted, and would never move to an earlier time. Beneath the clock was an enormous arrow, on which was printed: change here for Eastern trains. But time had no arrow, not here.
> Indeed, at the railway station in Treblinka, the four dimensions were intriguingly displaced. A place without depth. And a place without time. (143)

When modernist texts gestured toward the reversal, dislocation, or elimination of time, it was to explode standard time's commercial and imperial dictates from within and explore new depths of social temporality. When Amis explores alternate time, it is only an illusion, a deception, a painted surface. Timelessness is a temporary hoax in the boxcar ride to Auschwitz, the inevitable end destination for all grim views of a historicism that no one created and over which we have no control, like Amis's parasite narrator who views only (as does Benjamin's Klee angel) the horrors piled at his feet. The body owns time, and the state eliminates bodily time, replacing it with historicism. Negri's and Amis's visions coincide in this diagnosis of the temporal fabric of postmodernity.

The time against which Negri and Amis rail was not handed down from some nebulous source, but was constructed over the course of the first few decades of the twentieth century. Dissenting delegates at the Prime Meridian Conference struggled with the social construction of time and protested its enlistment into the commercial and scientific demands of empire. Their arguments were based not on the ontological purity of bodily time, but on the dictates of variable social, national, and cultural identities. For a brief moment modernist experiments with time attempted to explore and enact alternate social constructions of time buried in the conference debates. The postmodern, which finds any and all historical time fascistic and reverts to an interior, bodily time offering only fleeting pleasures in the face of inevitability, is light-years distant from those early temporal experiments. A politics of time in the age of prognoses of global instantaneity needs to resuscitate the temporal possibilities of the modernist aesthetic, to dismantle fatalistic views of history, and to find temporal regimes in socially specific solidarities rather than in isolated bodily pleasures. Whether or not such a resuscitation is possible depends on a recovery of the history of temporal politics, an aim to which this book has attempted to contribute.

Notes

INTRODUCTION

1. Developing conceptions of modernity in the eighteenth century necessitated a "changed relationship to historical time," as Alex Callinicos writes. Knowledge not only progressed in modernity, "but would continue to do so indefinitely into the future" (13).

2. The astronomer is Charles Piazzi-Smyth, whose remarks in 1879 on the relationship between standard time and nationalism I discuss in chapter 1.

3. Derek Howse provides a table that lists by year each nation's legal adoption of Greenwich-based time, from Japan in 1888 to Liberia in 1972, with the majority of adoptions occurring between 1892 and 1940 (154–55).

4. I discuss this critical tendency in some detail in chapter 2. As I suggest there, an understanding of modernist time as uncorrupted by materialism or public values derives in part from a persistent association of modernist temporality with the Bergsonian *durée*, which, as Bergson wrote in *Time and Free Will*, is "constantly changing" and exists in a "perpetual state of becoming" until corrupted by and confused with fixed and permanent objects (130). The identification of the modernist "time-mind" as Bergsonian was first made by Wyndham Lewis in *Time and Western Man*, but the notion of modernist temporality as detached from the shared, public sphere of the object world persists in contemporary criticism. See, for example, Sharon Stockton's reading of Virginia Woolf and her claim that a "hallmark" of modernism was that "the individual consciousness was inherently detached from public reality . . . brought closer to universal 'truth' by [the individual's] removal from shared space and time" (95).

5. In their introduction to a recently published collection of essays, *Modernism and Colonialism*, Richard Begam and Michael Valdez Moses identify the absence of and demand for "a sustained and comprehensive account of the relation of modernism to colonialism" (1).

6. In practice there are more than twenty-four zones, and there are exceptions to the whole-hour deviation, including India, Myanmar, Iran, Iraq, Central Australia, and Newfoundland (all deviating by half-hours from Greenwich Mean Time) and Nepal, which deviates by quarter-hour from Greenwich (by $5\frac{3}{4}$ hours, specifically). These irregular deviations were made to prevent the subdividing of one nation or territory into multiple zones. India, for example, should technically have had a western zone 4 hours ahead of Greenwich and an Eastern zone 5 hours ahead. The British, preferring to keep one time in the colony rather than two, compromised by adopting an average of $4\frac{1}{2}$ hours. When Pakistan was created it temporally seceded from Indian time, adopting the 4-hour zone.

7. In his book on Fleming and Standard Time, intended for a general readership, Blaise bluntly equates standard time with "reason," as when he writes, "The effect of standard time, that is to say 'reason,' on a non-Western culture has been explicitly captured in one novel, Chinua Achebe's *Arrow of God*" (174). Blaise reads Fleming as a truly progressive radical who, along with other revolutionary figures of his age, "did not build on previous knowledge or practice but, in effect, wiped them out." His list of innovators to place alongside Fleming include "Darwin, Pasteur, Edison, Seurat, Marx, James, Monet, and Van Gogh" (175).

8. I have in mind, of course, *Longitude,* Dava Sobel's 1995 best-seller biography of Harrison, the subtitle of which clearly expresses Sobel's view of the scientific autonomy of both Harrison and of the longitude problem: *The True Story of a Lone Genius Who Solved the Greatest Scientific Problem of His Time.*

9. Howse suggests that the magnitude of the 1707 "Clowdisley Shovel disaster," named after the admiral of a naval expedition that lost four ships and nearly two thousand men as a result of inaccurate positioning, directly contributed to the British government's receptivity to any innovation that might make navigation safer (45–47).

10. See, for example, an exchange between Sherlock Holmes and Dr. Watson in Arthur Conan Doyle's *The Valley of Fear* (1914), in which Holmes asks Watson to think of "standardized books which any may be supposed to possess." Watson proposes first the Bible, then Bradshaw's guide, then an almanac (21–22).

11. Cited in Royde Smith 52.

12. Ibid., 62.

13. The International Meter was installed in Paris in 1881; the British Standards Institute was established in 1901. See Wicke, "The Same and the Different," 575.

14. Howse, 116–51; Bartky, 147–54; Galison, 113–55.

15. Some of the more routinely cited book-length studies of time and modernism are Church, *Time and Reality;* Kern, *The Culture of Time and Space;* Ricoeur, *Time and Narrative* (especially vol. 2); Quinones, *Mapping Literary Modernism;* Schliefer, *Modernism and Time.*

16. See, for example, George Eliot's introductory chapter of *Felix Holt, the Radical* (1866), where the insularity of "slow old-fashioned" coach travel is nostalgically contrasted with the globalizing effect of train travel, which

unwholesomely confronts villagers with "that mysterious distant system of things called 'Gover'ment' " (4). In *Dombey and Son* (1848) Dickens represents, in Clark Blaise's words, the "literal demonstration of a railway's riding upon the back of a distraught, psychologically ruined Mr. Dombey" (37).

17. Wyndham Lewis's *Time and Western Man* (1928) is the key text in this tradition, discussed at some length in chapter 2. Among the more comprehensive and influential studies of Bergson and modernist time are Church, *Time and Reality;* Kumar, *Bergson and the Stream of Consciousness Novel;* Gillies, *Henri Bergson and British Modernism.* Church begins with a direct link between Bergson and Proust and then reads a discrepancy between lived and clock time in Bergsonian terms in chapters on Joyce, Woolf, and Aldous Huxley. Kumar also links Woolf and Joyce, along with Dorothy Richardson, to Bergsonian theory, asserting that the pervasive river imagery in modernism is the most viable symbol for the otherwise spatially unrepresentable durée. Gillies reads Woolf, Joyce, Richardson, and T. S. Eliot in relation not only to Bergson's theory of the durée, but also to his larger body of writings, including his essay on comedy.

18. See, for example, John G. Peters's discussion of Conrad's *The Secret Agent* in *Conrad and Impressionism* (86–122). Peters draws heavily on Kern's reading of the Washington conference and its relationship with modernist aesthetics. See also Whitworth, *Einstein's Clocks,* 172, and Daly, *Literature, Technology, and Modernity,* 46, both of which use Kern as their sole source on global standard time.

19. In *A Shrinking Island* Jed Esty nicely summarizes this model (105). The "anti-Bloomsbury" stance of the British left tradition has been notably attacked by Jane Marcus in her essay "Britannia rules *The Waves.*" Marcus claims that the "Leavisite legacy" has "indoctrinated" critics to radically suspect the "elite, effete English culture against which the democratic Great Tradition strenuously struggled" (152). For Marcus the leftist critique of modernism has been expressed in acutely gendered terms, with Lawrence and Orwell proving a masculine counter to the feminized, gentrified high modernist writers. Eagleton's *Exiles and Émigrés,* certainly a landmark text in this British left tradition, systematically exposes the class biases and political ambivalence among not only upper-class writers like Woolf and Evelyn Waugh, but also middle-class, ostensibly politically radical writers like Orwell and Graham Greene. As Jane Goldman notes, the battle between Marcus and the Leavisite tradition dates back to "ruptures" in the modernist period, such as the " 'rumpus' between Wyndham Lewis' Vorticists and the Bloomsbury Group" (10).

20. Blaise repeats the phrase "Time was in the air," which he borrows from a 1904 statement by a former president of the American Railroad Association, no fewer than eight times, also adopting it as the title of part 2 of his book, *Time Lord.*

21. This quote, from Eysteinsson's book, *The Concept of Modernism,* is cited in Chu (57) and Danius (33).

22. In addition to Danius's treatment of Kern, discussed in some detail here, both Mary Anne Doane and Mark Hama have raised this problem with Kern's oppositional approach.

23. Many of the contributors to Howard J. Booth and Nigel Rigby's collection, *Modernism and Empire,* take on Jameson's essay, sometimes aggressively. What largely rankles the critics Patrick Williams and Rod Edmond is Jameson's move early in the essay to disregard the "minor" writers of the "adventure" genre, such as Kipling, H. Rider Haggard, and Wells, on the grounds of their not being "modernist in any formal sense" (Jameson, "Modernism and Imperialism", 44). Booth and Rigby include essays that, by contrast, treat Kipling as a fellow modernist or, as in Edmond's essay on degeneration, attempt to isolate phenomena that demonstrate a common ground between "high" and "low" writers. Jameson has also been criticized for his textual analysis, which, overly dependent on Forster, curiously ignores *A Passage to India.* See, for example, P. Williams, "Simultaneous Uncontemporaneities," 21-22.

24. Stevenson writes, "When asked about the time, its hero cheerfully replies 'Hurray! Just half-past ten. Greenwich mean, eh Guv?'" ("Greenwich Meanings," 125).

25. In *Wars of Position* Timothy Brennan describes the turn to space or place in globalization theory as dependent on "the overcoming of temporality." The shift from the chronometric to the cartographic, for Brennan, is in part the manifestation of a worldview that "perceives the conflicts of history as being decisively decided," so that what matters is no longer "what will happen" but "when it will extend itself over a vast but finite territory" (136).

26. One of the more lasting effects of the theoretical shifts that followed the revolutionary hopes and frustrations of May 1968 has been a dramatic reevaluation of the categories of time and space. Prior to the 1970s time generally was considered inherently revolutionary—the locus of Bergsonian vitalism, or the force driving dialectical materialism. Space, on the other hand, was deemed a reactionary, counterrevolutionary category, embraced by protofascists such as Wyndham Lewis, who in his book *Time and Western Man* envisioned a static, spatial conception as a salutary counter to what he identified as the Bergsonian "fad" or "cult" of time worship. In the 1970s, though, a radical reorientation of the concept of space stood this state of affairs on its head. While Ernst Bloch could claim, in 1962, that "the primacy of space over time is an infallible sign of reactionary language," Foucault ten years later would reflect on having himself contributed to making such statements as Bloch's hopelessly passé (Fabian 37).

27. In an article in *Feminist Review* the social theorist Barbara Adam identifies this tendency to obscure the "taken-for-granted time politics" of globalization and argues for a realignment of a largely "spatial" discourse. Adam believes the absence of a time analysis in globalization removes a key strategic site for a potential solidarity and resistance in temporal terms. Her work on social time has been extensive; see *Time and Social Theory* and *Timescapes of Modernity.*

28. These terms come, respectively, from Harvey, *The Condition of Postmodernity;* Giddens, *The Constitution of Society;* and Castells, *The Rise of the Network Society.*

CHAPTER 1

1. Fredric Jameson calls the 1884 Berlin Conference "the codification of the new imperialist world system" in "Modernism and Imperialism" (44). Ngũgĩ wa Thiong'o in *Moving the Centre* calls the Berlin Conference "infamous" (88) and declares it the "external political expression" of the imperialist stage of capitalism (110). For a discussion of the Berlin Conference and its role in the "scramble for Africa," see Wesseling, *Divide and Rule*.

2. London *Times*, October 15, 1884, 9.

3. London *Times*. October 2, 1884, 9.

4. London Times, October 14, 1884, 9.

5. For a discussion of the role of time in these forms of cultural politics, see Ganguly, "Temporality and Postcolonial Critique."

6. In a letter to Fleming, Allen took issue with his claim in his essay "England and Canada" that the 1883 American adoption of time zones was not the result of an overwhelming sense of "emergency" among American railway managers. In the letter, dated July 19, 1884, Allen claimed, "The subject of the adoption of standard time had never been discussed . . . until April 1883 when my first report on the subject was made at the regular meeting. The meeting held in Chicago in October of the same year was called at the regular time and for the purpose of transacting the regular business of the convention. The standard time matter was taken up incidentally and not specially." Sandford Fleming Fonds, letter from W. F. Allen to Sandford Fleming, July 19, 1884, box 1, folder 6.

7. Fleming had a copy in his files of Noel's 1892 pamphlet, *International Time: A Scheme for Harmonising the Hour All the World Round*. Sandford Fleming Fonds, "Standard Time Miscellaneous," box 122, folder 48.

8. Clark Blaise invokes Kronos in his brief history of time in *Time Lord*: "Time is a bloodthirsty savage. None of us gets out alive, regardless of piety, decency, beauty, or innocence" (3).

9. See B. Adam, *Timewatch;* Urry, *Sociology beyond Societies*, 106.

10. This "task-centered" temporal orientation in agricultural labor is discussed by E. P. Thompson (60–63).

11. I have in mind a specifically temporal version of the general phenomenon of reification as discussed by Lukács in "Reification and the Consciousness of the Proletariat."

12. Fleming met Carlyle in 1877. He told his biographer, Lawrence Burpee, "I told Mr. Carlyle how impossible it was to say what pleasure it had given me to have the opportunity of talking to the author of *Sartor Resartus*." Fleming also presented Carlyle with a report on the Canadian Pacific railway (Burpee, 151).

13. "Science appears here only as the humble vassal of the powers of the day," Lefaivre had claimed at Washington, "to consecrate and crown their success. But gentlemen, nothing is so transitory and fugitive as power and riches" (quoted in Galison 152).

14. A copy of these remarks, dated September 5, 1879, is forwarded to the Marquis of Lorne by E. Hicks Beach, secretary of the governor general of

Canada; that forward is dated October 17, 1879. Sandford Fleming Fonds, "Lorne," box 30, folder 210.

15. Communication made to the "Geographic Society" by Comte Visconte, dated May 8, 1874, and included in Beach's report to the Marquis of Lorne. Sandford Fleming Fonds, "Lorne," box 30, folder 210.

16. "New Time Standards," *Sidereal Messenger* 2 (1884): 278. In fact Ian Bartky asserts that in America "between late 1853 and 1900 . . . no more than two timekeeping blunders resulted in passenger fatalities" (30). In both cases "unbelievably slow watches" (25 to 30 minutes slow) were to blame (221 n. 27).

17. Neither Blaise nor Galison counters Howse's statement that the conference recommended a Greenwich-based universal time (see my introduction, n. 14).

18. Sandford Fleming Fonds, letter from W. F. Allen to J. K. Rees (forwarded to Sandford Fleming), January 9, 1888, "Rees, J. K.," box 40, folder 286.

19. Bartky's accusation of the conference's "failure" stems from the fact that "no country's decision to adopt a meridian indexed to Greenwich can be traced back directly to the sessions in Washington." "Almost all English and American writers," Bartky writes, inaccurately "view the International Meridian Conference as a watershed event" (152).

20. All citations of the conference proceedings are from *International Conference Held at Washington*.

21. Sandford Fleming Fonds, box 106. Fleming's note to Rodgers immediately precedes the bound volume of the conference proceedings in the archive.

22. See Sobel, *Longitude*.

23. My attention was first drawn to this discrepancy by a series of letters between the Italian astronomer Tondini de Quarenghi and Sandford Fleming between 1889 and 1891. Fleming's claim that the conference had recommended universal time with "substantial unanimity," Tondini wrote, was a "mystification," given that "all European powers, Great Britain and Russia only excepted, either abstained from voting or voted against the Article V (specifying the parameters of the universal day)" Sandford Fleming Fonds, box 13, folder 85.

24. The reasons for this oversight vary. Howse, as head of navigation and astronomy at the National Maritime Museum located at the Greenwich Observatory, wrote *Greenwich Time and the Discovery of the Longitude* as a celebration of the venerable institution (as is clear by the glossy, coffee-table second edition). He thus suppresses this counterhistory of protest, which is simply ignored in his summary of the conference highlights (139–51). Blaise and Galison focus exclusively on the Anglo-French rivalry, which was most prevalent in the first two days of debates. They thus miss this larger base of protests from day three on.

25. Howse notes that Spain "abstained" from voting that day but does not discuss the reason (148).

26. See Piazzi-Smyth, 175–79.

27. Magda Abdelhadi, "Muslim Call to Adopt Mecca Time," *BBC News*, April 21, 2008, http://news.bbc.co.uk/2/hi/middle_east/7359258.stm.

28. The two resolutions in question were worded, "II: That the Conference proposes to the Governments here represented the adoption of the meridian passing through the centre of the transit instrument at the Observatory of Greenwich as the initial meridian for longitude" and "V: That this universal day is to be a mean solar day; is to begin for all the world at the moment of mean midnight of the initial meridian, coinciding with the beginning of the civil day and date of that meridian; and is to be counted from zero up to twenty-four hours."

29. Blaise and Galison describe only the debates over Resolution II, in which the French delegates took prominent part. Both critics ignore all other articles of the conference. Howse briefly mentions the Turkish delegate's insistence on preserving local time. Without discussing the context for Rustem Effendi's remarks, or the Spanish blockade that they supported, Howse neutralizes the relevance of Rustem's statements. See Howse, 148.

30. Sandford Fleming Fonds, letter from Ernst Pasquier to Sandford Fleming, March 12, 1891, box 38, folder 271.

31. Sandford Fleming Fonds, letter from Ernst Pasquier to Sandford Fleming, January 27, 1891, box 38, folder 271.

32. Sandford Fleming Fonds, letter from Ernst Pasquier to Sandford Fleming, May 26, 1890, box 38, folder 271.

33. Sandford Fleming Fonds, communication from William Miles to Colonial Secretary, February 23, 1891, forwarded by John Bramston to Lord Knutsford on January 28, 1892, "Lord Stanley of Preston," box 48, folder 328.

34. See Wheeler, *Report,* 23.

35. Sandford Fleming Fonds, card from Noel Fleming to Sandford Fleming, November 15, 1888, box 15, folder 107.

36. Sandford Fleming Fonds, memorandum to investors from the Para Transportation and Trading Company and the Goyaz Mining Company, "Kimball, R. J.," box 26, folder 185.

37. Sandford Fleming Fonds, forwarded to Sandford Fleming from R. J. Kimball on October 6, 1888, box 26, folder 185.

38. Sandford Fleming Fonds, communication dated December 19, 1888, and forwarded to Fleming by Kimball on December 28, 1888, box 26, folder 185.

39. Sandford Fleming Fonds, letter from J. J. C Abbot to Kimball, December 31, 1888, "Kimball, R. J.," box 26, folder 185.

40. Sandford Fleming Fonds. Kimball quotes Abbot's phrase "rascally Brazilians" in a letter from Kimball to Abbot which is stapled to a letter from Abbot to Fleming, May 13, 1889, "Abbot, J. J. C.," box 1, folder 1. The comments on the province's insufficient credit is from a letter from Kimball to Abbot, October 15, 1889, "Abbot, J. J. C.," box 1, folder 1.

41. Sandford Fleming Fonds, letter from Kimball to Fleming, November 1, 1889, box 26, folder 185.

42. Sandford Fleming Fonds, clipping dated October 14, 1889, stapled to a letter from Kimball to Fleming, November 14, 1889, box 26, folder 185.

43. Sandford Fleming Fonds. The plans generated from Louis J. Alloo, "a stockholder." His letter to Kimball is dated January 30, 1890, and is forwarded to Fleming on February 15, 1890, box 26, folder 185.

44. Sandford Fleming Fonds. The "Fleming vs. McNeill" case involving details on the anthracite are filed under "Lewis and Smellie 1902–1911" (Fleming's barristers), box 28, folder 202.

45. Sandford Fleming Fonds. See, for example, a letter from Hugh Fleming to Sandford dated August 11, 1908, and "inquiring into the possibility of exporting cement to Australia" (box 15, folder 105).

46. Sandford Fleming Fonds, letter from Clarence W. Ashford to Sandford Fleming, April 4, 1895, box 3, folder 13. Ashford was an attorney who had known Fleming since 1889 and was scouting out prospects for the Pacific cable through Hawaii. On March 14, 1890, Ashford wrote Fleming of the "late elections," in which the "entire opposition ticket" had been elected in Oahu on a platform "whose chief feature was hostility to any further tying up of Hawaiian affairs in American hands." In a letter of April 16, 1890, he writes that the "ways of Kalakaua, the king, are past finding out."

47. Sandford Fleming Fonds. Fleming's remarks come from an unlabeled news column stapled to a letter from the Hon. H. G. Joly de Lotbiniere to Sandford Fleming, December 28, 1905, box 24, folder 176.

48. Clark Blaise, however, asserts just the opposite about Fleming: "Fleming was always a government man, deeply suspicious of the motives of capital and profit" (188). Blaise's assertion is unsupported by evidence and seems particularly inaccurate in the light of Fleming's chief role in the Para venture.

49. Sandford Fleming Fonds, letter from H. M. Hozier to Sandford Fleming, May 13, 1897, "Lloyd's of London," box 29, folder 205.

50. "Thai Cabinet Wants to Shift Time Zone for Economic Gains," *Xinhua General News Service,* July 18, 2001.

51. Fleming's order of Frederick Taylor's *Concrete Costs* was sent on May 4, 1914, in response to a May 2, 1914, advertisement sent to him by the publishers, John Wiley and Sons. Sandford Fleming Fonds, "Wiley, John," box 53, folder 370.

CHAPTER 2

1. The larger political implications of the cosmopolitan worldview have been explored by Timothy Brennan in *At Home in the World: Cosmopolitanism Today.*

2. Martin Puchner comments on the interpretive fuzziness of time in Lewis's book, which "apparently refers not only to an obsession with memory but also to everything having to do with processes, transformations, instability, shapelessness, lack of formal discipline, and flux" (61).

3. For a discussion of the street itineraries of the characters in *Mrs. Dalloway,* see Andelys Wood, "Walking the Web in the Lost London of *Mrs. Dalloway.*"

4. Richard Begam has similarly argued about Joyce that his use of the "mythical method" and stream-of-consciousness device are not "vehicles for *escaping* cultural specificity and locality," but are used to "*undermine* ahistorical or transcultural aspirations" and to "deconstruct modernism's own universalist impulses" (186).

5. The great instance of this dialectical dynamic between nationalism and aestheticism in Joyce, an analysis of which makes for the most compelling of Nolan's chapters, is Bloom's confrontation with the nationalist citizen in the "Cyclops" chapter of *Ulysses*. For Nolan the critical paradigm that refuses to read any positive content in the citizen's litany of colonial abuse reveals the racial prejudice of Anglo critics more than the actual tone of the chapter. The citizen in fact, as Nolan skillfully demonstrates, recapitulates and echoes anticolonial essays Joyce himself had written in his early journalism. It is "strange and unlikely," Nolan argues, "that Joyce's massive creative effort in 'Cyclops' should ultimately be read as proposing the idea of the barbarism of the Irish, the hoariest stereotype in all of Irish colonial history, and one which he very frequently publicly attacked" (104). Bloom's quiet assertion of love as a foundation for human interaction, which most critics loudly proclaim as expressing Bloom's (and Joyce's) liberal and rational pacifism in the face of the barbaric citizen's rabid violence, is interrogated by Nolan. It is in fact Bloom's assertion of love that is savagely and potently satirized by the citizen, who immediately confronts Bloom with the counterimage of Cromwell slaughtering women and children with a cannon that reads "God is Love" (Nolan 102). Before the citizen and his cohort's bold and accurate imagery of an imperialism that consists of "flogging the natives on the belly to get all the red rubber out of them," Bloom's pacifism seems vague, inarticulate, and unconvincing.

Similarly Stephen's often cited comment on the "nightmare of history" is less an escape from particularity and more a confrontation of the distorted, sanitized, racist history proposed by Deasy in the "Nestor" chapter. Deasy's inaccurate denial of the killing of Catholics in the eighteenth century is protested, in Stephen's mind, by his evocation of images of "the Lodge of Diamond in Armagh the splendid behung with corpses of papishes." Stephen, Nolan argues, "seems to protest against the violence which is occluded by Deasy's narrative account of history, rather than deem historical fact uninteresting or irrelevant" (71). In comparing Stephen's confrontation with Deasy to Bloom's confrontation with the citizen Nolan perceptively notes that it is in fact Stephen and the citizen who use the same strategy of acknowledging the violence and suffering written out of the sanitized versions of history offered by Deasy and Bloom (102).

In a sense what Stephen and the citizen insist upon in their resurrection of political violence buried in the interstices of a confident liberal humanist narrative is the kind of redemption of the past represented in Walter Benjamin's famous use of the Klee angel in his "Theses on the Philosophy of History," who turns away from the future to arrest the wreckage of the past in a temporal confrontation of past and present. Ronald Schleifer, in his book on modernism and post-Enlightenment time, uses Benjamin's image of arrested temporality as a grid through which to read cultural modernism, quantum mechanics, and Saussurean linguistics alike, all of which refuse, in the early decades of the twentieth century, to engage with time as a kind of "ether" or an empty container of events, and instead fix it synchronically in a momentary halting of diachrony. For Joyce and T. S. Eliot, as for Bertrand Russell and Einstein, modernist aesthetic phenomena and mathematics alike derive from the "possibility of grasping phenomena whole, momentarily, in order to comprehend them and, as Benjamin says, by means of their enlarged wholeness to 'redeem' them" (Schleifer 182). Stephen's juxtaposition of slaughtered eighteenth-century Catholics with Deasy's racist monologue is hardly a retreat from historical particularity, but rather an arrested and conflicted insistence upon the dialectical image of the past that Benjamin advocates. Schleifer sees the same arresting of a past image in the curious section of *Mrs. Dalloway* in which the old woman beggar sings her ancestral song in front of the subway entrance. For Schleifer the old singer confronts the seamless continuities of present-day London with a momentarily disabling introduction of a prehuman landscape into the novel's texture, haunting the present as a ghost from the past (Schleifer 54).

6. The most "unabashedly partisan" of such readings, Joseph Brooker has argued in *Joyce's Critics,* is Len Platt's 1998 text, *Joyce and the Anglo-Irish* (Brooker 227).

7. For a thorough discussion of the modernist engagement with entropy, relativity, and radioactivity, see Michael Whitworth, *Einstein's Wake.*

8. In what has become a commonplace attack on Hegel's "world spirit," Osborne argues that "few would disagree" with Paul Ricoeur's characterization of the Hegelian project as having "totalized a few leading aspects of the spiritual history of Europe and of its geographical and historical environment." The substance of that totalizing move has "come undone" in that "difference has turned against development" (40). Osborne explains "difference" as the inability of humans to recognize themselves in the stages of unitary historical development. Setting aside Osborne's locution "few would disagree" (certainly a questionable phrase for a critic of totalization), it remains unclear how the European phenomenological tradition that occupies the bulk of *The Politics of Time* has more intellectual purchase on an ontological authentic humanity than does Hegelianism.

CHAPTER 3

1. Johannes Fabian, *Time and the Other.*
2. Haggard did not invent this story. Its original source is a possibly apocryphal tale of Christopher Columbus told by his illegitimate son, Hernando, in which Columbus predicted an eclipse in Jamaica in 1504 in order to awe the natives. Eclipse prediction is repeated in Mark Twain's *A Connecticut Yankee in King Arthur's Court* and in Hergé's Tintin adventure *Prisoners of the Sun,* among other texts.
3. As Stephen D. Arata has argued in his landmark essay, "The Occidental Tourist: Dracula and Reverse Colonization," Stoker used the Carpathians as a locale with a well-known history "linked to military conquest and to the rise and fall of empires" (627) in order to raise the specter of inevitable imperial decline for the dissolute 1890s. The warrior-like Dracula turns the mirror on "British imperial activities abroad" (633) with an "Occidentalism" that "both mirrors and reverses the more familiar Orientalism underwriting Western imperial practices" (634). Arata's essay rightly raised attention to the novel's politics of imperialism in a critical landscape understandably occupied with

questions of gender, sexuality, and Oedipal myth. Yet Arata is too eager to stress the "disquietingly familiar" affinities between British colonizer and colonized vampire, attesting a pure mirror image when the text's fabulous pleasures clearly depend on an ontological *difference* between human and vampire that, at base, cannot be reflected in any mirror. Navigating the imperial politics of Stoker's novel requires that we not lose sight of the glaring *inhumanity* of the vampire (expressed in temporal as well as bodily terms).

4. Arata highlights the oddity of Dracula's Bradshaw fixation in "The Occidental Tourist" and rightly asserts that it demonstrates both a parody of a generic convention of the travel narrative and also an insight into the complicity of knowledge and power (635–37). Yet the synchronization of time is not simply a generic convention or a stand-in for a generalized Orientalist knowledge, but is also and more importantly a very specific deployment of novel strategies of global conceptualization and control inaugurated at the 1884 International Prime Meridian Convention.

5. See, for example, Malley, "'Time Hath No Power Against Identity': Historical Continuity and Archaeological Adventure in H. Rider Haggard's *She*."

6. See also P. Williams, "*Kim* and Orientalism."

7. I follow Kipling's designation of "Anglo-Indian" as indicating a British person born or raised in India. As Geoffrey Moorhouse explains, the term changed its meaning at the census of 1911, when it was first used to indicate mixed-race or "half-caste" Indians (136).

8. In *Orientalism* Edward Said writes, "No Oriental was ever allowed to see a Westerner as he aged and degenerated, just as no Westerner needed ever to see himself, mirrored in the eyes of the subject race, as anything but a vigorous, rational, ever-alert young Raj" (42). Jed Esty characterizes the eternal youth of empire's agency as a "fantasy of perpetual emergence without closure" ("Virginia Woolf's Colony," 76). He argues that empire's limitless achronological temporality frustrates the familiar association between the Bildungsroman narrative and the demands of the nation state.

9. Helen Pike Bauer nicely captures Kipling's tone in the story, which is "jocular and knowing, told as if the worldly narrator were winking at us, inviting us into a circle where the wealthy and idle elbow for social position and the innocent and easily duped become fodder for dinner-table repartee. But Kipling's narrator is not entirely a member of the dominant social group; he is enough of an insider to know its manners and values, but stands sufficiently outside to mark its hollowness. This ambivalent stance, amused yet faintly repelled, characterizes many of the Simla stories" (30).

10. Steven Trout has argued that the text is as exemplary of imperialism as is Kipling's "The Mark of the Beast" or Conrad's *The "Nigger" of the Narcissus*, in that the Time Traveler applies the same rhetoric of degeneracy, logic of self-superiority, and propensity for violence to the Morlocks that an adventurer like Stanley would apply to tribes in the Congo. The novel's innovation is to apply the conventions of the overseas adventure tale to a temporally rather than spatially exotic culture.

11. It is not uncharacteristic of Wells to be skeptical of the unquestioned value of science and technology. As Hugh Kenner writes in *A Sinking Island*,

although Wells was "glib" with the "terminology" of science, "he would never share its official professions of confidence." Borrowing an image from *The Time Machine* Kenner writes, "Science lights a match, then sees its own hands, then darkness: that was the closing figure of the first piece Wells published for the world to see" (50). See also Philip Griffin on the significance of the warship in the final chapter of Wells's *Tono-Bungay* as an emblem of the final destructive end-point of an idealistic faith in technology.

CHAPTER 4

1. Certainly world standard time's treatment of temporality as infinitely measurable and manageable crucially informs H. G. Wells's *The Time Machine* (1895), as I discuss in chapter 3. If science fiction manifested anxiety over the manipulation and management of time, another strain within modernism placed the conception of time as an abstract and infinitely divisible quantum in tension with mythical, archaic, or primitive conceptions of temporality. Thomas Hardy's Wessex bears traces of an age when "one-handed clocks sufficiently subdivided the day" (20) even as it undergoes the transformations of mechanized agriculture with its "despotic demands" on the time management of farm laborers like Tess Durbeyfield. Similarly, D. H. Lawrence contrasts the "eternal, mechanical, monotonous clock-face of time," physically embodied in Gudrun's image of Gerald as a "chronometer-watch" (466), with Birkin's vision of an African or Egyptian time consciousness rooted in "thousands of years" of "mystically sensual" knowledge (253).

2. Rightly sensing an implicit condemnation of Greenwich in the novel, critics have nevertheless been at pains to agree on exactly what the Observatory symbolizes for Conrad. Stephen Kern states that Conrad uses the Observatory as a "graphic symbol of centralized political authority" with the embassy official Mr. Vladimir standing in for Conrad's "direct assault" on the "authority of uniform public time" (16). Kern's reading is echoed in Clark Blaise's *Time Lord* and in Peter Galison's *Einstein's Clocks, Poincaré's Maps*. Blaise calls *The Secret Agent* "the touchstone literary confirmation" of an artistic opposition to "the dreadful progress of Victorian will and order." Conrad offers, as a philosophical justification for the bombing, the "assassination" of a "single, unified time, everywhere and indivisible" (164). Galison's summation of the novel is the most accurate of the three in that he acknowledges that Bourdin's bombing remains, on Conrad's "canvas," the "murkiest" of actions, occurring in a milieu "from which no one emerges unsullied" (159–60).

For R. W. Stallman *The Secret Agent* dramatizes an attack on Time itself—history, narrative, chronology—all of which, in Stallman's reading, emanate from the Greenwich meridian. John G. Peters associates Greenwich with "civilization," scientific progress, and the Western impulse to abstractly organize human experience. Peters's reading renders Conrad's position an attack on the "Western worldview" (see 86–122). Provocatively frustrating these readings, Mark Hama argues that there has been no convincing evidence that Conrad was opposed to Greenwich at all. On the contrary, according to Hama, Greenwich represents for Conrad a stable principle for the human organization of time.

If Stephen Kern can read the Observatory as "a graphic symbol of centralized political authority" and Hama can read it as an embodiment of "the will of a society to organize its time in a particular way" (140), then surely the text supports wide latitudes of interpretation and embodies fundamental ambiguities.

3. Stevenson makes this point in his essay "A Narrow, Zigzag, and Secluded Path." See note 5 below for a thorough refutation of his argument.

4. London *Times,* February 27, 1894.

5. Randall Stevenson in "A Narrow, Zigzag, and Secluded Path" acknowledges the *Times*'s statement of motive but dismisses it as only one among many of the paper's "zanier" theories (39). Stevenson is incorrect. The *Times* correspondent does in fact hold consistently to the view of premeditated attack. This can be illustrated simply by looking at the coverage from the 16th (the day after the bombing) to the 20th (the 21st through the 26th are devoted to outrage over Bourdin's public funeral and offer no statements of motive). On the 16th two hypotheses are immediately offered. We can designate them as the "police surveillance" hypothesis and the "hide the evidence" hypothesis. The police, it is claimed, having "speedily discovered" plans for a bombing, had kept "special and very careful watch" on the Autonomie Club, which led Bourdin to flee for his safety. To "rid himself safely" of the explosives Bourdin attempted to hide them in the park, at which point he fell and triggered the explosion. In this first report the idea of a premeditated attack is dismissed. "At the last moment," the report states, Bourdin may have remembered that the Observatory was a "Government building" and tried to use the explosives against it, but this, we are told, "does not fit with facts."

On the very next day, in the first report from the special correspondent, the "hide the evidence" hypothesis is entirely refuted and the argument for a premeditated attack on the Observatory is strongly advocated. Bourdin, we are told, "was not merely seeking for a place in which to hide a store of explosives." The correspondent's own examination of the bomb materials leads him to "put an end conclusively to any theory that this was an accidental explosion of materials intended to be hidden." According to Colonel Majendie, head of the inquest, the report concludes, "all the indications pointed to the fact that Bourdin's intention was to use the explosive against the Royal Observatory." This, we are told, is "the solution of the mystery." The correspondent concludes the report with his own speculation on what the ideal escape route would have been had Bourdin not been injured. On the 19th we find Stevenson's other theories about punishing a comrade and taking a shortcut, but they are attributed to opinions other than those held by the *Times* correspondent and they never again recur in the paper. Note the placement of the clause in the sentence "Whatever Bourdin's design may have been, whether he meant to blow up the Observatory, or, *as some have it,* to punish a traitorous comrade or, to take a short cut across to Woolwich . . . " (emphasis added). The official statement remains a premeditated attack, with other hypotheses attributed to outside views. On the 20th, with the "hide the evidence" theory already defeated, the correspondent greatly discredits the "police surveillance" theory. The police, it must be admitted, "really knew very little about the Anarchical movement in England until the affair of Greenwich Park." In the same report the correspondent takes another look at the Observatory and notes the damage on the building's wall. A "wooden paling" near the wall is described as riddled with marks "similar to that of the ricochet marks made by bullets from the magazine rifle upon a wooden dummy." The image of the Observatory as a dummy under a barrage of machine-gun fire signals the extent to which the Observatory was understood as a target.

Far from a bewildering multitude of "zany" theories, then, the *Times* moved quite clearly from an initial assurance that the bombing was the result of police pressure on Bourdin, to a fairly consistent statement that Bourdin's attack was premeditated. Initially reassuring frightened readers of their safety in the hands of efficient police surveillance, the paper quickly found it more productive to suggest a governmental incompetence against a politically "educated" antagonist. By the time the paper makes an explicit connection between the bombing and the Prime Meridian Conference it has well refuted any alternate hypotheses and fully earned the right to its claim for a consistent view of premeditated attack.

6. See Norman Sherry and David Mulry for Conrad's reliance on the news coverage of the Bourdin bombing.

7. Coverage in the *Times* of the Prime Meridian Conference begins on October 2, 1884, with a lengthy description of the need for a global meridian and continues sporadically until the 22nd. French resistance to Greenwich was highlighted in reports on October 4, 8, 9, 11, 14, 15, and 16. The report on the 15th describes the response of the American press to the "puerile" arguments of the French delegates.

8. For example, the *Times* reported on anarchist papers seized in Brussels (February 21, 1894), trials of anarchists in Vienna (February 20) , a raid on an anarchist lodging in Cincinnati (February 20), and the arrest of anarchists in northern Austria carrying papers in French, Turkish, and Hungarian (February 22). Other examples include a report on a bomb in a Glasgow post office (February 20) and a description of a "large and well-organized Anarchist club" in Copenhagen (February 24).

9. London *Times*, February 18, 1894.

10. In suggesting that Conrad's text is engaged with alterity and imperialism I am sensitive to the fact that alterity in *The Secret Agent* is staunchly European rather than colonial (as was the laundry list of resident anarchists in the Autonomie Club). Yet although the novel refuses to narrate the encounter between colonizer and colonized (an encounter that preoccupies much of the rest of Conrad's oeuvre), this does not necessarily suggest that it is blind to the imperial function of Greenwich. As Fredric Jameson suggests in "Modernism and Imperialism" the term *imperialism* from 1884 to 1914 connoted relationships between First World powers rather than between First and Third Worlds. This intra-imperial rivalry "tended to repress the more basic axis of otherness, and to raise issues of colonial reality only incidentally" (48). As Jennifer Wenzel helpfully pointed out during the question and answer session of a panel at MLA (December 27, 2007, Chicago), alterity in *The Secret Agent* seems "longitudinal rather than latitudinal."

11. John G. Peters productively distinguishes between a range of temporal representations in Conrad's work (cyclical, regularized, private, anarchical). He schematically groups each of these temporal systems within three larger categories, which he labels "human," "mechanical," and "narrative" (86–122).

12. In this sense Conrad would have agreed with the argument of the superintendent of the U.S. Naval Observatory in 1881, John Rodgers, whose protest against standard time highlighted its usurpation of the sun's authority: "The Sun is the national clock used by many, and its position regulates the hour of rising, eating, working, and of going to rest. No other clock can supersede it, as it is the one ordained by Nature to regulate man's life" (Galison 122).

13. See, for example, Sharon Stockton's reading of Virginia Woolf and her claim that a "hallmark" of modernism was that "the individual consciousness was inherently detached from public reality . . . brought closer to universal 'truth' by his or her removal from shared space and time" (95).

14. See Whitworth, *Einstein's Wake* (58–82). Alex Houen has also written on the second law of thermodynamics and *The Secret Agent,* arguing that "images of thermodynamics" are "intrinsic" to the text's treatment of "stability and transformation" (999). In the dynamite novels of the late nineteenth century, Houen writes, the terrorist was often figured as a "renegade scientist," suggesting the extent to which the general public found "the social ramifications of thermodynamics" troubling (998).

15. Conrad's depiction of "darkest London" has attracted a great deal of productive critical attention, particularly in the essay collection *Conrad's Cities,* edited by Gene M. Moore. Robert Hampson, in his contribution to that collection, discusses the implicit mapping strategies Conrad brings to bear on metropolitan space in *The Secret Agent.* Beginning with clearly identifiable, specific places and names, the narrative gradually "shades from specificities to indeterminacies," ultimately conveying a city that, like the colonies, is "anonymous and unknown" (169). For Daphna Erdinast-Vulcan London is the organizing chronotope of the novel, which Conrad "sets out to destroy" over the course of the text, ceaselessly ironizing the city's function as a "shaping medium for human destiny" (213).

16. The connection between Winnie and a colonized subject has been made by Bev Soane, who argues that Winnie's domestic space is "a little 'colony' operating on the same principles governing actual colonies and subordinating them to imperial power" (46).

17. See Conrad, *Last Essays,* 1–17. Conrad criticizes the "geometric" rationality explicitly associated with longitudinal calculation. Geometry and geography, he argues, embody opposed principles of global conception. What is objectionable about geometry, he claims, is that it imposes a mathematical precision onto the mass of the Earth's features. It treats the Earth as if it were "a figure in a treatise on conical sections" (1). Favoring "trigonometrical surveys" and ludicrous notions of a mathematical "balancing of continents," the geometry taught him in his youth gave him only an "abstract formal" knowledge of, for instance, the poles, which for the geometer are "mere imaginary ends of

the imaginary axis upon which the earth turns" (17). Geography, in contrast, eschews theoretical purity and mathematical precision for what Conrad sees as the experiential, bodily explorations of adventurers who set out without preconceived notions, obeying only their own tactile impressions. The "accurate operations" of geometry, Conrad writes, "can never have for us the fascination of the first hazardous steps of a venturesome, often lonely explorer jotting down by the light of the camp fire the thoughts, the impression, and the toil of the day" (10). "The earth is a stage," but the "exact configuration" of that stage is far less important than "the drama of human endeavor that will be the thing" (2).

In a long excursus on the explorer Abel Tasman, Conrad explicitly links his critique of the precision of geometry to the spatial certitude of longitudinal orientation. Tasman's "problem" was, for historians, precisely his lack of longitudinal precision: "The early navigators had no means of ascertaining their exact position on the globe. They could calculate their latitude, but the problem of longitude was a matter which bewildered their minds and often falsified their judgment. It had to be a matter of pure guess-work. Tasman and his officers . . . did not know where any of the problematic places named in their instructions were, neither did they know where they themselves were" (10).

For Conrad, though, Tasman remains the consummate explorer who, despite (or even because of) his ignorance of the longitude, "discovered the island by which his name lives on the charts, took first contact with New Zealand (which was not seen again till one hundred and thirty years afterwards), sailed over many thousands of miles of uncharted seas, bringing back with him a journal which was of much value afterwards for his exploring successors" (11).

In Conrad's terms Tasman was a deficient geometer but a master geographer. As a geographer he is credited with propagating a benevolent colonialism in his "discovery" of New Zealand, "which is now the home of a very young commonwealth with all the possibilities of material and intellectual splendour still hidden in its future" (13). The great geographers founded noble imperial projects such as "commonwealths," a term suggesting a union with empire based on limited sovereignty and cultural difference. Geography, though the product of the confused, sometimes arrogant explorers in the wilderness, ultimately reaches outward to the corners of the globe in an imperial beneficence. Geometry, on the other hand, while purely objective and analytic, becomes ultimately a kind of blindness, a trope we see Conrad use in *The Secret Agent* when describing the characters of Sir Ethelred and Comrade Ossipon.

18. See Said, "Two Visions in *Heart of Darkness*," in *Culture and Imperialism*, 19–31.

19. Postcolonial readings of Joyce more generally have depended on a reevaluation of his attitude toward the politics of Irish nationalism, a project pursued by Emer Nolan and Len Platt. As Joseph Brooker writes in his recent overview of Joyce scholarship, challenges to the assertion that Joyce had no "genuine interest" in the "political present and future" of Dublin have been a "remarkably recent development" (219). Brooker marks the publication of Attridge and Howes's essay collection *Semicolonial Joyce* as a sign of the official "institutionalization" of postcolonialism in Joyce studies.

20. In his chapter "Colonial War and Mental Disorders" Fanon writes that for the colonized, "living does not mean embodying a set of values, does not mean integrating oneself into the coherent, constructive development of a world" (232). In *Orientalism* Edward Said writes that the "editing" of the Orient involves, in part, the reduction and domestication of the "eccentricities of Oriental life, with its odd calendars, its exotic spatial configurations, its hopelessly strange languages" (166).

21. In this episode, Trevor Williams writes, Joyce, though "no Marxist," demonstrates his ability "to represent the effects of alienated labor on the human body and mind" in his sustained engagement with the politics of consumption (172).

22. It is primarily Bergsonian readings of Joyce that tend toward this kind of dichotomy between a private interior temporality and a shared public space. See, as a founding text in this tradition, Shiv Kumar's *Bergson and the Stream of Consciousness Novel*.

23. Richard Begam similarly argues that Joyce's brand of modernism "deconstructs modernism's own universalist impulses" by using the familiar stream of consciousness and mythic methods to undermine "transcultural aspirations" (Begam 186).

24. Either Bloom is incorrect or Joyce is engaging in a historical anachronism. According to Patrick A. Wayman, Dunsink Observatory officials had resisted pressure (beginning in 1885) to set the Ballast Office time ball to Greenwich time because of its recognition of the "public's habit, when happening to pass over Carlisle (O'Connell) Bridge at 1 p.m., of checking their watch by the fall of the Time Ball." It was during the year 1914, not 1904, that the time ball began dropping at Greenwich time, only two years before the legal conversion of all Ireland to Greenwich time (138). See also Deborah Warner, "The Ballast Office Time-Ball and the Subjectivity of Time and Space."

25. Robert Ball, in his capacity as Andrews Professor of Astronomy at Dunsink Observatory, had resisted pressures by the principal officer of the Board of Trade and the harbor master in 1885 to set the ball to Greenwich time, arguing that "the time of Ireland has always been understood to mean the time of Dunsink" and that the control of the ball should thus remain with the Dunsink Observatory (Wayman 138). I have been unable to establish the extent to which Ball's objections were publicly known.

26. See Fleming, "Uniform Non-local Time," and Galison (153–55) for a discussion of Janssen's advocacy of the decimalization of time.

27. See, in particular, Whitworth, "Woolf's Web."

28. See, for example, Kenner, *A Sinking Island*, 179.

29. See, especially, Ricoeur, 2:101–12.

30. Phillips more generally presents Woolf's feminism as implicitly antiimperial, with patriarchy and empire mutually reinforcing one another. Other critics have been more circumspect in affirming Woolf's empathy for the colonized. *The Voyage Out* (1915), with its depiction of a reciprocal and mutually unsettling gaze between English tourists and South American women, has been the key text in examinations of Woolf's complex Orientalism. See, for example,

Cliff and Harwood on *The Voyage Out,* and Crawford on Orientalism in the character of Elizabeth Dalloway.

31. John Marx makes a similar argument in his reading of the novel. Clarissa uses Big Ben's chimes "as a guide," Marx writes: "They spark reflection about her capacity to organize the city" (182).

32. Clarissa's blush is of course homoerotically charged in its association with Sally Seton and with "yielding to the charm of a woman," in contrast to the sterile homogeneity of her heterosexual relationships with Richard and Peter. By evoking this passage in the context of standard time I do not mean to undercut its association of homoeroticism and creativity, but rather to suggest that for Woolf sexuality, female intimacy, and creativity are all intertwined in resistance to the kinds of rigidly standardized systems of power that I have been identifying. On the homoeroticism of this passage, see, for instance, Harrison, 292–99.

33. See I. Adam and Tiffin, ix, and also P. Williams's critique of their argument in "Simultaneous Uncontemporaneities," 25.

34. The cross-cultural potential of modernism's stylistic codes in the former colonies has recently been championed by Jahan Ramazani, who argues that the modernism of Christopher Okigbo, Kamau Braithwaite, or Agha Shahid Ali suggests that modernism is a "multifaceted and mutable resource, amenable to different localizing strategies and syntheses" (298).

CHAPTER 5

1. This tendency toward hyperbolic, quasi-mystical affirmations of postcolonial temporality celebrates the local, the heterogeneous, and the idiosyncratic: all of the details and textures that cannot be accounted for by the narratives of nation or history. Thus for Trinh T. Minh-ha time and space in a "remote village meeting" are not exterior forces, but are "built on infinitude" (1). "Headless and bottomless," postcolonial time embodies a truth that is "outside specific time, outside specialized space," and thus in between all "regimes of truth" (121). Dipesh Chakrabarty, borrowing from Heidegger, argues for a hermeneutic analysis of time that demonstrates a "loving grasp of detail" (18) in its celebration of "the temporal heterogeneity of the 'now'" (243). In contrast to this hermeneutic treatment of time, the Eurocentric analytic tradition, according to Chakrabarty, "evacuates the local by assimilating it to some abstract universal" (18). For Homi K. Bhabha the contrasting terms are "performative" and "pedagogical" rather than "hermeneutic" and "analytic," but the contrast remains the same. Whereas pedagogical time is "continuous" and "accumulative," the performative time of the postcolonial is "an insurgent act of cultural translation" (7), which is repetitive and recursive, refusing to fit neatly within nationalist narratives, remaining stubbornly and ecstatically "betwixt and between times and places" (158).

2. Timothy Brennan in *Wars of Position* labels this move toward ontology in postcolonial theory "the Heideggerian turn," a tendency that "floods postcolonial writing" and is characterized as a "highly structured discourse of authenticity, counter-Enlightenment, and sensuous 'peasant' consciousness

'thrown into' the world" (258). Largely informed by Bhabha's influential study of time in his essay "Dissemination," studies of ineffable postcolonial temporal difference have often explored the ways the pluralism and nonsynchronicity of the postcolonial have frustrated the narrative of the nation, characterized by homogeneous, empty time and a rational imperative to synchronize all human activity to Western clocks and calendars. In her essay "Temporality and Postcolonial Critique," however, Keya Ganguly challenges Bhabha's approach as merely a resurrection of an older discourse of "alterity" and "nativism," staged at the expense of any conversation about collective temporal experience across cultures. Ganguly accuses this strain within postcolonial theory of denying a common temporal experience, just as Johannes Fabian in the early 1980s accused structuralist anthropologists of denying "coevalness" in their construction of bordered cultural enclaves. As Ganguly argues, the very emphasis on time consciousness that enables Bhabha's critical interventions is itself borrowed from Kantian theory and other "philosophical and theoretical sources . . . not in themselves specifically of postcolonial provenance" (162). Grafting any notion of political praxis onto the postmodern philosophical assault on History, Reason, and Telos (an assault that, within the humanities at least, has itself become a tired master narrative), this tendency within postcolonial theory arguably blunts any uniquely critical edge it might bring to bear on contemporary colonial structures. Assaulting the "habits of mind and practice" that narrate the notion of the Other, colonial discourse analysis has tended to show, as Benita Parry argues, an "incuriosity about . . . enabling socio-economic and political institutions and other forms of social praxis" ("Problems in Current Theories," 43). Ganguly similarly argues that labeling "the rhetoric of otherness" the "main culprit" inevitably leads to an inattentiveness to the "material appetites of an emergent European bourgeoisie" with its attendant "imperial ambitions and sense of civilizational supremacy" (166).

3. R. D. Oldham, a geological surveyor, made the first attempt at civil time reform in India through the authority of the Asiatic Society of Bengal, which then proposed the reform to the governor-general. Despite the relatively low use of rails for passenger transport at the time (the English citizen in 1914 averaged roughly 27 railway trips a year, while in India the average was 1.4 [Westwood 84]), Oldham followed standard time architect Sandford Fleming's general rhetorical outline, beginning with accusations of the "barbarous" and uncivilized use of sundials and moving immediately to that hypothetical average traveler who had to alter his watch by a complex arithmetical sum. Oldham advocated Greenwich as a neutral time compared to that of Madras, Bombay, or Calcutta, each of which would cling jealously to its role as *"primus in Indus"* (Oldham 50). India's conversion to the Greenwich-based system was imminent, Oldham argued, as "the Indian railway system must inevitably become linked up, as has already happened to the telegraph system, with the railways of Europe and Western Asia on the one hand, and of the far East on the other" (52). The integration of India into a world system of transport and communication was at issue in time reform, and Oldham used a hypothetical "merchant in his office" to illustrate its desirability: "The merchant in his office, receiving a telegram from London, would know by a glance at his watch, exactly 6 hours fast of

Greenwich, how long the telegram had taken in transit. If it were from Berlin or Rome the difference in time would be five; if from New York, ten hours. The shipmaster in Hooghly, seeing the time-ball drop, would know that it was exactly 7 A.M. by Greenwich time, and determine the error of his chronometer at a glance, and without any need for calculation" (53).

The Society put Oldham's recommendations before the governor-general in May and received a reply in November: "The Government of India have come to the conclusion that the time has not yet arrived for action." Enforcing a standard time in "places like Bombay, Calcutta, Karachi, or Rangoon" would be immensely difficult, and "if it is not enforced in such places, it is not worth while enforcing it in such other places of minor importance as use the local time for other than railway time" (Oldham 111). On his receipt of the letter Oldham resigned his seat on the council of the Asiatic Society, presumably moving on to another outlet for the campaign. Even the Society had anticipated in its recommendations resistance to time reform at the major ports of Calcutta, Bombay, and Madras, where three independent astronomical observatories maintained discrepant time signals for rating chronometers. Given the structure of commercial transport in India, it was the ports that mattered most, and if the ports resisted the government saw no need to interfere.

By July 1905, though, the government had been sufficiently pressured to order the substitution of Greenwich for Madras time on all railways and telegraph offices. Again the seaports were considered exempt, as the *Times* reported: "In inland places it has been found convenient to generally follow railway time; but the great seaports of Calcutta, Bombay, and Karachi have followed the local time of their respective longitudes. The Government of India do not prescribe the new standard for these and other places following local time, as it is deemed desirable to leave the ultimate decision to local opinion" ("Standard Time in India," London *Times,* June 21, 1905).

It did not take long, however, for the seaports to follow suit. Bombay, expected to hold out the longest, adopted standard time only five months later, after a great deal of publicized debate in December. The reform went into effect in Bombay on January 1, 1906. By that date all of India had a uniform Greenwich-based civil time, with the exception of Calcutta (Howse 154).

4. In regard to Venkataramani, C.L. Khatri similarly argues that his work was not romantic, but "futuristic" in its realization of "a sense of the timeless as well as the temporal" (31–32).

5. See Ahmad's chapter "Indian Literature: Notes towards the Definition of a Category," in *In Theory,* 243–85.

6. On the "East-West encounter" in Indian fiction in English, see Mukherjee, 65–98.

7. For a discussion of the Indian railways and indentured railway workers at this time, see Metcalf and Metcalf, 126–31.

8. I am aware that the "art of dying" has a profound spiritual and philosophical significance in Vedantic belief and by no means wish to suggest that it or other Vedantic ideals are inherently politically reactionary. The art of dying signifies for Vedanta an orientation toward death that embraces its inevitability, actively intensifies spiritual life, and purifies mind, body, and ego. See Brah-

maprana, "Vedanta," for the application of this belief to the healing profession. My comments on the art of dying should be understood as strictly restricted to Ghosh's novel, in which Vedantic belief is explicitly used to justify a political capitulation to foreign rule. This is not to suggest that the art of dying, like the concept of karma itself, might not alternatively be mobilized in a stridently anti-imperialist discourse. See Josna E. Rege's *Colonial Karma,* for example.

9. See Brennan, *At Home in the World,* for a study of the discourse of cosmopolitanism and its relationship to political commitment.

10. Tara Sethia argues that in India in particular the imperial control of railway operation "frustrated industrial development and led to uneven economic growth of the Indian subcontinent" (103).

11. The major writers of "Gandhi literature" include, in addition to Venkataramani, Dhan Ghopal Mukerjee and K. Nagarajan. See Sharma, 75–123; Iyengar, 222–40.

CONCLUSION

1. My study of modernism clearly owes much, in this regard, to Jürgen Habermas's study of "modernity" in *The Philosophical Discourse of Modernity.* Just as Habermas argued that the central project of modernity—its reconciliation of subjectivity with the exterior world—remains a pressing problem, despite the Nietzschean (or Derridean, or Foucauldian) disavowals of the entire project, so my analysis of modernism as an aesthetic practice suggests that an unresolved project of temporal politics has been disavowed rather than extended in subsequent literary developments.

2. The master center is in Colorado Springs, and the other four are spaced at roughly equal intervals across the globe at sites controlled by the United States (Hawaii, Ascension Island, Diego Garcia in the Indian Ocean, and the Kwajalein Atoll in the western Pacific).

3. James Gleick, "A Switch in Time," *New York Times,* December 31, 1995, SM14.

4. I am thinking here not only of Deleuze and Guattari's "nomad" or "smooth" spaces in *A Thousand Plateaus,* but also of the influential heirs of their theories, Michael Hardt and Antonio Negri, in *Empire.*

5. As Timothy Brennan has demonstrated, arguments for the withering away of the nation-state perhaps surprisingly unite leftist humanities discourse with corporate and management practices, a trend culminating in Hardt and Negri's *Empire.* See Brennan, *Wars of Position.* Hardt and Negri's claims that empire is nationless have been challenged in a number of book-length studies, including Ellen Wood's *Empire of Capital.*

6. On the Galileo-GPS conflict, see Amodeo, "Satellites on Collision Course." Javier Benedicto, project manager of Galileo, has boasted that the European system "will provide an accuracy around one order of magnitude better than current open service GPS" ("Galileo and GPS Systems to Work Together," May 13, 2008, www.techworld.com/news/index.cfm?rss&newsid=101485). To allay U.S. fears the European Union has issued a cooperation agreement ensuring interoperability between GPS and Galileo. Russia and China are currently

developing their own alternatives to GPS. (Russia's Glonass and China's Beidou satellite networks are in preliminary development stages.)

7. "Statement by the President regarding the United States' decision to stop degrading global positioning system accuracy," The White House, Office of the Press Secretary, May 1, 2000.

8. The appropriation of positioning technology threatened by Galileo has also marked the legal disputes of disadvantaged North American communities. In her book on the Geographic Information System (GIS), a computer mapping technology that uses GPS for cartography, Karen Piper demonstrates how the Inuit and other First Nations of Quebec have appropriated GIS to fight the theft of their lands: "GIS was designed for the exploitative takeover of indigenous lands, the erasure of their history, and the occupation of the North. This became a way for Canada to manifest its sovereignty in areas that were 'scarcely' occupied, thus denying native sovereignty . . . but today First Nations are taking the maps back" (152).

While organizations like the Aboriginal Mapping Network share GIS information with Inuit so that they can "make their demands in a way that the courts understand," surveyors in Canada "have lobbied against the training of First Nations communities in GIS and GPS technology. The struggle over who has the rights to map land continues, whether it is by U.S. satellite, Hydro-Quebec, or Algonquin elders" (152). The Inuit's contest over space is not a quasi-mystical celebration of deterritorialized tundra in which, as in Deleuze and Guattari's schizoid evocation, sea and sky meld. Rather these "nomads" produced cartographic reproductions of space almost as accurate as any that could be produced with the best GPS-based cartography, as Piper demonstrates.

9. In his 1997 afterword to the English translation of *The Constitution of Time* Negri rejects these terms as too "aesthetic" and "ethical" for his present tastes (131), but the language of *Empire* does little to alter the basic impulse behind this terminology.

Bibliography

Adam, Barbara. "The Gendered Time Politics of Globalization: Of Shadowlands and Elusive Justice." *Feminist Review* 70 (Spring 2002): 3–30.
———. *Time and Social Theory*. Philadelphia: Temple University Press, 1990.
———. *Timescapes of Modernity: The Environment and Invisible Hazards*. London: Routledge, 1998.
———. *Timewatch: The Social Analysis of Time*. Cambridge, UK: Polity Press, 1995.
Adam, Ian, and Helen Tiffin. *Past the Last Post: Theorizing Post-colonialism and Post-modernism*. Calgary: University of Calgary Press, 1990.
Ahmad, Aijaz. *In Theory: Classes, Nations, Literatures*. London: Verso, 1992.
Allen, W. F. "The Reformation in Time-Keeping." *Popular Science Monthly* 26 (1885): 145–52.
Althusser, Louis, and Etienne Balibar. *Reading "Capital."* London: NLB, 1970.
Amis, Martin. *Time's Arrow*. New York: Vintage, 1991.
Amodeo, Christian. "Satellites on Collision Course." *Geographical* 76, no. 5 (May 2004): 12.
Anand, Mulk Raj. *Untouchable*. London: Penguin, 1935.
Anderson, Benedict. *Imagined Communities*. London: Verso, 1991.
Arata, Stephen. "The Occidental Tourist: Dracula and Reverse Colonization." *Victorian Studies* 33, no. 4 (1990): 621–45.
Ashcroft, Bill, Gareth Griffiths, and Helen Tiffin. *The Empire Writes Back: Theory and Practice in Post-Colonial Literatures*. London: Routledge, 1989.
Attridge, Derek, and Marjorie Howes, eds. *Semicolonial Joyce*. Cambridge: Cambridge University Press, 2000.
Auerbach, Nina. *Woman and the Demon: The Life of a Victorian Myth*. Cambridge, MA: Harvard University Press, 1982.

Awasthi, Aruna. *History and Development of Railways in India.* New Delhi: Deep & Deep Publications, 1994.
Ball, Robert S. *The Story of the Heavens.* London: Cassell, 1905.
Bartky, Ian R. *Selling the True Time: Nineteenth-century Timekeeping in America.* Stanford: Stanford University Press, 2000.
Bauer, Helen Pike. *Rudyard Kipling: A Study of the Short Fiction.* New York: Twayne, 1994.
Bauman, Zygmunt. *Globalization: The Human Consequences.* New York: Columbia University Press, 1998.
———. "Time and Space Reunited." *Time and Society* 9, nos. 2–3 (June 2000): 171–86.
Bayly, C. A. *Empire and Information: Intelligence Gathering and Social Communication in India, 1780–1870.* Cambridge: Cambridge University Press, 1996.
Begam, Richard. "Joyce's Trojan Horse: Ulysses and the Aesthetics of Decolonization." In *Modernism and Colonialism: British and Irish Literature, 1899–1939,* ed. Richard Begam and Michael Valdez Moses. Durham, NC: Duke University Press, 2007.
Begam, Richard, and Michael Valdez Moses, eds. *Modernism and Colonialism: British and Irish Literature, 1899–1939.* Durham, NC: Duke University Press, 2007.
Benjamin, Walter. *Illuminations.* New York: Schocken Books, 1968.
Bergson, Henri. *Duration and Simultaneity.* Indianapolis: Bobbs-Merrill, 1965.
———. *Time and Free Will.* New York: Humanities Press, 1971.
Bernstein, Stephen. "Politics, Modernity, and Domesticity: The Gothicism of Conrad's *The Secret Agent.*" *CLIO* 32, no. 3 (2003): 285–301.
Bhabha, Homi K. *The Location of Culture.* London: Routledge, 1994.
Bimber, Bruce. "Three Faces of Technological Determinism." In *Does Technology Drive History? The Dilemma of Technological Determinism,* ed. Merritt Roe Smith and Leo Marx. Cambridge, MA: MIT Press, 1994.
Bivona, Daniel. *Desire and Contradiction: Imperial Visions and Domestic Debate in Victorian Literature.* Manchester, UK: Manchester University Press, 1990.
Blair, Sara. "Local Modernity, Global Modernism: Bloomsbury and the Places of the Literary." *ELH* 71 (2004): 813–38.
Blaise, Clark. *Time Lord: Sir Sandford Fleming and the Creation of Standard Time.* New York: Pantheon Books, 2000.
Bloch, Ernst. *Heritage of Our Times.* Berkeley: University of California Press, 1991.
Booker, M. Keith. *Ulysses, Capitalism and Colonialism: Reading Joyce after the Cold War.* Westport, CT: Greenwood Press, 2000.
Booth, Howard J., and Nigel Rigby, eds. *Modernism and Empire.* Manchester, UK: Manchester University Press, 2000.
Bourdieu, Pierre. "Time Perspectives of the Kabyle." In *The Sociology of Time,* ed. John Hassard. New York: St. Martin's Press, 1990.
———. "Uniting to Better Dominate." *Items and Issues* 2, nos. 3–4 (2001): 1–6.

Brahmaprana, Pravrajika. "Vedanta: Death and the Art of Dying." *Cross Currents* 51, no. 3 (2001): 337–46.
Brantlinger, Patrick. *Rule of Darkness : British Literature and Imperialism, 1830–1914*. Ithaca, NY: Cornell University Press, 1988.
Brennan, Timothy. *At Home in the World: Cosmopolitanism Now*. Cambridge, MA: Harvard University Press, 1997.
———. *Wars of Position: The Cultural Politics of Left and Right*. New York: Columbia University Press, 2006.
Brooker, Joseph. *Joyce's Critics: Transitions in Reading and Culture*. Madison: University of Wisconsin Press, 2004.
Burpee, Lawrence. *Sandford Fleming: Empire Builder*. London: Oxford University Press, 1915.
Callinicos, Alex. *Social Theory: A Historical Introduction*. Cambridge, UK: Polity Press, 1999.
Cantor, Paul A., and Peter Hufnagel. "The Empire of the Future: Imperialism and Modernism in H.G. Wells." *Studies in the Novel* 38, no. 1 (2006): 36–56.
Castells, Manuel. *The Rise of the Network Society*. Oxford: Blackwell, 2000.
Chakrabarty, Dipesh. *Provincializing Europe: Postcolonial Thought and Historical Difference*. Princeton: Princeton University Press, 2000.
Chatterjee, Partha. "Anderson's Utopia." *diacritics* 29, no. 4 (1999): 128–34.
Cheng, Vincent J. *Joyce, Race, and Empire*. New York: Cambridge University Press, 1995.
Christie, W.H.M. "Universal Time." *Popular Science Monthly* 29 (1886): 796–802.
Chu, Patricia E. *Race, Nationalism, and the State in British and American Modernism*. Cambridge: Cambridge University Press, 2007.
Church, Margaret. *Time and Reality: Studies in Contemporary Fiction*. Chapel Hill: University of North Carolina Press, 1963.
Cliff, Michelle. "Virginia Woolf and the Imperial Gaze: A Glance Askew." In *Virginia Woolf: Emerging Perspectives*, ed. Mark Hussey. New York: Pace, 1994.
Cohen, Scott. "The Empire from the Street: Virginia Woolf, Wembley, and Imperial Monuments." *Modern Fiction Studies* 50, no. 1 (2004): 85–109.
Conan Doyle, Arthur. *The Valley of Fear*. New York: George H. Doran, 1914.
Conrad, Joseph. *Heart of Darkness and Other Tales*. New York: Oxford University Press, 1990.
———. "Karain." In *Tales of Unrest*. Garden City, NY: Doubleday, 1923.
———. *Last Essays*. London: J.M. Dent, 1926.
———. *Lord Jim: Authoritative Text, Backgrounds, Sources, Criticism*. New York: Norton, 1996.
———. *The Secret Agent: A Simple Tale*. Cambridge: Cambridge University Press, 1990.
———. *Three Plays: Laughing Ann, One Day More, and The Secret Agent*. London: Methuen, 1934.
Coroneos, Con. *Space, Conrad, and Modernity*. New York: Oxford University Press, 2002.

Crawford, Nicholas. "Orientalizing Elizabeth: Empire and Deviancy in *Mrs. Dalloway*." *Virginia Woolf Miscellany* 70, no. 20 (2006): 25–26.
Cwerner, Saulo. "The Chronopolitan Ideal: Time, Belonging, and Globalization." *Time and Society* 9, nos. 2–3 (2000): 331–46.
Daly, Nicholas. *Literature, Technology, and Modernity, 1860–2000*. Cambridge: Cambridge University Press, 2004.
———. *Modernism, Romance, and the Fin de siècle: Popular Fiction and British Culture, 1880–1914*. New York: Cambridge University Press, 1999.
Danius, Sara. *The Senses of Modernism: Technology, Perception, and Aesthetics*. Ithaca, NY: Cornell University Press, 2002.
Davis, Alex, and Lee M. Jenkins, eds. *Locations of Literary Modernism: Region and Nation in British and American Modernist Poetry*. New York: Cambridge University Press, 2000.
Debord, Guy. *The Society of the Spectacle*. New York: Zone Books, 1994.
De Carle, Donald. *British Time*. London: Lockwood, 1947.
Deleuze, Gilles, and Félix Guattari. *A Thousand Plateaus: Capitalism and Schizophrenia*. London: Athlone Press, 1988.
DiBernard, Barbara. "Parallax as Parallel, Paradigm, and Paradox in *Ulysses*." *Eire-Ireland: A Journal of Irish Studies* 10, no. 1 (1975): 69–84.
Doane, Mary Anne. *The Emergence of Cinematic Time: Modernity, Contingency, the Archive*. Cambridge, MA: Harvard University Press, 2002.
Duffy, Enda. *The Subaltern Ulysses*. Minneapolis: University of Minnesota Press, 1994.
Eagleton, Terry. *Exiles and Émigrés: Studies in Modern Literature*. New York: Schocken Books, 1970.
Edmond, Rod. "Home and Away: Degeneration in Imperialist and Modernist Discourse." In *Modernism and Empire*, ed. Howard J. Booth and Nigel Rigby. Manchester, UK: Manchester University Press, 2000.
Eliot, George. *Felix Holt, the Radical*. London: Penguin Books, 1995.
Engler, Edmund. "Time-Keeping in Paris." *Popular Science Monthly* 20 (1882): 304–12.
Erdinast-Vulcan, Daphna. "'Sudden Holes in Space and Time': Conrad's Anarchist Aesthetics in *The Secret Agent*." In *Conrad's Cities*, ed. Gene M. Moore. Amsterdam: Rodopi, 1992.
Esty, Jed. "The Colonial Bildungsroman: *The Story of an African Farm* and the Ghost of Goethe." *Victorian Studies* 49, no. 3 (2007): 407–30.
———. *A Shrinking Island: Modernism and National Culture in England*. Princeton: Princeton University Press, 2004.
———. "Virginia Woolf's Colony and the Adolescence of Modernist Fiction." In *Modernism and Colonialism: British and Irish Literature, 1899–1939*, ed. Richard Begam and Michael Valdez Moses. Durham, NC: Duke University Press, 2007.
Eysteinsson, Astradur. *The Concept of Modernism*. Ithaca, NY: Cornell University Press, 1992.
Fabian, Johannes. *Time and the Other: How Anthropology Makes Its Object*. New York: Columbia University Press, 1983.
Fanon, Frantz. *The Wretched of the Earth*. New York: Grove Press, 1963.

Fleming, Sandford. "Longitude and Time-Reckoning." In *Papers on Time-Reckoning from the Proceedings of the Canadian Institute, Toronto,* vol. 1. Toronto: Copp, Clark, 1879.
———. "Time-Reckoning for the Twentieth Century." In *Annual Report of the Board of Regents of the Smithsonian Institution (1886).* Washington, DC: Government Printing Office, 1889.
———. "Uniform Non-local Time (Terrestrial Time)." 1800. Reprint, Ottawa: Canadian Institute of Historical Microreproductions, 1980.
Fox, Susan Hudson. "Woolf's Austen/Boston Tea Party: The Revolt against Literary Empire in Night and Day." In *Virginia Woolf: Emerging Perspectives,* ed. Mark Hussey. New York: Pace, 1994.
Froula, Christine. *Virginia Woolf and the Bloomsbury Avant-garde: War, Civilization, Modernity.* New York: Columbia University Press, 2005.
Gadgil, D.R. *The Industrial Evolution of India in Recent Times.* London: Oxford University Press, 1924.
Galison, Peter. *Einstein's Clocks, Poincaré's Maps: Empires of Time.* New York: Norton, 2003.
Gandhi, Mohandas K. *Hind Swaraj and Other Writings.* Cambridge: Cambridge University Press, 1997.
Ganguly, Keya. "Temporality and Postcolonial Critique." In *The Cambridge Companion to Postcolonial Literary Studies,* ed. Neil Lazarus. Cambridge: Cambridge University Press, 2004.
Gąsiorek, Andrzej. "War, 'Primitivism,' and the Future of 'the West': Reflections on D.H. Lawrence and Wyndham Lewis." In *Modernism and Colonialism: British and Irish Literature, 1899–1939,* ed. Richard Begam and Michael Valdez Moses. Durham, NC: Duke University Press, 2007.
Ghosh, S.K. *The Prince of Destiny: The New Krishna.* London: Rebman, 1909.
Giddens, Anthony. *The Consequences of Modernity.* Stanford: Stanford University Press, 1990.
———. *The Constitution of Society: Outline of the Theory of Structuration.* Berkeley: University of California Press, 1984.
———. *Modernity and Self-Identity: Self and Society in the Late Modern Age.* Stanford: Stanford University Press, 1991.
Gillies, Mary Ann. *Henri Bergson and British Modernism.* Montreal: McGill-Queen's University Press, 1996.
Goldman, Jane. *Virginia Woolf: To the Lighthouse, The Waves. Columbia Critical Guide.* New York: Columbia University Press, 1998.
Griffin, Philip. "'X2': The Final Chapter of *Tono-Bungay.*" *Critical Survey* 13, no. 3 (2001): 78–88.
Habermas, Jürgen. *The Philosophical Discourse of Modernity.* Cambridge, MA: MIT Press, 1990.
Haggard, H. Rider. *King Solomon's Mines.* London: Cassell, 1885.
———. *She.* Oxford: Oxford University Press, 1991.
Hall, Stuart. *Modernity and Its Futures.* Cambridge, UK: Open University Press, 1992.
Hama, Mark. "Time as Power: The Politics of Social Time in Conrad's *The Secret Agent.*" *Conradiana* 32, no. 2 (2000): 123–43.

Hampson, Robert. "'Topographical Mysteries': Conrad and London." In *Conrad's Cities,* ed. Gene M. Moore. Amsterdam: Rodopi, 1992.

Hardt, Michael, and Antonio Negri. *Empire.* Cambridge, MA: Harvard University Press, 2001.

Hardy, Thomas. *Tess of the D'Urbervilles.* New York: Norton, 1965.

Harootunian, H. D. "Ghostly Comparisons: Anderson's Telescope." *diacritics* 29, no. 4 (1999): 135–49.

———. "Some Thoughts on Comparability and the Space-Time Problem." *boundary 2* 32, no. 2 (2005): 23–52.

Harris, Wilson. *History, Fable and Myth in the Caribbean and Guianas.* Georgetown, Guyana: National History and Arts Council, 1970.

Harrison, Susan. "Playing with Fire: Women's Sexuality and Artistry in Virginia Woolf's *Mrs. Dalloway* and Eudora Welty's *The Golden Apples.*" *Mississippi Quarterly* 56 (2003): 289–313.

Harvey, David. *The Condition of Postmodernity: An Enquiry into the Origins of Cultural Change.* Oxford: Blackwell, 1989.

Harwood, June. "Bloomsbury and the Literature of Empire: Virginia Woolf and Her Voyage Out." *Virginia Woolf Bulletin* 17 (2004): 27–34.

Henke, Suzette. "De/Colonizing the Subject in Virginia Woolf's *The Voyage Out*: Rachel Vinrace as La Mysterique." In *Virginia Woolf: Emerging Perspectives,* ed. Mark Hussey. New York: Pace, 1994.

Henry, Holly. *Virginia Woolf and the Discourse of Science: The Aesthetics of Astronomy.* Cambridge: Cambridge University Press, 2003.

Heusel, Barbara Stevens. "Parallax as a Metaphor for the Structure of Ulysses." *Studies in the Novel* 15, no. 2 (1983): 135–46.

Hobsbawm, Eric J. *The Age of Empire: 1875–1914.* New York: Pantheon Books, 1987.

Houen, Alex. "*The Secret Agent*: Anarchism and the Thermodynamics of Law." *ELH* 65 (1998): 995–1016.

Howse, Derek. *Greenwich Time and the Discovery of the Longitude.* Oxford: Oxford University Press, 1980.

Hutcheon, Linda. "The Post Always Rings Twice: The Postmodern and the Postcolonial." *Textual Practice* 8, no. 2 (1992): 205–38.

International Conference Held at Washington. For the Purpose of Fixing a Prime Meridian and a Universal Day. Washington, DC: Gibson Bros., 1884.

Iyengar, K. R. S. *Indian Writing in English.* New Delhi: Sterling, 1983.

James, C. L. R. *The Case for West-Indian Self Government.* London: Hogarth Press, 1933.

Jameson, Fredric. "Modernism and Imperialism." In *Nationalism, Colonialism, and Literature.* Minneapolis: University of Minnesota Press, 1990.

———. *The Prison-house of Language: A Critical Account of Structuralism and Russian Formalism.* Princeton: Princeton University Press, 1972.

Joyce, James. *Ulysses.* New York: Random House, 1961.

Kaplan, Caren. *Questions of Travel.* Durham, NC: Duke University Press, 1996.

Karlin, Daniel. Introduction to *Rudyard Kipling.* New York: Oxford University Press, 1999.

Kenner, Hugh. *A Sinking Island: The Modern English Writers.* New York: Knopf, 1988.
Kern, Stephen. *The Culture of Time and Space 1880–1918.* Cambridge, MA: Harvard University Press, 1983.
Kertzer, J.M. "Joseph Conrad and the Metaphysics of Time." *Studies in the Novel* 11 (1979): 302–17.
Khatri, C.L. *Indian Literature in English: Critical Discourses.* Jaipur: Book Enclave, 2003.
Kipling, Rudyard. *Kim: Authoritative Text, Backgrounds, Criticism.* New York: Norton, 2002.
———. *Plain Tales from the Hills.* London: Macmillan, 1960.
Kittler, Friedrich. *Discourse Networks 1800/1900.* Trans. Michael Metteer, with Chris Cullens. Stanford: Stanford University Press, 1990.
Kumar, Shiv. *Bergson and the Stream of Consciousness Novel.* London: Blackie, 1962.
Lawrence, D.H. *Women in Love.* London: Penguin, 1920.
Lefebvre, Henri. *The Critique of Everyday Life.* New York: Verso, 1991.
———. *Key Writings.* Ed. Stuart Elden and Elizabeth Lebas. London: Continuum, 2003.
———. *The Production of Space.* Oxford: Blackwell, 1991.
———. *Rhythmanalysis: Space, Time and Everyday Life.* London: Continuum, 2004.
Lewis, Pericles. *Modernism, Nationalism, and the Novel.* Cambridge: Cambridge University Press, 2000.
Lewis, Wyndham. *Time and Western Man.* Santa Rosa, CA: Black Sparrow Press, 1993.
Lukács, Georg. *The Historical Novel.* Lincoln: University of Nebraska Press, 1962.
———. *The Meaning of Contemporary Realism.* London: Merlin Press, 1963.
———. "Reification and the Consciousness of the Proletariat." In *History and Class Consciousness.* Cambridge, MA: MIT Press, 1971.
Lütticken, Sven. "Suspense and . . . Surprise." *New Left Review* 40 (2006): 95–109.
Malley, Shawn. " 'Time Hath No Power against Identity': Historical Continuity and Archaeological Adventure in H. Rider Haggard's *She.*" *English Literature in Transition* 40, no. 3 (1997): 275–97.
Marcus, Jane. "Britannia Rules *The Waves.*" In *Virginia Woolf: To the Lighthouse, The Waves. Columbia Critical Guide,* ed. Jane Goldman. New York: Columbia University Press, 1998.
Marx, John. *The Modernist Novel and the Decline of Empire.* Cambridge: Cambridge University Press, 2005.
Marx, Karl. *Capital: A Critique of Political Economy.* Vol. 1. Trans. Ben Fowkes. London: Penguin, 1990.
Matin, A. Michael. " 'We Aren't German Slaves Here, Thank God': Conrad's Transposed Nationalism and British Literature of Espionage and Invasion." *Journal of Modern Literature* 21, no. 2 (1997–98): 251–80.

Metcalf, Barbara D., and Thomas R. Metcalf. *A Concise History of Modern India*. Cambridge: Cambridge University Press, 2001.

Misa, Thomas J. "Retrieving Sociotechnical Change from Technological Determinism." In *Does Technology Drive History? The Dilemma of Technological Determinism*, ed. Merritt Roe Smith and Leo Marx. Cambridge, MA: MIT Press, 1994.

Monsman, Gerald. *H. Rider Haggard on the Imperial Frontier: The Political and Literary Contexts of His African Romances*. Greensboro, NC: ELT Press, 2006.

Moore-Gilbert, Bart. "Imagining Independent India: Japan as a Model for Indian Nationalism." *Journal of Commonwealth and Postcolonial Studies* 9, no. 2 (2002): 123–34.

Moorhouse, Geoffrey. *India Britannica*. Chicago: Academy Chicago Publishers, 1983.

Moses, Michael Valdez. "Disorientalism: Conrad and the Imperial Origins of Modernist Aesthetics." In *Modernism and Colonialism: British and Irish Literature, 1899–1939*, ed. Richard Begam and Michael Valdez Moses. Durham, NC: Duke University Press, 2007.

Mukherjee, Meenakshi. *The Twice Born Fiction: Themes and Techniques of the Indian Novel in English*. New Delhi: Arnold-Heinemann, 1971.

Mulry, David. "Popular Accounts of the Greenwich Bombing and Conrad's *The Secret Agent*." *Rocky Mountain Review of Language and Literature* 54, no. 2 (2000): 43–64.

Murphy, Patricia. *Time Is of the Essence: Temporality, Gender, and the New Woman*. Albany: State University of New York Press, 2001.

Negri, Antonio. *The Constitution of Time*. In *Time for Revolution*. London: Continuum, 2003.

Newton, Michael. "Four Notes on *The Secret Agent*: Sir William Harcourt, Ford and Helen Rossetti, Bourdin's Relations, and a Warning against Δ." In *The Secret Agent: Centennial Essays*, ed. Allan H. Simmons and J. H. Stape. Amsterdam: Rodopi, 2007.

Ngũgĩ wa Thiong'o. *Moving the Centre: The Struggle for Cultural Freedoms*. London: J. Currey, 1993.

———. *Petals of Blood*. New York: Penguin, 2002.

Noel, E. *International Time: A Scheme for Harmonising the Hour All the World Round*. Pamphlet. London: Edward Stanford, 1892.

Nolan, Emer. *James Joyce and Nationalism*. New York: Routledge, 1995.

Oldham, R. D. "On Time in India: A Suggestion for Its Improvement." In *Proceedings of the Asiatic Society of Bengal*. Calcutta: Asiatic Society, 1899.

Osborne, Peter. *The Politics of Time: Modernity and Avant-garde*. New York: Verso, 1995.

Pang, Alex Soojung-Kim. *Empire and the Sun: Victorian Solar Eclipse Expeditions*. Stanford: Stanford University Press, 2002.

Parkinson, Bradford, and James J. Spiker Jr., eds. *Global Positioning System: Theory and Application*. Vol. 1. Washington, DC: American Institute of Aeronautics and Astronautics, 1996.

Parry, Benita. *Conrad and Imperialism*. London: Macmillan, 1983.

———. "The Institutionalisation of Postcolonial Studies." In *The Cambridge Companion to Postcolonial Literary Studies,* ed. Neil Lazarus. Cambridge: Cambridge University Press, 2004.
———. "Problems in Current Theories of Colonial Discourse." *Oxford Literary Review* 9, no. 1–2 (1987): 27–58.
Partington, John S. "The Time Machine: A Polemic on the Inevitability of Working-class Liberation, and Plea for a Solution to Late-Victorian Capitalist Exploitation." *Cahiers Victoriens et Edouardiennes* 46 (1997): 167–79.
Peters, John G. *Conrad and Impressionism.* Cambridge : Cambridge University Press, 2001.
Phillips, Kathy J. *Virginia Woolf against Empire.* Knoxville: University of Tennessee Press, 1994.
Piazzi-Smyth, Charles. "Memorandum Requested by the Committee on Kosmic Time and Prime Meridian, appointed by the International Institute for Preserving and Perfecting Weights and Measures." *Sidereal Messenger* 2 (1884): 175–79.
Piper, Karen. *Cartographic Fictions: Maps, Race, and Identity.* New Brunswick, NJ: Rutgers University Press, 2002.
Platt, Len. *Joyce and the Anglo-Irish: A Study of Joyce and the Literary Revival.* Amsterdam: Rodopi, 1999.
Puchner, Martin. "The Aftershocks of *Blast*: Manifestos, Satire, and the Rear-Guard of Modernism." In *Bad Modernisms,* ed. Douglas Mao and Rebecca L. Walkowitz. Durham, NC: Duke University Press, 2006.
Quinones, Ricardo J. *Mapping Literary Modernism: Time and Development.* Princeton: Princeton University Press, 1985.
Ramazani, Jahan. "Modernist Bricolage, Postcolonial Hybridity." In *Modernism and Colonialism: British and Irish Literature, 1899–1939,* ed. Richard Begam and Michael Valdez Moses. Durham, NC: Duke University Press, 2007.
Rao, Raja. *Kanthapura.* London: New Directions, 1963.
Redfield, Marc. "Imagi-Nation: The Imagined Community and the Aesthetics of Mourning." *diacritics* 29, no. 4 (1999): 58–83.
Rege, Josna E. *Colonial Karma: Self, Action, and Nation in the Indian English Novel.* New York: Palgrave, 2004.
Ricoeur, Paul. *Time and Narrative.* 3 vols. Chicago: University of Chicago Press, 1984.
Rip, Michael Russell, and James Hasik. *The Precision Revolution: GPS and the Future of Aerial Warfare.* Annapolis, MD: Naval Institute Press, 2002.
Rosenfield, Claire. *Paradise of Snakes: An Archetypal Analysis of Conrad's Political Novels.* Chicago: University of Chicago Press, 1967.
Royde Smith, G. *The History of Bradshaw: A Centenary Review of the Origin and Growth of the Most Famous Guide in the World.* London: Henry Blacklock, 1939.
Rushdie, Salman. *Midnight's Children.* New York: Random House, 1981.
Said, Edward W. *Culture and Imperialism.* New York: Knopf, 1993.
———. *Orientalism.* New York: Vintage Books, 1979.

Schivelbusch, Wolfgang. *The Railway Journey: The Industrialization of Time and Space in the 19th Century.* Berkeley: University of California Press, 1986.
Schleifer, Ronald. *Modernism and Time: The Logic of Abundance in Literature, Science, and Culture, 1880–1930.* New York: Cambridge University Press, 2000.
Schotz, Myra Glazer. "Parallax in Ulysses." *Dalhousie Review* 59 (1979): 487–99.
Schwarz, Roberto. *Misplaced Ideas: Essays on Brazilian Culture.* London: Verso, 1992.
Sethia, Tara. "Railways, Raj, and the Indian States: Policy of Collaboration and Coercion in Hyderabad." In *Railway Imperialism,* ed. Clarence B. Davis and Kenneth E. Wilburn Jr. New York: Greenwood Press, 1991.
Sharma, Saroj. *Indian Elite and Nationalism: A Study of Indo-English Fiction.* Jaipur: Rawat Publications, 1997.
Sherry, Norman. "The Greenwich Bomb Outrage and *The Secret Agent.*" *Review of English Studies* 18, no. 72 (1967): 412–28.
Singh, Kushwant. *Train to Pakistan.* New York: Grove Press, 1956.
Smith, Merritt Roe. "Technological Determinism in American Culture." In *Does Technology Drive History? The Dilemma of Technological Determinism,* ed. Merritt Roe Smith and Leo Marx. Cambridge, MA: MIT Press, 1994.
Smith, Vincent A. *Oxford History of India.* London: Oxford University Press, 1958.
Soane, Bev. "The Colony at the Heart of Empire: Domestic Space in *The Secret Agent.*" *Conradiana* 30, no. 1 (2005): 46–58.
Sobel, Dava. *Longitude.* New York: Walker, 1995.
Sonn, Richard D. *Anarchism and Cultural Politics in fin de siècle France.* Lincoln: University of Nebraska Press, 1989.
Squillace, Robert. *Modernism, Modernity, and Arnold Bennett.* Lewisburg, PA: Bucknell University Press, 1997.
Stallman, R. W. *The Art of Joseph Conrad: A Critical Symposium.* East Lansing: Michigan State University Press, 1960.
Stanley, Henry Morton. *The Autobiography of Sir Henry Morton Stanley.* London: Adamant Media, 2005.
Stevenson, Randall. "Greenwich Meanings: Clocks and Things in Modernist and Postmodernist Fiction." *Yearbook of English Studies* 30 (2000): 124–36.
———. "A Narrow, Zigzag, and Secluded Path: Conrad, Clockwork, and the Politics of Modernism." In *Aspects of Modernism,* ed. Andreas Fischer, Martin Heusser, and Thomas Hermann. Tubingen: Narr, 1997.
Stewart, Susan. *On Longing: Narratives of the Miniature, the Gigantic, the Souvenir, the Collection.* Durham, NC: Duke University Press, 1993.
Stockton, Sharon. "Public Space and Private Time: Perspective in *To the Lighthouse* and in Einstein's Special Theory." *Essays in Arts and Sciences* 27 (1998): 95–115.
Stoker, Bram. *Dracula: Authoritative Text, Contexts, Reviews and Reactions, Dramatic and Film Variations, Criticism.* New York: Norton, 1997.

Suleri, Sara. *The Rhetoric of English India*. Chicago: University of Chicago Press, 1992.
Thompson, Edward. *The Other Side of the Medal*. London: Hogarth Press, 1926.
Thompson, E.P. "Time, Work-Discipline, and Industrial Capitalism." *Past and Present* 38 (1967): 56–97.
Trinh T. Minh-ha. *Woman, Native, Other: Writing Postcoloniality and Feminism*. Bloomington: Indiana University Press, 1989.
Trout, Steven. "Narratives of Encounter: H.G. Wells' *The Time Machine* and the Literature of Imperialism." *Journal of Commonwealth and Postcolonial Studies* 5, no. 1 (1997): 35–45.
Urry, John. *Sociology beyond Societies: Mobilities for the Twenty-first Century*. New York: Routledge, 2000.
Venkataramani, K.S. *Murugan, the Tiller*. London: Simpkin, Marshall, Hamilton, Kent, 1927.
Vonnegut, Kurt. *Slaughterhouse Five*. New York: Delta, 1969.
Warner, Deborah. "The Ballast-Office Time Ball and the Subjectivity of Time and Space." *James Joyce Quarterly* 4, no. 1 (1998): 861–64.
Wayman, Patrick A. *Dunsink Observatory, 1785–1985: A Bicentennial History*. Dublin: Dublin Institute, 1987.
Wells, H.G. *The Time Machine*. London: Charles E. Tuttle, 1995.
———. *Tono-Bungay*. London: Penguin Books, 1909.
Wesseling, H.L. *Divide and Rule: The Partition of Africa, 1880–1914*. Westport, CT: Praeger, 1996.
Westwood, J.N. *Railways of India*. London: David and Charles, 1974.
Wheeler, George M. *Report upon the Third International Geographical Congress and Exhibition at Venice, Italy, 1881*. Washington, DC: Government Printing Office, 1885.
Whitworth, Michael H. *Einstein's Wake: Relativity, Metaphor, and Modernist Literature*. Oxford: Oxford University Press, 2001.
———. "Woolf's Web: Telecommunications and Community." In *Virginia Woolf and Communities*, ed. Jeanette McVicker and Laura Davis. New York: Pace University Press, 1999.
Wicke, Jennifer. "The Same and the Different: Standards and Standardization in Thomas Hardy's *Tess of the D'Urbervilles*." In *Tess of the D'Urbervilles*, ed. John Paul Riquelme. New York: Palgrave, 1998.
———. "Vampiric Typewriting: *Dracula* and Its Media." In *Dracula*, ed. John Paul Riquelme. New York: Palgrave, 2002.
Williams, Patrick. "*Kim* and Orientalism." In *Kim*. New York: Norton, 2002.
———. "'Simultaneous Uncontemporaneities': Theorising Modernism and Empire." In *Modernism and Empire*, ed. Howard J. Booth and Nigel Rigby. Manchester, UK: Manchester University Press, 2000.
Williams, Raymond. *The Politics of Modernism: Against the New Conformists*. London: Verso, 1989.
Williams, Trevor. *Reading Joyce Politically*. Gainesville: University Press of Florida, 1997.

Wilson, Edmund. *Axel's Castle: A Study in the Imaginative Literature of 1870–1930.* New York: C. Scribner's Sons, 1931.
Wood, Andelys. "Walking the Web in the Lost London of *Mrs. Dalloway.*" *Mosaic* 36, no. 2 (2003): 19–31.
Wood, Ellen. *Empire of Capital.* New York: Verso, 2003.
Woolf, Leonard. *Empire and Commerce in Africa: A Study in Economic Imperialism.* London: Allen and Unwin, 1919.
———. *Imperialism and Civilization.* London: Hogarth Press, 1928.
Woolf, Virginia. *Mr. Bennett and Mrs. Brown.* London: Hogarth Press, 1928.
———. *Mrs. Dalloway.* New York: Harcourt, 1925.
———. *Night and Day.* London: Hogarth Press, 1960.
———. *Orlando: A Biography.* New York: Harcourt Brace Jovanovich, 1928.
———. *Virginia Woolf's "The Hours": The British Museum Manuscript of* Mrs. Dalloway. Ed. Helen M. Wussow. New York: Pace University Press, 1996.
———. *A Writer's Diary: Being Extracts from the Diary of Virginia Woolf.* New York: Harcourt, Brace, 1954.

COLLECTIONS CITED

Sandford Fleming Fonds, Library and Archives Canada, Ottawa.

Index

Abbot, J.J.C., 47, 48, 51
Aboriginal Mapping Network, 192n8
Abyssinia, 140
accumulation, flexible, 154, 156
Achebe, Chinua, *Arrow of God*, 172n7
Acts of Union (1707), 5
Acworth, William, 143
Adam, Barbara, 30, 174n27
Adam, Ian, 128
Adams, J.C., 41
aestheticism, 167; of Joyce, 68, 179n5; of Woolf, 123
aesthetics, 9, 14, 82, 192n9; antimodern, 154; modernist, 2, 4, 8, 12, 15–17, 54, 60, 66, 98, 128, 165, 169, 191n1; politics and, 54, 65, 73; postmodernist, 154, 155, 160, 165; space and, 76, 95, 155
Ahmad, Aijaz, 133
Ahmedabad, 143
Airy, George, 34
Algeria, 30
Ali, Agha Shahid, 188n34
Allen, W.F., 27, 35–36, 44, 175n6
Alvensleben, Baron H. von, 39
American Metrological Society, 35
American Railroad Association, 173n20
Amis, Martin, *Time's Arrow*, 160–61, 165–69
Amritsar massacre, 144
Anand, Mulk Raj, 132; *Untouchables*, 147

anarchists, 25, 102–4, 107, 111, 162, 163, 184n8, 184n10
Anderson, Benedict: *Imagined Communities*, 159; *The Spectre of Comparisons*, 159–60
Anglo-Catholicism, 62
Anglo-Indians, 93–96, 181n7
Anticosti Island, 50
Apollo 9 astronauts, 70–71
Arata, Stephen D., 180n3, 181n4
Arthur, Chester A., 28
Ashford, Charles W., 178n46
Asiatic Society of Bengal, 131, 189n3
Asquith, Henry, 104
atomic clocks, 157
Auerbach, Nina, 87
Auschwitz, 167–69
Australia, 49, 172n6
Austria-Hungary, 43
Autonomie Club, 104, 183n5, 184n10
Awasthi, Aruna, 143, 144

Ball, Robert, 115, 187n25
Bartky, Ian, 6, 36, 176n16, 176n19
Bauer, Helen Pike, 181n9
Bauman, Zygmunt, 1
Bayly, C.A., 144
Begam, Richard, 171n5, 178n2, 187n23
Belgium, 45
Benedicto, Javier, 191n6
Benjamin, Walter, 160, 169, 179n5

Bergson, Henri, 2, 8–12, 54–67, 73, 111, 130, 161, 163, 164, 173n17, 174n26, 187n22; *Duration and Simultaneity*, 58–59; *Time and Free Will*, 11, 55, 60, 171n4
Berlin, 55, 78, 190n3; Conference on West Africa (1884), 16, 17, 23, 24, 75, 175n1
Bernstein, Stephen, 110
Bhabha, Homi K., 188n1, 189n2
Bhagavad-Gita, 133
Bimber, Bruce, 27
Bivona, Daniel, 82
Blair, Sara, 66
Blaise, Clark, 4, 15, 41, 172n7, 173n16, 173n20, 175n8, 176n17, 176n24, 177n29, 178n48, 182n2
Bloch, Ernst, 73–74, 174n26
Bloomsbury Group, 66, 173n19
Bombay, 143, 189n3
Bourdieu, Pierre, 7, 30, 51
Bourdin, Martial, 18, 102–4, 182n2, 183n5
Bradshaw's guide, 5–6, 14, 85–86, 99, 107, 121, 122, 172n10, 181n4
Braithwaite, Kamau, 188n34
Brantlinger, Patrick, 75–76
Brazil, 7, 46–51
Brecht, Bertolt, 62
Brennan, Timothy, 174n25, 188n2, 191n5
British Empire, 2, 14, 19, 29, 83, 99, 127, 149–52, 184n10; Africa and, 23–25; India in, 77, 89, 91–96, 132, 134, 136–38, 143–47, 150, 172n6; narratives of, 13, 75–77, 91, 93; Pacific Cable and, 49–50; Prime Meridian Conference and, 26–27, 36, 39, 42, 45, 50–51, 103–4, 176n23; Royal Navy, 4, 39, 152, 172n9; science and, 98
British Home Office, 18
British Museum, 124
British Standards Institute, 172n13
Brooker, Joseph, 186n19
bureaucracy, 69, 78, 84, 89, 107, 127, 163. *See also* technobureaucracy
Burpee, Lawrence, 175n12

Calcutta, 143, 144, 189n3
Callinicos, Alex, 171n1
Canada, 1, 7, 31, 42, 45, 47–51, 119, 123; First Nations of, 192n8
Canadian Pacific Railway, 175n12
Cantor, Paul A., 98
Carlyle, Thomas, 31, 175n12
Casablanca, 104

cartography, 1, 16–17, 34, 53, 76, 79, 88–91, 111, 192n8
Chakrabarty, Dipesh, 188n1
Chaplin, Charlie, 164
Chatterjee, Partha, 160
Chatterjee, Sarat Chandra, *Pather Dabi*, 133–34
Chaucer, Geoffrey, 66
Cheng, Vincent J., 113
China, 191n6
Christianity, 81, 94
Christie, W. H. M., 35
chronometry, 88, 89
Chu, Patricia E., 15
Church, Margaret, 173n17
Civil War, American, 143
Clinton, Bill, 158
clocks, 9, 30, 34, 142, 159, 168; in adventure fiction, 78, 80, 89; atomic, 157; Bergson on, 56, 58, 59, 173n17; coordinated, 4, 5, 15, 58, 59, 100, 101, 123; cosmopolitan, 31, 32, 51; decimal, 119, 120; Einstein on, 58, 59; factory, 5, 162; in India, 26, 89, 128, 129, 140, 149, 151; in modernist literature, 46, 67, 100–101, 107, 111–16, 118–21, 123–24, 182n1; in postmodernism, 165–66; Stanley on, 78–79; synchronized, 8, 59, 76, 123, 189n2; twenty-four-hour, 52, 119, 120
Clowdisley Shovel disaster, 172n9
Columbus, Christopher, 180n2
Congo, 24, 76, 181n10
Congress, U.S., 37
Conrad, Joseph, 3, 8, 14, 18, 68–69, 98, 112, 117–19, 127, 154, 185nn11–12, 185n17; *Heart of Darkness*, 69, 75, 76; *Lord Jim*, 108, 109, 112, 163; *The "Nigger" of the Narcissus*, 181n10; *Nostromo*, 50; *The Secret Agent*, 25, 100–111, 163, 165, 182n2, 184n10, 185nn14–15
cosmopolitanism, 54, 61–62, 65–69, 106; in Eastern culture, 19, 136, 141–42; temporal, 1–2, 9–12, 31–33, 36, 42–43, 50–53, 55, 102, 112, 152, 159
Crawford, Robert, 66
Curzon, Lord, 135

Dakar, 104
Dalhousie, Lord, 142–43
Danius, Sara, 16
Darwin, Charles, 4, 172n7
Darwinian evolution, 136, 139

Davis, Alex, 66
"Day of Two Noons," 35
Defense Department, U.S., 157
Deleuze, Gilles, 20, 161, 192n8
Delhi, 148–49
determinism, technological, 27
diacritics (journal), 159
Dickens, Charles, *Dombey and Son*, 8, 173n16
Doane, Mary Anne, 6
Doyle, Arthur Conan, 75, 172n10
Dreyfus Affair, 9, 69
Dublin, 9, 25, 60, 62, 64, 66, 112, 115, 186n19; Dunsink Observatory, 25, 113, 115, 116, 187n24, 187n35
Duffy, Enda, 113
Dutt, R.C., 144

Eagleton, Terry, 10, 173n19
East India Company, 90
Eddington, Arthur, 70, 71
Edison, Thomas, 4, 172n7
Edmond, Rod, 174n23
Einstein, Albert, 11, 55, 58–59, 63, 179n5
Eliot, George, 172n16
Eliot, T.S., 62, 173n17, 179n5; *The Waste Land*, 66
Enemy, The (magazine), 63
England, 8, 23, 39, 61, 91, 121, 124, 133, 139, 153; class in, 65; ontological purity of, 87, 100; racialized national character in, 69, 70; rail travel in, 5–6, 111, 122, 189n3; rivalry between France and, 6, 7; standard time measurement in relation to (*see* Greenwich Mean Time); technological capacity of, 91; *See also* British Empire; London
Engler, Edmund, 35
Enlightenment, 4, 23, 27, 69, 155
Erdinast-Vulcan, Daphna, 185n15
Esty, Jed, 88–89, 181n8; *A Shrinking Island*, 61, 173n19
Eurocentrism, Marxist, 162
European Union, 158, 191n6
Evans, Admiral F.J.O., 39, 57, 88–89
Eysteinsson, Astradur, 15

Fabian, Johannes, 76, 188n2
famine, 143–44
Fanning Islands, 49–50
Fanon, Frantz, 113, 187n20
fascism, 12, 62, 73, 161
feminism, 187n30
Flaubert, Gustave, *Salammbô*, 61

Fleming, Sandford, 4, 7, 14, 15, 28, 45, 74, 172n7, 175nn6–7, 175n12, 178n46, 189n3; cosmopolitan time of, 31–36, 43, 50, 52, 53, 55, 159; at International Prime Meridian Conference, 1, 35–40, 42–44, 46, 53, 119, 176n23; "Longitude and Time-Reckoning," 32–33; and Para syndicate, 47–50, 178n48; Taylorism advocated by, 51–52; "Time Reckoning for the Twentieth Century," 28, 71–72; twenty-four hour clock designed by, 52, 119, 120
flexible accumulation, 154, 156
Ford, Ford Madox, 69, 112
Fordism, 154
Foresta, Albert de, 40
Forster, E.M., 17, 174n23
Foucault, Michel, 20, 174n26
France, 6–7, 24, 42, 46, 50, 119; delegation to Prime Meridian Conference of, 37, 40, 43, 48, 103–4, 120, 177n29, 184n7
Freemasons, 114
French Revolution, 120

Gadgil, D.R., 142–43
Galileo System, 158, 191n6, 192n8
Galison, Peter, 5, 6, 34, 40, 59, 176n17, 176n24, 177n29, 192n8, 182n2
Gandhi, Mohandas K., 135, 144–45, 149; *Hind Swaraj*, 144
Ganguly, Keya, 188n2
Geographic Information System (GIS), 192
Germany, 7, 24, 42, 45; delegation to Prime Meridian Conference of, 39, 40, 43
Ghosh, Sarath Kumar, 20, 130–33, 146, 150–52; *The Prince of Destiny*, 19, 130, 132, 135–42, 144, 191n8
Giddens, Anthony, 23
Gillies, Mary Ann, 173n17
Gladstone, William, 137
Gleick, James, 157
globalization, 3, 20–21, 105, 172n16, 174n25; collective solidarity of work and, 164; economic, 154; temporal, 23, 31, 51, 75, 79, 105, 155, 174n27
Global Positioning System (GPS), 29, 128, 154, 156–59, 191n6, 192n8
Gokhale, Gopal Krishna, 143
Goldman, Jane, 173n19
Gothic literature; horror, 92, 94; imperial, 13, 75–77, 91, 93
Grand Trunk Road, 91
Great Game, 77

208 | Index

Great Indian Peninsula Railway, 143
Greene, Graham, 173n19
Greenwich Mean Time (GMT), 3–4, 8, 18, 28, 107, 171n3, 172n6, 187n25; cultural construct and technological infrastructure of, 29; India and, 20, 96, 130, 153, 189n3; modernist literary references to, 14–15, 25, 78, 100–102, 104, 112, 113, 115–19, 128, 187n24; in nineteenth-century adventure novels, 76–79, 87, 110; Prime Meridian Conference and, 1–2, 6–7, 17, 26, 35–44, 53, 88–89, 176n17, 176n19, 177n28, 184n7; social time versus, 30–31
Greenwich Royal Observatory, 2, 4, 14, 15, 18–19, 24, 34, 37, 40, 110, 157, 177n28; attempted bombing of, 18, 25, 102–4, 107, 182n2, 183n5; National Maritime Museum in, 176n24
Guattari, Félix, 20, 192n8
Gujarat, 143
Gulf War, 157

Habermas, Jürgen, 191n1
Haggard, H. Rider, 14, 75–77, 79–83, 87, 89–91, 93, 99, 174n23; *King Solomon's Mines*, 79–80, 110, 180n2; *She*, 13, 77, 80–82
Hall, Stuart, 128
Hama, Mark, 182n2
Hampson, Robert, 185n15
Hardt, Michael; *Empire*, 161, 191n5; *Multitude*, 161
Hardy, Thomas, 182n1; *Jude the Obscure*, 89
Harootunian, Harry, 160
Harris, Wilson, 152
Harrison, John, 4, 25, 39, 172n8
Harvey, David, 10, 154–55
Hasik, James H., 158
Hawaii, 49, 178n46
Hegel, Georg Wilhelm Friedrich, 180n8
Heidegger, Martin, 61, 72–73, 188nn1–2
Henry, Holly, 70–71
Hergé, 180n2
Hinduism, 133, 136, 139, 140, 144, 148
Hong Kong, 51
Hooker, G.W., 47
horror, Gothic, 92, 94
Houen, Alex, 185n14
Howse, Derek, 6, 36, 41, 171n3, 172n9, 176n17, 176nn24–25
Hufnagel, Peter, 98
Huk, Abdul, 137–38

humanism, liberal, 10, 69, 70, 179n5
Huxley, Aldous, 173n17
hybridity, 26, 92
Hyderabad, 137–38, 143

imperial Gothic, 13, 75–77, 91, 93
India, 26, 89–90, 128–53, 172n6, 189n3, 191n10; British Raj in, 77, 89, 92–96, 132, 134, 136–37, 150; in imperial Gothic fiction, 75–76; modernization in, 19, 129, 135, 148–50; National Congress of, 135; Partition of, 147–50; Woolf on, 123
instantaneity, 20, 154, 156
International Prime Meridian Conference (Washington, D.C., 1884), 5, 22, 31, 52, 75, 78, 175n13, 176nn23–25, 177n29, 181n4; Bergson's theories versus, 11, 55, 57; clock-face reform and, 119, 120; Einstein's theories versus, 11, 59; GPS as descendent of, 156–57; Greenwich Mean Time and, 1–2, 6–7, 17, 26, 33, 35–44, 53, 88–89, 176n17, 176n19, 177n28, 184n7; London *Times* coverage of, 18, 23–27, 184n5, 184n7; Para syndicate and, 48, 50; railroads and, 85; resistance to unification of global time at, 53–54, 159, 169
Inuit, 192n8
Iran, 172n6
Iraq, 172n6
Ireland, 25, 113, 115; nationalism and, 62, 65, 68, 186n19
Islam, 42, 54, 144, 148
isolationism, temporal, 9–11, 60, 62, 67, 73–74, 152, 154
Italy, 42, 64, 65, 140; delegation to Prime Meridian Conference of, 39, 40, 43

James, William, 172n7
Jameson, Fredric, 16–17, 76, 174n23, 175n1, 184n10
Janssen, Jules, 37, 38, 119, 120
Japan, 135–36
Jean, James, 70, 71
Jenkins, Lee M., 66
Jerusalem, 41, 62
Jinnah, Muhammad Ali, 149
Joly, Charles Jasper, 117
Joyce, James, 12, 14, 63–69, 118–19, 127, 128, 154, 161, 164, 165, 172n17, 178n4, 186n19, 187n21–24; *Dubliners*, 66; *A Portrait of the Artist as a Young Man*, 65, 68, 69; *Stephen Hero*,

68; *Ulysses*, 3, 9, 25, 60, 62, 64, 67, 68, 101, 112–18, 179n5
Judeo-Christian tradition, 41

Kabyle people, 30
Kant, Immanuel, 60, 188n2
Karachi, 190n3
Kenner, Hugh, 181n11
Kern, Stephen, 8–10, 16, 113, 182n2
Kertzer, J.M., 108
Keynesianism, 155
Khatri, C.L., 190n4
Kikuyu people, 30–31
Kimball, R.J., 47, 48, 51
Kipling, Rudyard, 14, 89–96, 174n23, 181n7, 181nn9–10; *Kim*, 14, 77, 89–93, 96, 147; *Plain Tales from the Hills*, 93–96
Kittler, Friedrich, 84
Klee, Paul, 169, 179n5
Korean Air Lines Flight 007, 158
Kumar, Shiv, 173n17

Lahore, 148–49
Lawrence, D.H., 67, 173n19, 182n1
leap second, 157
Lefaivre, Albert, 33, 40, 175n13
Lefebvre, Henri, 22, 26–27, 154
Lewis, Pericles, 69
Lewis, Wyndham, 10, 62, 173n19; *Time and Western Man*, 12, 54, 62–67, 171n4, 173n17, 174n26, 178n4
liberalism, 10, 69, 70, 179n5
Lloyd's of London, 50
London, 5–6, 8, 19, 76–77, 139; Conrad's depiction of, 100, 103–7, 109–10, 112; cosmopolitanism of, 55; Wells's Time Traveler in, 97; in Woolf's novels, 66, 67, 123–26
London *Times*, 18, 23–27, 103, 183n5, 184nn7–8
Longitude Act (England, 1714), 4
Lukács, Georg, 57, 62–64; *The Historical Novel*, 61; *The Meaning of Contemporary Realism*, 12, 60
Lütticken, Sven, 104

Macaulay, Thomas Babington, 144
MacDiarmid, Hugh, 66
Madras, 143, 189n3; Law College at, 145
Majendie, Colonel, 183n5
Marcus, Jane, 173n19
Marx, John, 188n31
Marx, Karl, 160–62, 164, 172n7
Marxism, 10, 161; Eurocentric, 162

Mecca, 42
metropolitan modernism, 61, 62
Middle Passage, 152
Military Affairs, Revolution in, 158
Minh-ha, Trinh T., 188n1
Misa, Thomas, 28
Mitra, Siddha Mohana, 132
modernity, 1–2, 19–21, 23, 42, 72, 111–12, 171n1, 191n1; capitalist, 160; industrial, 5, 50, 109, 136; Lefebvre on, 22; literature and, 84, 87; periodization between postmodernity and, 155; railway, 148; social time and, 23, 36, 128; technological, 16, 130–31; temporal dynamics of, 87, 88; urbanization and, 5, 55
modernization, 87, 88, 128; in India, 19, 125, 129, 148–50
Modern Times (film), 164
Monet, Claude, 172n7
Moore-Gilbert, Bart, 135
Moorhouse, Geoffrey, 181n7
Moses, Michael Valdez, 98, 171n5
Mukherjee, Meenakshi, 137; *The Twice Born Fiction*, 19, 132–33
Murphy, Patricia, 27
Muslims, 42, 54, 148
Mussolini, Benito, 64, 65
Myanmar, 172n6

Narayan, R.K., 132
nationalism, 24–26, 33, 54, 62–65, 67, 70–71, 133, 159, 188; aestheticism and, 155, 179n5; anticolonial, 135, 136, 142, 144, 147; fascism and, 12, 73, 161; industrial, 136; Irish, 62, 65, 68, 186n19
Naval Observatory, U.S., 157, 185n12
Nazis, 160, 165, 167, 168
Negri, Antonio, 168, 169; *The Constitution of Time*, 160–65, 192n9; *Empire*, 161, 191n5, 192n9; *Marx beyond Marx*, 161; *Multitude*, 161
Negritude, 147
Nehru, Jawaharlal, 135
Nelson, Admiral Horatio, 152
neoliberalism, 66, 155
Nepal, 172n6
Newfoundland, 172n6
Newton, Isaac, 25, 58
Newton, Michael, 18
New York, 105, 190n3
New Zealand, 186n17
Ngũgĩ wa Thiong'o, 175n1; *Petals of Blood*, 29, 31

Nigeria, 23
Noel, Major E., 28, 175n7
Nolan, Emer, 67, 179n5, 186n19

Okigbo, Christopher, 188n34
Oldham, R.D., 131, 188n3
ontology, 73, 87, 100, 151, 162, 164, 168, 169, 188n2
Orientalism, 90, 133, 181n4, 187n30
Orwell, George, 173n19
Osborne, Peter, 72–73, 180n8
Other, 93–94, 99, 189n2; temporal, 100, 126
Ottoman Empire, 7, 42–45, 53–54, 177n29

Pacific Cable, 49–50, 178n46
Pakistan, 26, 149–50, 172n6
Pang, Alex Soojung-Kim, 71
parallax, 115–18, 164, 165
Para Transportation and Trading Company, 47–51, 178n48
Paris, 62, 66, 139; cosmopolitanism of, 55; International Meter in, 172n13; Observatory, 157
Parkinson, Colonel B.W., 157–58
Parliament, British, 4; House of Commons, 78–79
Parnell, Charles Stewart, 69
Parry, Benita, 188n2
Partington, John S., 97
Pasquier, Ernst, 45
Pasteur, Louis, 4, 172n7
Paulin, J.R., 47
Pentagon, terrorist attack on, 104
Peters, John G., 182n2, 185n11
phenomenology, 72–73
Phillips, Kathy, 123, 187n30
Piazzi-Smyth, Charles, 34, 41, 45, 171n2
Picasso, Pablo, 62
Pinero, Arthur Wing, *The Magistrate*, 18
Piper, Karen, 18, 192n8
Platt, Len, 186n17
Poincaré, Henri, 139
Poona, 143
Popular Science Monthly, 35
Poulkova Observatory, 34
Pound, Ezra, 12, 62, 63, 68
Pritchard, Charles, 71
Proust, Marcel, 9, 12, 57, 63, 65, 108, 173n17; *The Guermantes Way*, 69
Puchner, Martin, 178n2
Punch magazine, 6
Puritanism, 5
purity, ontological, 87, 100, 169

Qaradawy, Sheikh Youssef al-, 42
Qatar Conference (2008), 42
Quinones, Ricardo J., 67

race-consciousness, 147
railroads, 71, 162; in Canada, 49; in England, 5–6, 8, 67, 85, 97, 110–11, 121, 172n16; in Europe, 83, 85, 97; in India, 90–91, 131, 142, 145–51, 157; in Para syndicate scheme, 47–49; standard time and, 14, 34, 40
Railway Time Convention, 27
Ramazani, Jahan, 188n34
Rao, Raja, 132, 150; *Kanthapura*, 134–35
Reagan, Ronald, 158
Redfield, Marc, 160
Rees, J.K., 35–36
Rege, Josna E., 133
Renaissance, 66
Reykjavik, 105
Richardson, Dorothy, 173n17
Ricoeur, Paul, 73, 128, 180n8
Rio News, 48
Rip, Michael Russell, 158
Rodgers, Admiral C.R.P., 38, 43
Rodgers, John, 185n12
Rome, 190n3
Rosenfeld, Claire, 110
Ruiz del Arbol, Emilio, 41, 42
Rushdie, Salman, *Midnight's Children*, 26, 128–29, 136, 151
Russell, Bertrand, 179n5
Russia, 34, 42, 135, 176n23, 191n6
Rustem Effendi, 42, 43, 88–89, 177n29
Rutherford, Lewis, 37, 43–44

Said, Edward, 89, 90, 112, 181n8, 187n20
San Domingo, 46
Scandinavia, 42
Schleifer, Ronald, 179n5
Schreiner, Olive, 88
Schwarz, Roberto, 29
Scotland, 5
Scotland Yard, 18, 103, 105
Scott, Ridley, 155
Senghor, Leopold Sedar, 147
Sethia, Tara, 137–38, 191n10
Seurat, Georges, 172n7
Shakespeare, William, 66
Sidereal Messenger, The, 35
Sikhs, 148
simultaneity, 20, 39, 58–59, 156, 165
Singh, Kushwant, 132, 162; *Train to Pakistan*, 147–51

slavery, 152
Smith, Merrit Roe, 27
Soane, Bev, 185n16
Soble, Dava, 172n8
Sorabji, Cornelia, 132
Spain, 7, 42; delegation to Prime Meridian Conference of, 39–42, 54, 57, 176n25
Spanish succession, war of, 5
Stallman, R.W., 182n2
Stanley, Henry Morton, 78–79, 181n10
Stein, Gertrude, 12, 63, 65
Stevenson, Randall, 18, 103, 174n24, 183n5
Stevenson, Robert Louis, 99
Stewart, Susan, 86
Stockton, Sharon, 171n4, 185n13
Stoker, Bram, 14, 75, 89, 90, 96; *Dracula*, 3, 13, 77, 82–87, 92, 101, 104, 107, 121, 180n3, 181n4
Strachey, General Richard, 41–44
Struve, Otto, 34
Suleri, Sara, 87–89
Suri dynasty, 91
Sweden, 43
Switzerland, 43

Tasman, Abel, 186n17
Taylor, Frederick, 51–52
Taylorism, 5, 52, 162
technobureaucracy, 57, 76, 84
technology, 14, 16–17, 21, 29, 46, 85, 127, 130–31, 157, 181n11; communications, 5, 48, 51, 53, 59, 82, 108, 131; determinism and, 27; GPS (*see* Global Positioning System); in India, 19, 135, 145–48, 150, 151; synchronized, 71, 151; temporal, 82, 89, 96–98, 123; transport, 39, 48, 53, 82, 91, 108, 131
telecommunications, 49, 59, 108, 142
Teske, Charles, 34
Thailand, 51
Thompson, E.P., 5, 23
Thompson, Francis, 139
Tiffin, Helen, 128
Tondini de Quarenghi, Cesare, 176n23
trains, *See* railroads
transnationalism, 11, 34, 54, 61, 71, 159; temporal, 9–10, 67, 73–74, 152
Treblinka, 168
Trinidad, 45–46
Trout, Steven, 181n10
Turkey. *See* Ottoman Empire
Twain, Mark, 180n2

United States, 1, 39, 42, 45, 176n16, 178n46; "Day of Two Noons" in, 35; delegation to Prime Meridian Conference of, 37, 38, 43–44, 53; foreign investment of capital from, 47, 48, 51; GPS technology, 157–59, 191n2, 191n6, 192n8
Universal Coordinated Time (UCT), 157
Urry, John, 30

Valera, Juan, 39
Van Gogh, Vincent, 172n7
Vedanta, 190n8
Venkataramani, Kaneripatna Sidhanatha, 20, 130–33, 146–47, 150–52, 162, 190n4; *Murugan, the Tiller*, 3, 19, 130, 132–33, 144–47
Victoria, Queen, 50, 136–37
Vonnegut, Kurt, 160; *Slaughterhouse Five*, 165–67
Vorticists, 173n19

Waldo, Leonard, 34
Waugh, Evelyn, 173n19
Wayman, Patrick A., 187n24
Weber, Max, 84
Wells, H.G., 75, 96, 174n23, 181n11; *The Time Machine*, 96–98, 182n1
Wenders, Wim, 155
Wenzel, Jennifer, 184n10
Western Canada Cement and Coal Company, 49
Whitworth, Michael, 15, 59, 109, 165
Wicke, Jennifer, 6, 84, 87
Wilde, Oscar, 9, 94
Williams, Patrick, 174n23
Williams, Raymond, 10, 12, 65, 66; *The Politics of Modernism*, 61, 62
Williams, Trevor, 187n21
Wood, Ellen, 191n5
Woolf, Leonard, 70
Woolf, Virginia, 2, 3, 14, 70–71, 88, 120–28, 161, 164–66, 171n4, 173n17, 173n19, 185n13, 188n32; *The Hours*, 126; *Mrs. Dalloway*, 46, 66, 67, 71, 99, 101, 119–20, 122–26, 163, 180n5; *Night and Day*, 120–22, 127; *Orlando*, 125; *The Voyage Out*, 187n30; *The Waves*, 67
World Trade Center, terrorist attack on, 104
World War I, 16

Yeats, William Butler, 62

Zeno of Elea, 11, 57

TEXT
10/13 Sabon
DISPLAY
Sabon
COMPOSITOR
Toppan Best-set Premedia Limited
INDEXER
Ruth Elwell
PRINTER AND BINDER
IBT Global

www.ingramcontent.com/pod-product-compliance
Lightning Source LLC
Chambersburg PA
CBHW031550300426
44111CB00006BA/247